FLYING TIGER
MEMORIES

Guy Van Herbruggen

designed by Simon De Rudder

edited by Charles Kennedy

astral
HORIZON

Acknowledgements

I have to start by thanking the Belgian Tiger, Rudi Kohlbacher, for the idea of developing a third book on the Flying Tiger Line geared towards its people, their souvenirs and stories.

Thank you to everyone at the Flying Tiger Club who helped so much by opening their unique archives at LAX, and for the encouragement, patience and contributions to this book, in particular Fran Thompson, Archives Director; Helena Burke, Membership Director; Margi Falk, Secretary; John Burke, Vice President and Halli Gudmundsson, President. With them I discovered another family of Tigers next to the FTLPA who share the same unconditional passion for their airline.

To everyone at the Flying Tiger Line Pilots Association (FTLPA) with a very special thanks to Captain John Dickson, FTLPA President for his unique support, encouragement and commitment to this book. John was always there, he never stopped me; he only encouraged me; he always found answers. His true Can-Do Spirit helped me to get through the times when success seemed a long way off. Amongst the Flying Tiger Line Pilots Association staff, special thanks to Peter Okicich, Secretary/Treasurer; George Gewehr, Historian; Joyce Danielsen Dalbey, Flight Attendant Representative and Eliot Shulman, Photographer.

Writing this book was a team effort. To those I like to express my thanks for their contributions, for their patience and commitment: John Dickson, George Gewehr, Helena Herceg Burke, John Burke, Dwight Small, Starr Thompson, Catherine Nau, Patti Bliss, Kristi Bliss Peake, Paul and Susan Rebscher, Tom Constable, Garry Duff, John "Dizzy" Dziubala and his son Toby, Leigh-lu Prasse, Charles "Chuck" Marshall, Dick Feuerherm, Gael Okicich, Bob Baird, Ralph F. Mitchell, Dennis Flanagin, Guy López, Diana Smith Nagatani, Sharon Schlies, Joe Crecca, Carole and Rex Cotter, Kathy Smith, Reyné O'Shaughnessy, Mark Hunt, Dr. Cameron Byerley, Michael S. Prophet, Deborah Paul (McCoy), Al Hader, Doug Happ, Curt Dosé, Bob Stickler, Thomas Pierchala, Ted Loubris, Rudi Kohlbacher, Cathy Fune-Schinhofen, Robin Burkey Pestarino and Glenn Van Winkle.

Writing this book gave us the opportunity to connect or reconnect with some historical Tiger figures like Lydia Rossi, widow of AVG Captain Dick Rossi, Virginia (Ginny) Dixon, secretary and administrator of the offices of the chairman and the president of Flying Tigers from 1968 to 1986; Ann Ludwig, early stewardess and loyal friend of Bob Prescott till his last day or Kirchy Prescott, last surviving child of Bob Prescott.

For supplying photographic material, providing information or sharing some of their personal archives: Annette and Dave Lusk, Kenneth Barton, Frances Drew, Juanita Danewitz Hennessey, Dave Stratton, Robert Ruggiero, Jacques Barbé, Frank de Koster, Jason Pineau, Jacques Guillem, Ed Kushins, Peter van Leeuwen, Jo Nell Kocisko, Guy Viselé, Art Chin, Nissen Davis, Dave Gilmore, Alain Chaillé, Sheree Weber, John Hazlet, John Tymczyszyn, Jeanne Dickson, Kip Cutting, Doug Shaw, Erich Krueck and Anatole J. "Frenchy".

At my publisher Astral Horizon Press, I would like to thank Emma Entero, Bhavna Vadher and Steve Finnigan.

Thank you Katie and Jean-Claude Démirdjian who opened their home in Los Angeles while I was digging in the archives of the Flying Tigers Club and the Flight Path Museum. Merci.

Finally I am forever indebted to my best friend, Charles Kennedy for his precious editorial help, keen insight, and ongoing support in bringing the stories to life. That is true friendship. It is because of his efforts, passion and commitment that we have a legacy to pass on to future generations.

Also special thanks to Simon de Rudder for his hard work in the design of this book.

Last but not least, I have to thank my awesome wife, France and my kids Maria and José. From reading early drafts to keeping the house and garden in order so I could work on the book. France was as important to this book getting done as I was. Thank you so much, my dear.

Thank you all for letting me serve the legacy of the Flying Tiger Line.

Contents

FLYING TIGER **MEMORIES**

Guy Van Herbruggen

ISBN 978-0-9932604-8-3

© 2019 Astral Horizon Aviation Press. All rights reserved.

27 Meadow Road Claygate Surrey KT10 0RZ United Kingdom

www.theairlineboutique.com

Bob & Peter Prescott in Burbank on September 27, 1965

Tribute to Robert W. Prescott

Captain John F. Dickson,
President, Flying Tiger Line Pilots Association

It is an honour for me to write this first chapter as a tribute to our company's founder. Bob Prescott succumbed to cancer in 1978, three months before I was hired as a pilot for the Flying Tiger Line, so I never had the opportunity to thank him personally for creating the organization that would allow me to forever call myself a Flying Tiger. However, I have since expressed my gratitude to him numerous times in thought and prayer. I suspect that most of my colleagues have done so as well, one time or another in their own lives.

There is a strong feeling of family among the Flying Tigers and an almost spiritual connection with the brave men and women of the American Volunteer Group (AVG) whose heritage and name we proudly embrace. This connection probably comes from the strong dedication, work ethic and camaraderie exhibited by the early investors of the airline, most of whom were former AVG pilots. Possibly this sense of purpose was deliberately promoted by Mr. Prescott in an effort to maintain the same esprit de corps that led to their success in a strange and hostile fight in Rangoon. Prescott once said, "Whether or not tigers like to be called people, people seem to like being called tigers. This airline has always attracted unusual personalities - men and women with more than the normal amount of imagination, energy, ingenuity - and guts." All former Flying Tiger Line employees, from every department throughout our airline's history, possess an ingrained feeling that we have always proudly referred to as the Tiger Spirit. Many came wondering if they were accepting second best to the glamour airlines. They left knowing they were the cream of the crop. The military elite snubbed the AVG until those original Tigers mounted the only successful attack on the Japanese during the first months of the Pacific War. Indeed, the word legacy can be a powerful noun.

There isn't much about Robert Prescott that has not been well documented. The quick success of the Flying Tiger Line in the mid 1940s can only be explained by the fortitude, charisma, and drive of its founder and his ability to share his dream with early employees to the extent that they didn't work for the Flying Tiger Line, they were Tigers. The team work ethic and camaraderie that Prescott created, the Can-Do spirit that he so often touted, continued right up to T-Day, the date when the Flying Tiger Line and Federal Express merged their operations in 1989. The Prescott version of corporate culture at Tigers demanded hard work, open doors, and an unspoken but absolute requirement to have fun and enjoy the ride that being a part of the world's largest air cargo company offered. A good boss makes others realize they have more ability than they think they have so they can consistently do better work than they thought they could. There is little doubt that Prescott surrounded himself with such prodigies and mentored them well. What Bob Prescott created was so special that it survived years of assault by corporate orthodoxy and an aggressive Wall Street raider. The fates must have smiled on Bob's dream when another magician that turns dreams into reality took over Bob's creation.

EARLY DAYS

To really pay tribute to Robert W. Prescott, it's necessary to explore the earlier days leading up to his success as president of the world's largest air cargo airline – the founder of an entirely new industry in America.

Prescott was born on May 5, 1913, in Fort Worth, Texas. A typical kid born into a depression-era family, he was forced to grow up quicker than those in most other generations. He matured into a tall, handsome, good-natured young man, deceptively easy-going on the outside but with an internal restlessness that was more physical than emotional. The only business experience that the young Prescott ever had was watching his father, a fairly successful auctioneer and warehouseman, lose the family's entire worth in a trucking venture while Prescott was in high school. This threw the family into a loop, one which they apparently never really recovered from.

The seventh of eight children, in age as well as family importance, his childhood possessions were hand-me downs. He inherited all his older siblings' toys, schoolbooks and clothes. During high school he was distinguished more by the varied pieces of wardrobe that he inherited from his six older brothers than by his grades. The tone was set; and he turned out to be no scholar. At high school graduation, his mathematics teacher told him that he was lazy, inattentive and did not have the right attitude to ever amount to anything. He helped his father at home as much as he could, pumped fuel in a gas station, sold milk by driving a truck door to door, and worked other odd jobs as they came along.

His first attempt at entrepreneurship was to manage a schoolmate who had a talent for boxing. In 1931, after graduating from high school, he bought his first suit, presumably the first outfit that had not been passed down, and moved to St. Louis to promote his boxing buddy. Unfortunately, his promoting career was very short; a one-fight bout that ended in defeat for his client. Prescott remained in St. Louis and worked as an usher in a vaudeville theatre. His bad luck continued as he was quickly fired for his uncontained and hilariously loud laughter that disrupted performances. His boyish sense of humor apparently couldn't be daunted and he wore that perpetual grin for all his life.

Penniless, he decided to return to Fort Worth by jumping on a freight train for a free ride home. While making the jump into the moving boxcar he cut his knee badly and ripped his new suit before rolling onto the dirty floor. Still wearing his bloodstained, filthy suit, he was greeted by his mother who said, "Now that you know what it's like to shift for yourself, maybe you'll settle down." That wasn't going to happen.

He tried to follow in one of his older brother's footsteps as an engineer. He was twenty-one when he left home once more, bound for Los Angeles with a goal to attend California Institute of Technology. Once in L.A. he worked odd jobs during the day and took night classes in mathematics to prepare for the tough entrance exams. He was unable to complete even one of many tests, his dreams of becoming an engineer quickly shot down, as if in some pre-ordained manner.

Next, Prescott decided to switch gears and explore the career route that another successful brother took: the field of law. He enrolled at Compton Junior College and supported himself by working midnight to six in a distribution warehouse at Goodyear Tire and Rubber Company. His bare hands were rubbed raw at times from handling the rubber stock all night. He would complain of a tingling in his fingertips for the rest of his life. Returning to his dorm room each morning, he would clean up, gather his books, eat breakfast and usually make the 8 o'clock class on time. It was the hardest work he had ever done and he put everything he could into it. It was during these days that he discovered something about himself: he liked to learn.

He earned his Associate degree and promptly applied, and was subsequently accepted, to attend law school at Los Angeles' Loyola University. Finally breaking through and succeeding at something for the first time in his life, Prescott began to find that he could accomplish anything he really put his mind to. His Can-Do Spirit started becoming a reality.

FROM PEACE TO WAR

In 1936 there were unimaginable tensions and conflicts developing around the entire globe. By the time Prescott was in his second year at Loyola, an obscure Army Air Corps Captain, Claire Lee Chennault, had retired from the Army and found employment as a civilian in the military service of Nationalist China under the leadership of Chiang Kai-shek. Coincidentally, or possibly equally pre-ordained, Prescott found himself caught up during this time in the exciting shop talk of fellow students, novice flyers who had enrolled in a Naval Reserve training course offered at Loyola. One weekend he followed them to the Long Beach airport, a location that would figure prominently in his life a decade later. He immediately enrolled in the course and eventually finished with marks high enough to win him an appointment to the Navy's air training center at Pensacola, Florida.

In 1939, with war breaking out in Europe, a twenty-five-year-old Prescott put his law career on hold and left Loyola to enlist in the Navy. His self-confidence and enthusiasm for life grew even larger during training as an aviation cadet. From the original group of twelve that had accompanied him from California, he was one of only three who graduated and won the gold wings of a Naval aviator. It was while in Pensacola that Prescott became good friends with John R. "Dick" Rossi, a cocky and confident Californian from Placerville who would be at Prescott's side to his very last days. For two years he and Rossi became primary flight instructors for other youths entering as cadets.

Then, one afternoon in the spring of 1941, their executive officer entered the barracks with a completely unexpected announcement. President Roosevelt had personally authorized the early resignation and discharge of a limited number of naval aviators to fly fighter planes in China and Burma in an effort to protect the Burma Road from Japanese aggression. Those wishing to apply would be civilians employed at high pay with a contract that allowed them to return, after one year, to their branch of the military, with no loss of seniority. For this they would receive high pay, adventure, and get to fly a "hot" fighter plane. Their commander would be a man unknown to any of them at the time, Claire Chennault. Anyone wanting to interview was encouraged to report immediately. A boisterous Rossi proclaimed, "Hell, nobody ever gets out of the Navy this easy." Rossi and Prescott both signed the secret contract and were shortly thereafter given cryptic orders to report to San Francisco.

Once recruited and assembled, this diverse group of military-trained men from throughout the country were given passports that identified them as skilled laborers, missionaries and teachers. They then boarded a Dutch ship, the Bosch Fontein, bound for Asia. They unknowingly had become members of one of the soon-to-be best-known air combat units ever assembled, and were soon to distinguish themselves as unique in the history of modern warfare. They were the American Volunteer Group, the Flying Tigers!

Bob Prescott in the early 1940s   photo Flight Path Museum Archives

Prescott, Rossi and the others on their ship were late arrivals when they disembarked in Rangoon on November 11, 1941. That was Armistice Day, a day when the Japanese were putting the finishing touches on a scheme all their own. Volumes have been written of the successes achieved by the three Flying Tiger squadrons. There have been multiple and differing accounts of the AVG and Prescott's participation. Bob did leave an unpublished diary and it, along with the testimony of actual participants, tells the story of the making of a Tiger.

Two weeks changed a life and eventually changed an industry, and inspired thousands of lives. Bob joined the AVG to fly 1,000-horsepower fighters in combat. Thus far he had only flown 200-horsepower biplanes on training flights. After only a few hours checking out in the P-40 with its panel of instruments and its throttle, boost, prop pitch, trim, gun arming, landing gear and fuel controls, he sortied looking to challenge the Imperial Japanese Air Force. The greenest of the AVG pilots, he was on the wing of the most experienced. Greg Boyington had been a Marine Corps fighter pilot that had won many dog fight contests.

At 10 AM January 26, 1942, Prescott, Boyington and six others were late getting off and were led by a green pilot directly up under the Japanese force. When the Japs came down, guns ablaze, the six dove in all directions. Boyington made two attempts to fight the nimble Nakajima Nates before diving and running himself. Bob Prescott alone, feeling cowardly and thinking of going home, landed to find that everyone had run. Boyington said, "We sure screwed that up partner!" Ironically the only fatality was a man named Cokey Hoffman, the oldest, most veteran of the group.

Two weeks later, February 6, Bob was again late getting off, and he went solo looking for a fight. He found Link Laughlin and joined up. They attacked six I-97 Nates from altitude. Bob shot a Jap off Link's tail while being shot at himself. With his first kill of an eventual five, Bob went from zero to hero in two weeks, and the Can-Do spirit was firmly imprinted. Interestingly, the same month Bob scored his first kill, his future partner's oil facility in California was attacked by a Japanese submarine.

Robert W. Prescott AVG ID card signed by General Claire Chennault
photo Flying Tigers Club Archives

P-40 aerial – The single engine Curtiss P-40 with distinctive tiger shark markings was the aircraft of the American Volunteer Group, better known as the "Flying Tigers" of General Claire Lee Chennault. (1941-1942)
photo Flying Tigers Club Archives

JANUARY, 1942

日期 Date	飛機式樣 Type of Plane	任務記號 Mission (Code No.)	任務概 A BRIEF STATEMENT	略 OF MISSION	FLYING TIME 任飛駛員 As pilot Hrs.	Min.	任觀察員 As Observer Hrs.	Min.
3	P-40	O-7				35		
5	"	A-2				45		
4	"	A-2				35		
8	"	A-4	POUSHAN		1	00		
9	"	A-4	LOCAL		1	00		
10	"	A-3	MENGTSE PATROL		1	15		
12	"	O-7	LOCAL			30		
15	"	A-4	PATROL LOCAL	(NITE) KUNMING		45		
17	"	A-4	PATROL LOCAL	(NITE) KUNMING		45		
18	"	A-4	PATROL LOCAL	(NITE) KUNMING		40		
19	"	A-3				45		
24	"	A-2				30		
25	"	B-5	KUNMING - LASHIO		2	00		
25	"	B-5	LASHIO - RANGOON		2	00		
26	"	B-8	FIRST FIGHT HOFFMAN	KILLED	2	00		
26	"	B-11	THAILAND		2	00		
27	"	B-10	SITANG RIVER			30		
27	"	B-1	NIGHT PATROL		1	00		

FEBRUARY, 1942

日期 Date	飛機式樣 Type of Plane	任務記號 Mission (Code No.)	任務概 A BRIEF STATEMENT	略 OF MISSION	FLYING TIME As pilot Hrs.	Min.	As Observer Hrs.	Min.
1	P-40	B-10						
2	"	B-10						
4	"	B-11						
5	"	B-10						
5	"	B-11						
5	"	O-7	TEST		1	30	1	
5	"	B-1				30	1	
6	"	B-10				30	1	
6	"	B-1	MOULMEIN STRAFE			30	2	
6	"	B-10	FERRY		2	00	1	
7	"	B-1	ESCORT ALEXACINI	STRANGH POSITIONS		15	1	
7	"	B-10			1	45	1	
8	"	B-10	SECOND FIGHT - GOT FIRST	CONFIRMATION		15	1	
8	"	B-1	SIGHTED BOMBERS -	COULDNT CATCH AT MOULMEIN	1	15	1	
9	"	B-16			1	30	1	
9	"	B-1				45	2	
9	"	B-11	PA-AN ESCORT		1	40	1	
10	"	B-10	FERRY			45		

Bob's pilot's logbook extract showing his first fight on January 26, and his first confirmed kill on February 8, 1942   Flight Path Museum Archives

Robert W. Prescott (second from left) was co-pilot of the famous "Mission to Moscow" flight of Ambassador Joseph E. Davies in 1943
photo Flying Tigers Club Archives

Hero at war workers' canteen. Mrs. James H. Doolittle' wife of Major General Doolittle, shown at canteen program with flight leader Robert Prescott   Star Staff Photo / Flight Path Museum Archives

Quick to catch Chennault's eye, Prescott became a P-40 Flight Leader for the 1st Squadron, Adam and Eves, and contributed his part by recording 5 ½ air victories against Japanese aircraft. At the age of twenty-nine, he was the oldest ace to come out of the AVG.

Pearl Harbor had been bombed, war declared on Japan, and on July 4, 1942, after an honorable discharge from the disbanded AVG, Prescott had choices to make. He could join the newly-created 14th Army Air Force, a move unpopular with those loyal to "the old man" (Chennault) whom most felt had been treated unfairly when the Army Air Corps took over command of his unit. Prescott could have also joined the twenty-two Flying Tigers flying as civilian Hump pilots for the non-combat outfit, China National Airways Corporation (CNAC). He turned both opportunities down, opting instead to return to Washington D.C. and fly for the international division of Trans World Airlines (TWA).

Prescott wasn't with TWA very long. His most notable flight was as co-pilot on the aircraft that took Joseph E. Davies, U.S. Ambassador to the Soviet Union, on his second 'Mission to Moscow' trip, at the request of Roosevelt in May 1943. It was also during this period that Prescott was interviewed by a sassy reporter for the Washington Daily News, a woman named Helen Ruth Verheyden. She wanted to learn more about the wartime hero that chose to come to D.C. Prescott, on the other hand, fell in love.

It wasn't long before the tedium of transatlantic long haul flying at TWA bored the restless Prescott. Letters from his old pals flying the Hump in China tempted him with stories of the high pay they were receiving. In 1943, at thirty-years old, he promised his new gal that he would return, and flew to Assam, India, to join his AVG buddies, including his good friend Dick Rossi. CNAC, operated by Pan American Airways for the United States Air Transport Command, was another example of America's tendency toward quasi-covert operations during wartime periods.

After the demise of the Burma Road due to Japanese successes, the air routes that CNAC flew became logistically important to Chiang Kai-shek. For the pilots flying the surplus C-46 Commandos, the environment was often the most challenging they had ever experienced. The shortest route between eastern points in the rarified high plateaus of China, through the frigid windy passes of the Himalayan peaks (the C-46s had no heaters) to the unbearably humid Indian plain was over 500 miles. The air routes flown were often referred to by the crews as "skyways over hell."

Despite the horrible weather conditions, logistical handicaps, and proximity to enemy planes, the Hump route proved to be an effective supply line which inevitably focused attention on the airplane as a freight carrier rather than as a war machine. Prescott added his 300 Hump flights to the CNAC's 35,000 before growing restless yet again. Cargo and aircraft formally met on a huge scale for the first time in history, and Prescott was there to witness it all firsthand. It would be easy to assume that imaginative seeds for the creation of a profitable cargo airline in the U.S. were sewn during this time.

In November of 1944, while losing in a poker game on a hot sweaty night in his Indian barracks, Prescott threw down his cards in frustration proclaiming, "I'm going home to get married." He stormed out, resigned from CNAC and returned to Washington to marry Helen Ruth. As did a lot of veterans from the world's greatest war, he contemplated his future with a burning desire to create rather than destroy.

THE TIGERS FLY AGAIN

Based on his experiences in hauling freight for TWA and CNAC, Prescott soon formed the business model for what a transcontinental freight service would look like. He imagined it as a kind of tramp-steamer line that would be capable of flying anything, anytime, anywhere, a unique and catchy marketing slogan that would be used heavily as his future endeavor developed.

Prescott wasted no time getting some of his Flying Tiger buddies involved, soliciting initial investments of $10,000 each. He also reached out to four businessmen on the West Coast with whom he had become acquainted during an earlier failed venture to start an airline in Mexico, Aerovias Azteca, which was going to transport freight from Tijuana to Mexico City utilizing the Budd Conestoga. One of these gentlemen was Samuel B. Mosher, founder of Signal Gas and Oil, who promptly advised Prescott that he would match, dollar for dollar, any funding that Prescott could independently raise himself. Prescott was able to gather up $90,000 from his AVG pals, a significant amount of money in that day (about $1.16 million in 2019). This amount was matched by Mosher and a the new company was incorporated as the National Skyways Freight Corporation. Prescott was elected president and Mosher became the chairman of the board.

Although incorporated on June 25, 1945 in Teterboro NJ, National Skyways' first headquarters was a suite within the Los Angeles Biltmore Hotel, where long lines of employment applicants began crowding the elegant lobby and hallways to the dismay of the hotel's management. Prescott quickly chose Long Beach Municipal Airport to base his operations after finding a hangar with a partitioned office and garage. While Prescott tried to drum up business opportunities, his new wife, Helen Ruth was the sole, unpaid, office staff, utilising a borrowed typewriter that sat on a stark metal desk.

Prescott had purchased a fleet of twelve (of only seventeen ever produced) big twin-engine Budd Conestoga cargo planes, which sat idle on a ramp in Atlanta, Georgia. Originally built for the Navy, he was able to purchase his new fleet with $320,000 of credit from the Surplus War Property Board ($4.1 million in 2019). Four were sold for a profit, one crashed while being ferried, and another never made it off the ground and was presumably scavenged for parts.

From all of this, only enough money remained to buy the gas to fly four of the aircraft from Atlanta to his new ramp at Long Beach. The Budd Conestoga was an unusual looking stainless-steel craft with a bulging nose and high-perched tail from which a ramp could be lowered enabling trucks to drive right into the empty interior. Within this aircraft, 10,000 pounds of cargo could be stowed in all types of configurations. A mechanic's nightmare and already a collector's item in a short period of time, nothing quite like the Budd had ever flown before. Experts would later claim the aircraft to be one of the most unusual aircraft experiments of the war.

Once flights were sold and operations began, the airline's first pilot/investors such as Robert 'Duke' Hedman, Cliff Groh, Bob 'Catfish' Raines, Link Laughlin and Joe Rosbert were all met with the same question, "What in the hell is that?" Prescott had flown the Budd during the Aerovias Azteca startup attempt and believed them to be steady, reliable aerial boxcars, an extremely timely notion during a period when American business

'Prairie Schooner' of the sky. Showing the large cargo dimensions of the Budd Conestoga airfreight transport, Robert W. Prescott, president of National Skyway Freight Corp., drives a car right into the payload space of big twin-engine plane. His passengers, left to right, are Mrs. Dorothy Tutt and Mrs. Helen Ruth Prescott.   photo Flying Tigers Club Archives

and manufacturing were about to explode with post-war expansion. It was really of no great importance what model aircraft was used during these early flights; and in any case the Budds were quickly replaced with surplus C-46s and C-47s. Prescott's vision was the concept that changed transportation history and created an entirely new industry – airfreight.

Prescott's first break came one afternoon when Ralph E. Meyers, a big-time West Coast produce shipper, called on August 21, 1945 from Bakersfield, California, to inquire about the shipment of four tons of

With a Budd Conestoga in the background, this is Duke Hedman on the right next to an unknown lady   photo Flying Tigers Club Archives

grapes the next day to Atlanta. Prescott's hands were reportedly shaking but his voice steady when he replied. "I'll have to look at the flight charts." He shuffled a pile of papers in front of the phone, mostly bills, came up with a figure out of the blue, took a breath, and replied, "I'm sorry, we have only one airplane available tomorrow. But you can have that one and we'll carry as much as we can." The flight operated the very next day. One of the grocers to receive the grapes advertised, "By special plane they come to you still fresh with California dew." That grocer was able to charge 43 cents a pound, three times the price of locally-grown grapes. Soon Meyers was frantically demanding as many airplanes as National Skyways could provide, declaring that every grocer in the country was screaming for fresh fruit.

Although history records the Bakersfield-Atlanta grape charter as the first revenue flight, it went down in the books as Trip No. 2, flown by Paul Kelly, a fellow AVG pilot on thirty days leave from the Air Transport Command and still in military uniform. As quickly as Helen Ruth penciled in Meyer's flight, two other opportunities were phoned in that same day. Trip No. 1, flown by John Gordon, was a planeload of flowers requiring immediate shipment from Long Beach to Detroit. Trip No. 3 was scheduled out of the miniscule New York office. Duke Hedman flew this trip west, unloading the 10,000-pound load of uncrated furniture in Long Beach without a scratch. During a twenty-four-hour period National Skyways had made history by moving 30,000 pounds of commercial freight by air. That night everyone celebrated at the Hilton Skyroom by toasting each other and listening to every detail of Hedman's trip westbound. A new industry was born and the word 'airfreight' was added to the dictionary.

The following day was met with misfortune when Bob and Helen Ruth arrived at the hangar to find Hedman and Rosbert with heads in their hands and solemn looks on their faces. John Gordon, who flew the flowers to Detroit, was able to book another planeload of furniture out of Detroit to Long Beach. "Backhaul" had become a very important word. Once at their destinations, pilots were expected to act as salesmen for the new airline

and hustle up any type of business in order to fill the aircraft for the return trip. Unfortunately, on August 23rd Trip No. 4, with its load of furniture, crashed on takeoff at Detroit. Luckily Gordon and his crew were OK, but the aircraft and cargo were destroyed.

Despite the setback, opportunities to fly cargo developed quicker than Prescott could keep up with. Soon, National Skyways was hauling everything imaginable, from kitchen stoves to family pets. Prescott was awakened at all times of the night by the likes of worried poultry-men with 8100 newly-hatched chicks that would perish unless quickly shipped to brooders in L.A the next day; florists who received the first post-war shipments of tulip and hyacinth bulbs from Europe and were frantic for quick delivery to buyers on the West Coast; an oil-company official calling in the middle of the night to request a noon delivery of a large heavy turbine for one of its steamers that was disabled in Galveston, TX. Prescott had a plane on the way within an hour and the turbine was delivered before noon, as needed. Soon they were flying fashion garments, Roy Roger's horse, Borden's Elsie the Cow, football teams, and every other oddity imaginable. Prescott was proving to the world that airfreight was the best way to transport anything. His airline would pick it up anywhere and get it to its destination on time, for little more than it would cost by truck. Anything, Anywhere, Anytime was catching on and quickly became the company's mantra.

These days continued, hectic and wild, and the revenue began to pour in. Unfortunately, with no real plan the money disappeared just as quickly as it was made. Prescott and his pilots were all still a bunch of flyboys, rowdy and just as irreverent as they had been in Rangoon. They lacked all financial sophistication for handling money in the amounts of which they were now dealing. It's been written that when Prescott was handed one of the company's first financial statements he nodded earnestly as if comprehending, while others noted that the paper was completely upside down.

It was Sam Mosher who finally stepped in and offered the advice that helped move the fledgling company towards a more secure financial footing.

William F. Bartling, an extremely intelligent fellow AVG pilot and investor, became assistant general manager, choosing to work behind the scenes with logistics and schedules rather than fly. Former Army Air Corps Captain, Fred Benninger, was a German-born wizard at figures and a tough-minded watchdog at different auditing posts in the military. He was recruited by Mosher to become the corporation's first treasurer. When Benninger asked to have a look at the books Prescott laughed, responding, "What books?"

Bob was a social type, laid back but always ready for a good time. He was a dreamer who would roll up his sleeves and load an aircraft when the need arose. With his innate charm, he partnered with a self-made industrial millionaire, acquired capital from fellow pilots, and hired the sharpest "bean counter" in the country. His accomplishment was similar to fellow Texan Carroll Shelby.

Fred Benninger, Executive Vice-President, Treasurer and Chairman of the Executive Committee. A graduate of the University of Southern California in accounting, Benninger joined The Flying Tiger Line shortly after its formation in 1945 and has since headed up the administrative, contract and treasury functions of the airline

photo Flying Tigers Club Archives

Bob Prescott and Bill Bartling in the office at the Lockheed Air Terminal in Burbank   *photo Flying Tigers Club Archives*

The industrialist was Sam Mosher. Sam was a young farmer in Downey, CA when the oil began to gush from the top of Signal Hill. He thought flaring the gas was wasteful, so he contracted to capture the gas, dry it by extracting the natural gasoline, and sell both; the gasoline at Signal Gasoline stations and the gas to pipelines. Signal's facility near Goleta, CA was shelled by the Japanese submarine in February 1941. After the war, Mosher saved his friend Cliff Garrett's company from a corporate raider. Signal and Garrett AiResearch became a major aerospace supplier of turbojet engines. The name changed to Allied Signal, and today it's Honeywell.

Fred Benninger, hired as the fledgling Flying Tigers' bean counter, soon became the general business manager and may have been the most important executive. He and his wife Esther became close friends of Bob and his family. Benninger kept Tigers flying until

Bob Prescott with his son Peter and Helen Ruth, Bob's first wife in the cockpit of the first Boeing 707 delivered on September 27, 1965 in Burbank   *photo author's collection*

it acquired the Transpacific Route award, and Wayne Hoffman arrived. In 1967, Kirk Kerkorian showed up with a few million dollars and made an offer Fred couldn't refuse. Together they bought Western Airlines, then MGM, and topped it all off by creating MGM Grand in Las Vegas.

Benninger was never a publicity hound, but he was inducted into the Gaming Hall of Fame, and Kerkorian, in a memoir said, "Fred made my money for me." Kerkorian's fortune topped at 16 billion dollars!

EXPANSION

In their promotional material, National Skyways soon began subtitling itself 'The Line of the Flying Tigers.' The general public was similarly unable to refrain from constantly referring to the pilots as "those Flying Tigers guys". In 1947, the name of the airline was wisely changed to The Flying Tiger Line, with the permission and good graces of General Chennault.

The Flying Tiger Line continued to grow in size and profitability; eventually it was awarded Route #100 on April 24, 1949, which stretched from coast to coast.

It was the first-ever all-cargo certificate awarded by the CAB. Prescott's dream had become a solid reality.

Unfortunately, one of the largest failures in his life came while the airline was experiencing rapid expansion. His marriage to Helen Ruth was apparently unable to stand the stress of creating this entirely new industry, and they divorced. Prescott married Dr. Anne-Marie Bennstrom in July 1962, and they remained together until his death on March 3, 1978 at the age of 64.

Wayne Hoffman had come to Tigers in 1967. He was a decorated Silver Star and Purple Heart veteran of the Normandy campaign and one of the fiercest battles of the war, in the Hurtgen Forest near Aachen, Germany. He had become a lawyer and worked for North American Car, and then became number two at New York Central Railroad. He handled the Penn Central merger. Once at the Flying Tiger Line, with the Far East route in hand and the ensuing cash flow, he formed the holding company

Bob and Anne-Marie Prescott in 1970

photo Flying Tigers Club Archives

Bob Prescott with his daughters, Kirchy, left and French during a Christmas party in 1975   *photo Flying Tigers Club Archives*

Tiger International, downplayed the flyboy image, and began acquisitions.

Over the years, the company headquarters and base of operations had been moved from Long Beach, to Mines Field (now LAX) to Lockheed Air Terminal at Burbank, and back to LAX. In 1974, the parent company, the Flying Tiger Corporation that had been formed in 1969, was renamed Tiger International. It became a corporate umbrella for other interests that senior management at the time were interested in pursuing. These ventures away from the company's core included aircraft leasing, computers, executive charters, home mortgages and an FBO. As well as the challenge of making such a diverse portfolio of interests profitable, the airline had to deal with rising fuel prices, deregulation spawning new competitors, and an army of senior management using a revolving door at Hi-Tiger to cut golden deals, with matching colored parachutes included. And then Bob Prescott died. It was the era of corporate raiders and, without its original founder around, it soon became the beginning of the end, as was the case at many other legacy carriers.

The irony of Tigers' demise is that had Hoffman pushed hard in Congress for deregulation. When it was

achieved, he sent a cadre of his young vice presidents out to get tough with customers, threatening to buy Tigers' own trucks. The major customers, freight forwarders, responded in turn by purchasing their own airplanes.

In 1978, when Prescott finally Flew West (a more poetic term that fellow airmen use to describe our final journey) he left behind his wife, Anne-Marie Prescott and two daughters, French and Kirchy from his first marriage to Helen Ruth. His only son Peter, the third child from his former marriage, was tragically killed in 1965 at age 11 when the private jet he was traveling in crashed into the mountains outside of Palm Springs during climb out killing all onboard. Prescott received the tragic news in London on the famous Pole Cat transpolar flight during this time. Those close to him would all later comment that it took a huge toll on him, both physically and emotionally, and that he never quite recovered from the loss.

WEARING DIFFERENT HATS

During his life, Prescott was a man who delighted in wearing many different hats, rubbing elbows with politicians and golfing with corporate moguls. His best-known antics are the undocumented yet infamous stories that would leak out after mixing it up with the Hollywood elite, especially while in Palm Springs. He worked tirelessly at making business connections, what we now refer to in business as networking. Almost to a fault, he rewarded himself by playing just as hard.

There is a non-descript room, almost a vault, on the ground floor of the original LAX flight training building, which is now owned by FedEx Express. To the credit of FedEx, they allow the room and the important contents within to be exclusively controlled by a group of former Flying Tiger employees that make up the board of directors for the Flying Tigers Club (formerly established as the Tiger Retirement Club). Within it are artifacts, memorabilia, pictures and other documentation of Flying Tigers' earliest years.

A recent visit by researchers found seven framed displays that apparently hung on the walls of Prescott's office, each holding a montage of pictures

Mosher and Prescott with CL-44 model

Meeting JFK in 1963 photos Flying Tigers Club Archives

Prescott captures a Tiger Girl

Prescott and Rossi carrying Hollywood star Rhonda Fleming in 1959

Prescott flies the DC-8 on March 2, 1959   photo Douglas

Reception with President Lyndon B. Johnson

April 3, 1966 - Little Chapel of the West, Las Vegas. Bob Prescott, Dick Rossi, Lydia Rossi and Mary Lynn Elliott (Lydia's sister)

photo Lydia Rossi

showing the different types of men that Bob Prescott was apparently proud of portraying. One is labeled PRESCOTT - The Military Man, showing various shots of him sharply dressed in his Navy and AVG uniforms. In turn, The Pitchman shows him with various clients and business contacts. The Sportsman shows him fishing, playing tennis, and golfing, the latter being a passion of his. The Transportation Expert displays early pictures of he and Mosher, along with aircraft, various cargo loads, and a picture of him sitting in a new 747 cockpit. The Man In Politics shows Prescott with different dignitaries, at functions with John Kennedy, and rubbing elbows with fellow Texan Lyndon B. Johnson. With too many images to display, it took two framed displays to hold all the photos of PRESCOTT - The Harem Man. They show some very heartwarming pictures of Prescott with Anne-Marie and his two daughters. And a good many of them also show Prescott, Rossi, and his Hollywood pal, Art Linkletter, in various poses with some of Hollywood's most beautiful movie actresses.

I had the very good fortune of interviewing three colleagues of Prescott's for this tribute, all who became good personal friends of his to the very end.

LYDIA ROSSI INTERVIEW

Lydia Rossi is the widow of Prescott's best friend, Dick Rossi, and probably offers the best perspective of what Prescott was like, away from the pressures of the company and out of the spotlight. Lydia, a former stewardess for Tigers, and Dick fell in love in 1964 and were married in Las Vegas on April 3, 1966, with only twelve people in attendance. Prescott flew them over in a company airplane and was the best man at their wedding. A strong friendship soon developed between the Rossis and the Prescotts.

Lydia first met Bob in his office at LAX. Before they were to marry, Dick took her to meet him and to ask Bob for permission that she should still be allowed to work for the airline even though they had a rule that all stewardesses had to quit when they got married. This was an industry-wide rule with all the airlines and there were never any exceptions. Most women kept their marriage a secret for as long as possible. Bob called up the man in charge of all stewardesses and told him to change company policy. When the man objected, citing the rule, Bob's answer was, "Well, I'm changing that – make it so."

The Rossis lived close to Bob and Anne-Marie in the Los Angeles area, and socialised with them many times throughout the years. They cruised with them to Catalina Island a couple of times on the company yacht, the Sea Tiger, attended baseball games, football games, and had dinners at their home in Beverly Hills and Palm Desert where Dick also had a home. Dick and Bob, along with others, subsequently founded a chain of

Hoffman and Prescott at Douglas Long Beach plant in June 1968
photo Air Transport World / Flying Tigers Club Archives

restaurants, The Hungry Tiger. Whenever the American Volunteer Group had a reunion, or traveled together to such destinations as Taipei, Thailand, and Spain, Lydia and Anne-Marie accompanied the group.

When the stewardesses from the 1950s began retiring and having reunions and parties in Palm Springs, they named themselves the Clipped Wings, and invited Lydia to join. Bob came to many of their parties and hosted many in his home or restaurant.

According to Lydia, Bob was always a happy person with a very outgoing personality. He drew people to him with his intelligence, wit and humor. He was also a risk taker, as when he started up the airline with no money or airplanes, only a dream, and an ability to talk others into joining him. He invested in many projects over the years, some good, some bad, but he always kept his good humor. She remembers the last AVG reunion that he was able to attend. He was in a wheelchair, very thin, hardly able to talk due to the cancer, but smiling and pouring vodka down his feeding tube, laughing as he did so.

ANN LUDWIG PETERSON INTERVIEW

The second interview that I conducted was with Ann Ludwig, a fellow Texan from Buffalo Gap, just to the southwest of Fort Worth where Prescott was raised. She was hired by the Flying Tigers soon after the airline's base was relocated to the Lockheed Air Terminal in Burbank, now called the Bob Hope Hollywood Burbank Airport.

Her aspirations were to begin a nursing career for which she had already been trained and credentialed. Affectionately referring to Prescott as "Bobby", she began her employment in the late 1940s in the accounts receivable department as Ann Peterson, her married name at the time. She worked closely with Prescott as the company was still trying to find a bottom line that was profitable. It wasn't long before she won Prescott's confidence and was asked to join him and others in management on an exploratory flight to Asia to determine the customs and passport requirements of the different countries there. The Korean War was about to erupt, and Prescott wanted to assist America in the airlift of troops and supplies in this new theatre of conflict. Little did she know how much her life would change when they returned to the United States.

She soon found herself among a handful of early stewardesses in the back of C-47s and DC-4s flying American GIs in and out of Tokyo, Japan. She left Flying Tigers in the early 1950s but remained a loyal friend of Bob's, regularly attending meetings of the Clipped Wings, the group of former stewardesses more jokingly referred to as Bob's Girls, meeting regularly with Prescott in the well-known party oasis of Palm Springs, CA.

In the mid-1970s, the debilitating effects of Prescott's fast-growing cancer presented themselves and would go unabated during his two-year battle with

Ann Ludwig Peterson at her home in Murrieta, CA - August 2018

photo Jeanne Dickson

the disease, during which time he was subjected to painful surgery and upsetting chemotherapy. When it was apparent that he was going to require assistance around the house, he turned to his old friend Annie (as he called her), who lived near him in Palm Springs. Ann, who still held her nursing credentials, was asked to stay with him and assist Mondays through Fridays at his home in the desert. The last time she spoke to him was Friday, March 3, 1978. As she said goodbye for the week, Prescott thanked her for all she had done for him. Then he looked her in the eyes and said "Annie, I won't need you to return on Monday." She scoffed saying, "Of course, I'll be here Monday morning."

He passed away that Friday night. Ann joined more than 700 people the following Tuesday to attend the afternoon services at the Encino Community Church in southern California. Bob's favorite song, Frankie and Johnny, was played for him for the very last time. Asked to describe her friend, Ann smiled with obvious admiration and a twinkle in her eyes that only comes from knowing one of the greater men of our times. With a slight drawl reemerging in her voice she said, "Well, he was just a good ol' Texan!"

GINNY DIXON INTERVIEW

Ginny Dixon in 1972

My third interview was with Virginia (Ginny) Dixon who occupied a unique vantage point as secretary and administrator of the offices of the chairman and the president of Flying Tigers from 1968 to 1986. Asked to offer her written perspective on what it was like to know and work under Bob Prescott, the following was received:

In March of 1968, I was on a temporary job in Bob Six's office at Continental Airlines across the street from the Flying Tiger Line headquarters on World Way West, when a full-time executive secretary position opened at Tigers to work for Thomas Grojean, who was the new Vice-President Finance. About a year later Wayne Hoffman's secretary left and I decided a move across the hall would open the world to me. Tom tried to accuse me of disloyalty. I asked him if he would turn down a presidency to stick with me and he backed off.

In 1967, Bob Prescott had brought in Wayne Hoffman to be the Chairman after Samuel Mosher, who was co-founder of the company, resigned saying bluntly that he did not approve of changes in policy and personnel. Fred Benninger, who had been the executive vice president and general manager from 1946, also resigned in 1967. The timing of who-did-what and when is unclear. Benninger went on to great fame and fortune with Kirk Kerkorian.

Ellen Toney, Bob Prescott's long-time executive secretary/protector, and I worked side-by-side covering for each other. Immediately I knew why Flying Tigers was such a great place to work. Bob Prescott, with his amiable ways, was the clue. The family atmosphere was obvious with company picnics, Christmas parties, bowling leagues, softball teams, etc for everyone. I participated in every activity I could along with my husband, John Dixon, who had an appreciation for the history of Tigers. John's father soloed in 1925, was in the RAF and retired from the USAF as a colonel. He had flown B-29s over the Hump into China, and Ed Pinke, Tigers' senior vice-president of flight operations, had been a young lieutenant in his outfit. Ed was an air force ferry command pilot and flew with my father-in-law who he called 'Pappy Dixon'.

My husband John's best Pinke story was when Ed flew a load of 3.5" bazookas to Japan. My father-in-law commanded combat cargo for the USAF. Normally Tigers off-loaded in Japan and the Air Force moved the cargo to Korea. This trip, the station manager met Ed at the ramp and told him, "Ed, grab a cup of coffee, you've got to take this load to Korea." Our troops were desperate because the 2.5" WWII bazooka wouldn't stop the Russian T-34 tank. Ed Pinke was a spit-and-polish veteran pilot who was extremely valuable to the company's flight operations during his tenure. This incident tells of Tigers' part in preventing the North Koreans from pushing us into the sea at Pusan.

Monday mornings were exceptionally exciting in our offices since you never knew where Bob had been over the weekend and who he had promised favors; free rides to somewhere, employment, shipments, and so on. Because of his good nature, he had trouble saying no to people so sometimes it needed to be said by Ellen or me. We loved our second floor Lo-Tiger offices. They were very handy, comfortable, workable and looked out to the hangar. But in 1971 ground was broken to build a new ten-story building and the four of us were to occupy the entire tenth floor.

Construction on the Hi-Tiger, as it was dubbed, is a story in itself. Sheldon Appel, a Prescott friend, was the contractor/designer, and Frank Toney, Ellen's husband, was the superintendent. My husband John came by for lunch one day and I showed him the plans. He noted that the building had uniform square windows.

Joe Healy, Wayne Hoffman and Bob Prescott in Prescott's tenth floor office in the Hi Tiger headquarters   photo Flying Tigers Club Archives

He was shocked that the executive offices on the 10th floor had no provision to take advantage of the view. The building was already in the skeletal stage and Frank took us to the top on the construction elevator. He proudly described their construction methods. The concrete had already been poured.

Back in the office, John and I questioned Wayne and Bob as to why the 10th floor would have the same peek-a-boo windows as the first-floor mailroom. That lit a fire! They got busy redesigning the 10th floor with floor-to-ceiling glass on the half of the building that faced northwest and northeast, along with an open balcony. Bob was going to occupy the northwest corner and Wayne the northeast corner.

Sheldon was angry that they were disrupting his uniform design. Frank was upset that he had to jackhammer pre-poured concrete and it disrupted his schedule. The change orders were costly.

Shortly after this eruption, John and I attended the opening of the new office/penthouse on Sunset Boulevard of our board member, prominent architect

Charles Luckman. His new complex was spectacular. Bob whispered, "Wait until you see ours!"

Well, when I saw my office design I stepped into the fight! Wayne had hired his home interior decorator, Maurice Martiné, to handle the décor, lay-out and furnishings. He had my office set-up with a magnificent but impractical desk, boudoir lighting, a plug for a coffee pot, no file cabinets, no copy machine. He wanted all the ugly necessities of an office on a different floor. His décor was paramount! I pointed out to Bob and Wayne that we needed office-specific items such as practical lighting above our desks, file cabinets, etc, and that along with the fancy bar they probably would want to serve some meals and have special events which would be impossible with a plug-in hot plate. After hassles with the health inspectors over a minimum service area, we ended up with a commercial kitchen and an on-call chef. As a result, we were able to host many staff and board meeting lunches, dinners, and other special events that impressed customers, government officials and investors. The tenth floor was impressive and beautiful to look at, but it was not as functional as our offices in Lo-Tiger.

After Ellen Toney retired, her office was occupied by many different people which is another story. However, I was there to help the short-timers and Bob and his family when needed.

By the time Bob Prescott was found to have cancer, Wayne Hoffman was spending more and more time at his Tiger International office in Century City and I was given more responsibilities at the airline offices, including special projects such as designing and staffing the Peter Prescott Scholarship Program for Tiger employees' children. I managed the campaign for the Vietnam War Memorial and was rewarded with a trip to Washington and a meeting with Tip O'Neill, Barry Goldwater and other government officials. I served on the board of the Aero Club of Southern California and set up their scholarship program. I was also on the boards of United Way, the Great Western Council of the Boy Scouts of America, and headed the charitable and political contribution committee for Tiger International

The race is almost run. Bob Prescott sitting with AVG pilot, Robert C. Moss at the Ojai Valley Inn, California, in Spring 1978

photo Flying Tigers Club Archives

and Flying Tiger Line. A perk of the Aero Club was trips to Prague, Istanbul, and Toulouse, France as guests of their national FAI clubs. Another part of my job was representing Tigers at many Beverly Hills banquets.

Bob Prescott and Wayne Hoffman were quite the opposites as executives, a true odd couple. Bob was a very laid back and casual Texan, while Wayne was a prim and proper Easterner. However, the two men were fond of each other and interestingly, their traits complimented each other. Bob was a Democrat who was able to visit LBJ's ranch and secured our Transpacific route award, Flying Tigers' cash cow, from his fellow Texan, President Johnson. When Nixon was elected and tried to cancel what LBJ had given, Wayne, as a New York Republican,

was able to save the day with his political connections. The effort got Hoffman appointed to Nixon's Finance Committee and I got a direct line to the president!

It was devastating to all of us when Bob became ill to the point he could no longer come to work in the office. Even when he was already eating through a tube, he would come to the office at noontime and sit with Wayne and eat his liquid lunch. John and I last saw him at his desert home shortly before he passed away.

Following an elaborate public memorial service in a packed church in Encino, where John and I sat between Jimmy Doolittle and Bob Hope, his ashes were scattered at sea. It was a private ceremony aboard the Sea Tiger skippered by Al Cormier, Bob's long-time, "take no prisoners" fixer. We were buzzed by a low-flying P-40 flown by famed stunt pilot Frank Tallman, a friend of Bob's. Tallman lost his life the following month when, in bad weather, he flew into a peak in the Santa Ana Mountains.

My choice to turn down a job for the president of a glamorous airline (Continental) was because John knew that Flying Tiger Line was more than just a cargo carrier. He had spent 36 hours on a Tigers' C-54 flying to the war in Korea. Little did we realize that Robert W. Prescott would change our lives and fulfill our dreams of travel. It was his manner that brought international celebrities and common folk of exceptional talent to Tigers, and we were able to work with, socialise and travel the world with many of them. The list includes two presidents of the United States, senators, congressmen, generals, movie stars, a knight of Monaco, war heroes, and many simply good people.

CONCLUSION

There have been many posthumously dedications to the memory of Robert W. Prescott since he flew west. The 10-storey building at LAX, the final location of the airline's headquarters and informally known as Hi-Tiger, was named after him. His name was written on the side of the airline's first Boeing 747 cargo aircraft, as well as a fully restored P-40 Warhawk purchased in his honour and currently on display at the Pearl Harbor Aviation Museum in Honolulu. Two museums have exhibits dedicated to both the man and his airline, the Flight Path Museum and Learning Center on the south side of Los Angeles International Airport, and the Palm Springs Air Museum. Probably the most significant dedication can be found by the existence of two associations with hundreds of members carrying on the Flying Tiger Line legacy even after all of these years.

The Flying Tiger Line Pilots Association is a group that consists of pilots and other Tigers employees, dedicated to preserving the legacy of the great airline as well as to those who served in China and World War 2. An average of 300 members and their guests gather each year for a reunion. Not surprisingly, the Flying Tiger

Line Pilots Association (FTLPA) was formed by Prescott's old buddy, Dick Rossi, when he retired as a senior Boeing 747 captain in 1974. Since then, there have been forty-four consecutive annual reunions. The association's logo is a reprint of the prominent cover of Tiger Spirit, April 1978, which pays visual tribute to Prescott, the P-40, the Budd, and the 747.

Another group of former Tiger employees, the Flying Tigers Club (formerly the Tiger Retirement Club), meets regularly at LAX for the same purpose – to celebrate the good fortune of working for such a great company. The home page of their website reminds us all that being an employee for the Flying Tiger Line was so much more than a job; it was a place we went to every day and worked hard, played hard, and made lifetime friendships.

Shortly before he died, Prescott said, "It is difficult for me to express the pride I feel at what has happened to a struggling idea I had so many years ago." As explained in the special February/March 1978 edition of Tiger Review, there is really no way to accurately pay tribute to the man his friends and colleagues knew; the living, giving, one-of-a-kind human being with an obsession for life, relentless drive, inexhaustible optimism, side-splitting sense of humor and genuine love for his fellow man and woman. During his eulogy, Wayne Hoffman, CEO of Tiger International, explained that Prescott never once uttered the words, "Why me?" while going through his battle with cancer. To the contrary, Hoffman said that his final words were "The world does not owe me a thing. I had my allotted time, and I made the most of it."

My life was charted in a significant direction that day in 1978 when I became a Tiger. I would join most of my colleagues at Flying Tigers in disagreeing with Prescott's final sentiment. Our world, the one that the Tiger family knows, does owe him a tremendous amount of gratitude. I will always be in awe of the man that I never got the opportunity to look in the eye, shake hands, and thank personally. For the Tiger Spirit that he magically instilled in all of us lucky enough to call ourselves Tigers, Robert W. Prescott will always be alive.

2

Bob Prescott And Hollywood

Captain John F. Dickson, President, Flying Tiger Line Pilots Association

Bob Prescott had attended college in Southern California before entering the Navy. He was well aware of the hold Hollywood had on the American public. When he founded National Skyway Freight Corporation, and throughout his life-long position as the president of The Flying Tiger Line, Bob Prescott had a special regard for and developed special relationships with those involved in the Hollywood film industry.

In June of 1945, with a sense of showmanship and intent to hit the deck running, he chose the luxurious Biltmore Hotel in Los Angeles as the fledgling airline's first employment office. (On the practical side, flight operations were set up at the Long Beach Municipal Airport.) The hotel had served as a military rest and recreation facility during World War II, with the entire second floor set up with cots for military personnel on leave.

At that time, downtown Los Angeles was a bustling American city and the hotel had been an early venue for the Oscar awards' ceremonies at the Biltmore Bowl, the hotel's auditorium. The Academy of Motion Pictures Arts and Sciences was created in its Crystal Ballroom in 1927. From 1945 to 1949, in a post-war boom for the film industry, Hollywood had experienced the most stable and lucrative years in its history. In 1946, when two-thirds of the American population went to the movies at least once a week and the studios earned record-breaking profits, Bob Prescott was busy creating a whole new industry of his own – airfreight.

During the war there were many films made about American air power used to defeat Germany and Japan. One in particular, Flying Tigers starring John Wayne, dramatized the exploits of the famed American Volunteer Group (AVG, the official name of the Flying Tigers) of which Prescott and his fellow pilot/investors were a part.

Flying Tigers movie poster   *Republic Pictures*

The country welcomed the returning flyboys, as they were called then, with open arms as true American heroes. The pilots of National Skyway Freight were constantly referred to as "those Flying Tiger guys" so in 1947 Prescott changed the name of the company to The Flying Tiger Line to take advantage of their fame and to set them apart from the many other GI start-ups. Although always the modest soft-spoken boy from Texas, Prescott sensed the value of this goodwill directed towards him and his fellow AVG buddies. He used this to advantage when schmoozing with the Hollywood elite – networking, as we call it today – in its purest form.

Prescott's affinity for the Hollywood elite was affirmed by the many beautiful movie actresses and actors he was photographed with. There are many archived public relations prints of Prescott and various celebrities such as Bob Burns (the "Arkansas Traveler"

Camille Joseph Rosbert with Marilyn Maxwell at Long Beach in 1946
photo Flying Tigers Club Archives

Bob Burns and Helen Ruth Prescott

photo Jack Birns / Flying Tigers Club Archives

Bob Hope in 1946 promoting his Capitol Records album 'I Never Left Home' with four women on the tarmac in front of a Flying Tigers C-47 cargo aircraft. Hope was on a promotional tour for Capitol Records
photo Flying Tiger Line Pilots Association Archives

Bob Prescott helps the star pass out pledge cards to (left to right) John Stowell, looking over Prescott's shoulder; "Rod" Rodriguez; Manny Bernal; Frank Simpkins; John Kuncewitch; Harley Chambers and Tony Kovacs, looking over Miss Jayne Mansfield's shoulder. Burbank Tigers spearhead their area Chest drive for 1960

photo The 6 Watson Bros / Flying Tigers Club Archives

who played an instrument that he called the "Bazooka" which is where the military rocket launcher got its name), Marilyn Maxwell, Jayne Mansfield, Susan Hayward, Bob Hope and Art Linkletter, to name a few. Over the ensuing years many were invited as special guests to annual reunions for the AVG. Bob's second wife, Anne-Marie Bennstrom (1930-2018), was a Swedish health guru to the stars with one of her spas, the Sanctuary on Hollywood Boulevard, across from Grauman's Chinese Theatre. Howard Hughes mixed Hollywood and aviation, and Bob took note.

As the airline was gaining success and notoriety, Palm Springs had become Hollywood's desert playground for celebrities to relax and escape from the hustle and bustle of showbiz. The legendary 'two-hour rule' of Hollywood studios put Palm Springs on the map as a perfect getaway. Actors under contract had to be within two hours of the studio in case they were needed for last minute filming or photo shoots. Famous celebrities eventually built hideaway Palm Springs homes and golf courses, and called the desert home.

Much of America's business is conducted on the golf course and in the 19th hole (to be clear, a golf course only has 18 holes; the 19th is the clubhouse). Prescott wasted no time remaining in close proximity to the friendships and contacts that he had developed by purchasing a home and opening a branch of his Hungry Tiger restaurant chain in Palm Springs.

Of the many relationships that developed over the years, one celebrity in particular became a close friend. Radio and television personality Art Linkletter can be seen in many photos and early movies with Bob. Linkletter remained a close friend and confidant to the very end and was one of many who attended his memorial services in 1978. The church was packed with Hollywood, military, and business celebrities, including Bob Hope, Jimmy Doolittle and the heads of every major aerospace company. The packed church was a testament to how highly respected and loved Bob Prescott had become.

Susan Hayward supporting a Korean Gift Lift flight

photo Flying Tigers Club Archives

3

A Story Of A Redhead

Captain George Gewehr, Historian, Flying Tiger Line Pilots Association

"I'm running out of gas," she told her husband over the radio. She and her husband were operators of a freight service in Long Beach, California. Her name was Dianna Cyrus Bixby. She was born in Ventura County, California on September 30, 1922 and was killed off the coast of Baja California, Mexico on January 2, 1955.

Loreto was her destination, but the visibility was poor so she was circling out over the Gulf of California in a twin-engined Douglas A-20 Havoc bomber converted into a corporate transport. Navy divers recovered her body a day after the crash. Why is Dianna Bixby being mentioned in a book about the Flying Tiger Line? because she was closely connected to the Flying Tiger Line at one time. You might say she was the first redheaded woman pilot to work for Flying Tigers.

Dianna Bixby was five feet two inches tall and weighed 110 pounds with blue eyes. She was a fast walker, typical of her boundless energy, as was the big friendly smile she flashed at familiar faces. Born in Santa Paula California, she was the mother of two children, four-year-old daughter Lillian and year-old son Bobby. Dianna came from a line of pioneers, descended from a blue-blooded family which came to America in the 17th century, settling in New England. Her grandmother, Mary (Parker) Converse was the only woman who ever received full papers as a captain in the merchant marine. Mary's father in-law and Dianna's great grandfather Elisha S. Converse founded Boston Rubber Shoe Company, later named the U.S. Rubber Company, famous for making Converse shoes, a rock n roll fashion staple and acquired by Nike in 2003.

Aviation intrigued Dianna as a little girl and Amelia Earhart set her to dreaming. Her family didn't encourage her flying so she wasn't able to pursue her dream. She later married a man named John Cyrus, an Army Air Force pilot during World War II. She learned to fly while traveling with him to air bases. In 1945 he was

shot down in the Battle of the Bulge, also called Battle of the Ardennes (Belgium) and was killed. She kept flying, landing a job with Eagle Air Freight in California and flew east as far as Texas and Oklahoma. There she met Bob Bixby, a 10,000-hour war time Air Transport Pilot who was also flying freight. In 1948 they were married and when Eagle discontinued flying operations, Bob and Dianna acquired two C-47s which they used for charter operations. By 1949 Dianna had logged 3,000 hours.

Dianna Bixby flew the New-York Boston route in a C-47 for the Flying Tiger Line in 1949   photo Flying Tigers Club Archives

During this time, she and her husband came to the Flying Tigers with an interesting proposition. "You need the air lift and Dianna wants to fly the airplane". The company came to an agreement. Flying Tigers would lease the C-47s for three months and Dianna could fly

Diana Bixby preparing for the round the world flight

photo Coy Watson / Flying Tigers Club Archives

one of them with the stipulation she had to have a Tiger as her copilot. The company chose Dick Stratford since he was a copilot at the time. Dianna flew for the three months and then she went back to the west coast. She had been flying the busy Boston - Newark segment of Tiger's route system. You could say Dianna was the first female airline captain flying on any Part 121 airline operation, not unlike her merchant marine grandmother. At the end of the three months Dianna left Tigers but she came back later on with another quest.

This time it was an attempt to fly around the world with her husband. The airplane she chose was a de Havilland DH.98 Mosquito, a British twin-engine shoulder-winged multi-role combat aircraft constructed almost entirely of wood. It was a fast airplane and widely used by the Royal Air-Force during the Second World War.

Dianna's Mosquito was white and maroon with Tiger teeth, with her name and Flying Tigers titles. The company provided all of the maintenance and support for the around-world record attempt, starting at San Francisco at 10:30 local time on April 1 1950. Mrs and Mr Bixby made it as far as Karachi but engine trouble caused the flight to be terminated.

Diana Bixby and her Mosquito named Miss Flying Tiger

photo Coy Watson / Flying Tigers Club Archives

two others had done before: a record-breaking solo flight around the world. The first man to do it was Wiley Post in 1937 with a Lockheed Vega aircraft, the Winnie Mae, followed by Bill Odum in 1947 who had set a record of 73 hours and five minutes. The only other woman to try it back then was Amelia Earhart, but she was lost in the Pacific in 1937.

On April 16, 1954, the modified Mosquito, B 25 now named Miss Flying Tiger, roared out of San Francisco on the way to Newark. Somewhere along her route, she ran into bad weather and technical problems which caused her to abandon the whole effort. Before she lost her life in the A-20, she did some racing cross country in a B-26, plus she also flew for the Hollywood studio's on occasion. Who knows what else she would have achieved as an early female aviation pioneer if she had lived longer?

After this attempt Dianna wasn't seen for a while. She probably kept in touch with Tigers because she returned in 1954. Dianna got wind Tigers had the Mosquito back in their hangar, so she went to Burbank to investigate. As she walked into the hangar, she spotted it under the wing of a C-54. She went to Bob Prescott's office. "I see you've got the Mosquito". Prescott smiled and waited for her to continue. "I'd like to try it again, this time solo." Prescott looked at her a moment. "Sure, why not?"

So it was, 31 year old Dianna Bixby, 110 pounds of five feet two with eyes of blue tried to do what only

---

Flight Plan for Bixby Round-the-World-Flight

Pilot — Dianna C. Bixby, 2195 E. Spring St., Long Beach, Calif.

Aircraft — British DeHavilland Mosquito, twin engine. Identification Number—N1203V.

Colors — White trimmed with red and blue. Nose and wing-tank bear shark's mouths.

Ship named "Miss Flying Tiger."

Engines — Two Packard-Merlin V-type liquid-cooled. Type — V 1650-9. Horsepower — 1600 each.

Range — 4,000 miles. **Fuel capicity** — 1,325 gallons.

FLIGHT SCHEDULE

City	Miles	Flying Time at 385 MPH	Greenwich Mt. Time	Local Time	Take off or Landing
San Francisco	0	0:00 hrs.	1500 hrs.	0700 hrs.	Time off
Newark	2532	6:35	2135	1635	Landing
			2235	1735	Take-off
Paris	3642	9:25	0800	0800	Landing
			0900	0900	Take off
Basra	3000	7:15	1615	1915	Landing
			1715	2015	Take off
Karachi	1250	3:15	2030	0230	Landing
			2130	0330	Take off
Calcutta	1361	3:35	0105	0705	Landing
			0205	0805	Take off
Tokyo	3204	8:20	1025	1925	Landing
			1125	2025	Take off
Midway Island ..	2532	6:35	1800	0700	Landing
			1900	0800	Take off
San Francisco	3204	8:20	0320	1920	Landing
Totals	20,525	60:20 Hrs.			

Flight schedule follows route officially approved by the National Aeronautics Association and flight will be timed by the NAA.

Flight Plan for Bixby Round-the-World Flight

photo Flying Tigers Club Archives

A sister ship of the ill-fated N90433 is prepared for flight

photo Don Downie Star News Pasadena / Flying Tigers Club Archives

4

The Tigers And The Sharks

Edward Peary Stafford

"IN THE EMPTY NIGHT SKY ABOVE A VACANT SEA, THE FLYING TIGER CREW BEGAN A BATTLE FOR THEIR LIVES."

From the surface of the empty sea, the plane would have looked like a slow-moving star. Then as it crossed the sky, an observer could have seen the shifting red and green flashes of its running lights and could have heard the high hum of its engines.

It was September 24, 1955. A Flying Tigers DC-4 airliner was on a routine transpacific flight with a crew of five and a cargo of jet engines destined for Tokyo. But man's incredible conquest of time and distance still hangs on the twin threads of mechanical reliability and human skill, and no flight across an ocean is ever really routine.

Yet aboard the DC-4 it certainly seemed that way. In the cockpit, Captain Tony Machado monitored the rows of red-lighted gauges from his usual left seat. To his right, First Officer Warren Gin made minor adjustments on the auto-pilot knobs to keep the plane on course at its assigned 8,000-foot altitude.

Behind the two pilots were navigator Dominic Ventresca and radio man Richard Olsen. Ventresca kept the plane's position pinpointed, giving the pilots heading changes as necessary to keep the plane on the flight planned course from Honolulu to Wake Island, about 2600 statute miles to the west. Machado knew exactly where he was. The flight was 1,000 nautical miles west of Oahu, with Wake Island, their immediate destination, 1,000 nautical miles to the west. Midway Island was some 600 miles to the north and Johnston Island 500 miles southeast.

Machado had started his rest period an hour after take-off, when the flight was well underway and all was going well. He had slept for five hours while First Officer Warren Gin took command and the young co-pilot, Bob Hightower, rode the right seat. Machado had

been back on the job for just ten minutes and, with the help of black coffee, was returning to full alertness. Gin had moved to the right seat, replacing Hightower, when one of the threads on which man's mastery of the elements depends began to fray.

Near the center of the instrument panel, a needle on the left-hand gauge of a group of four wavered uncertainly and then fell until it rested against a tiny peg labelled "zero". Number one engine had lost fuel pressure! The silent flicker and fall of that one slim needle was like the clang of an alarm bell in the minds of Machado and Gin. They saw it instantly and reacted instantly. All the crew felt the DC-4 swerve slightly to the left as the left outboard engine stopped and its windmilling prop dragged against the airstream. Almost imperceptibly at first the plane began to lose altitude as a quarter of its horsepower was lost.

DC-4 cockpit similar to N90433   *author's collection*

Captain Machado immediately rammed the throttles forward on the other three engines while Gin snapped off the auto-pilot and took the control wheel in his hands and the rudder pedals under his feet. The plane levelled off and Machado went to work to find and correct the trouble. Ventresca automatically rechecked the flight's position while Hightower and Olsen crowded anxiously into the cockpit. So it was that, in the empty night sky above a vacant sea, the Flying Tiger crew began a battle for their lives.

A minute after the number one engine failed, the number three engine coughed and stopped. Now, two of the four red fuel pressure gauge needles had collapsed to zero. Olsen sat down at the radio position and began to click his key. His SOS crackled over the hemisphere of water: dit dit dit, dah, dah, dah, dit, dit, dit. He knew, at least he hoped, that dozens of receivers on sea, land and air would hear his distress call. After sending an SOS twice he proceeded with the message: "Flying Tiger November 90433 is going down. Standby for lat-longs", he clicked. Ventresca then handed him a position report form and said, "This is my best guess, should be fairly close." Olsen went back to work with the morse code key. "Flying Tiger 433 position is 21 degrees, 21 minutes North; 176 degrees West, losing altitude, unable to return to HNL."

280 miles from where Tony Machado's men fought to stay out of the patient Pacific, the steamship Steel Advocate rolled and lifted in gentle swells, bound for Honolulu on the next-to-last leg of a round the-world voyage. There had been a shift change; the men on the new watch had just settled down to their duties when the radio speaker guarding aircraft distress frequencies began a staccato chirping. The radioman clapped on his earphones, fine-tuned his receiver, and began to tap the keys of his typewriter. He listened for a minute and when the message was over he pulled the paper from its roller and ran along the boat deck to the bridge. He handed the message to Dick Rausch, navigator and chief officer of the watch.

It was Olsen's Mayday. The message said that Flying Tiger Flight 433, now with three dead engines, was losing altitude rapidly and preparing to ditch. The aircraft's position followed. Rausch plotted it quickly and found that it lay 280 miles to the south of the Steel Advocate's location. Rauch called the captain, and seconds later, the merchantman's high bow swung southward and her deck began to tremble as the Advocate's two huge steam-turbine engines went to full power. They would be at full power for the next 14 hours pushing the huge 492-foot ship at nearly 20 knots. Help was on the way and Tony Machado needed it!

Jesus, the ships cook, had just finished feeding the oncoming watch and hungry off duty crewmembers were arriving in his galley. He was near the door to the pantry when he noticed unusual vibrations and he felt himself being pushed against a bulkhead as if the ship were listing to port, or as if the ship was making a big course change. Big course changes in the middle of the ocean are very unusual, he thought. Vibrations in the deck plates became intense and he could feel a buzz in his feet that he'd never experienced. What is going on, he wondered? His question was soon answered when the captain's voice came over the speaker. "Men, we have just received a distress message from an aircraft that has gone down 280 miles south of us. We are the closest surface vessel so I've directed a course change and we are proceeding at full speed. We can be at the scene of the ditching in about 10 or 11 hours. I'm asking that every crew member get as much rest as possible because when we arrive at the scene we will need every available crewmember to be at the rails scanning the sea for survivors." The race was on!

Aboard the faltering DC-4, all five men were desperately busy. Machado and Gin tried various positions of fuel selector valves, cross-feeds, and boost pumps, attempting again and again to restart the dead engines. Only number four was still operating. One engine cannot maintain an empty plane in level flight so Machado's DC-4, heavily loaded with cargo and fuel, was doomed. Hightower, in the jump seat between the two pilots, worked frantically with them to locate and remedy the trouble.

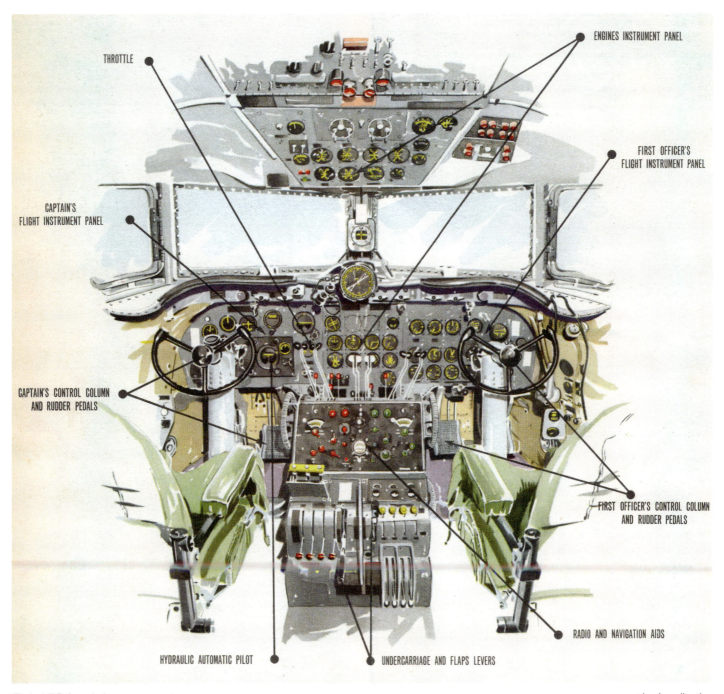

ENGINES INSTRUMENT PANEL

THROTTLE

FIRST OFFICER'S
FLIGHT INSTRUMENT PANEL

CAPTAIN'S
FLIGHT INSTRUMENT PANEL

CAPTAIN'S CONTROL COLUMN
AND RUDDER PEDALS

FIRST OFFICER'S CONTROL COLUMN
AND RUDDER PEDALS

RADIO AND NAVIGATION AIDS

HYDRAULIC AUTOMATIC PILOT

UNDERCARRIAGE AND FLAPS LEVERS

Typical DC-4 cockpit arrangement

author's collection

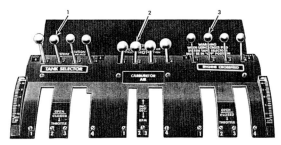

FORWARD PEDESTAL — SIX WING TANK FUEL SYSTEM

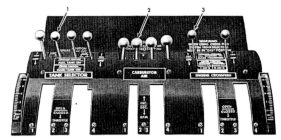

FORWARD PEDESTAL — EIGHT WING TANK FUEL SYSTEM

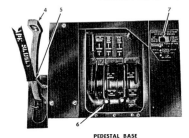

1. FUEL TANK SELECTOR LEVERS (MAIN FOR SIX-TANK, MAIN AND AUX FOR EIGHT TANK)

2. CARBURETOR AIR LEVERS

3. CROSS FEED SELECTOR LEVERS

4. GUST LOCK HANDLE

5. GUST LOCK PIN

6. AUXILIARY FUEL TANK SELECTOR LEVERS (SIX-TANK)

7. HYDRAULIC SYSTEM BYPASS VALVE HANDLE

PEDESTAL BASE

The fuel system controls are located forward of the pedestal. After the failure of engine number one, the crew placed the numbers two and three fuel selectors to the near-empty auxiliary tanks. The numbers two and three engines then also stopped.

USAF C-54 manual / author's collection

Olsen clacked steadily away on his key while, back in the cargo compartment, Ventresca struggled to get the lashings off heavy wooden boxes so that he could jettison them to lighten the ship. All the while the altimeter implacably unwound and the dark face of the sea loomed closer.

At 6,000 feet, Machado punched the red feathering buttons for number one, two and three engines, The big propellers twisted their blades to the feathered position and were now slicing knife-edge through the airstream. The windmilling engines stopped turning, reducing drag and slowing the descent dramatically. The plunging descent was now 500 feet a minute instead of nearly 800, but still the descent continued.

Gin attempted to hold the plane's direction straight and at optimum speed but it wasn't possible. With only the right-outboard engine producing power, the plane was turning to the left. The unwanted turn was somewhat more than expected because Machado, in an attempt to buy time, had pushed the number four throttle forward to what is called "firewall power". This is beyond maximum power and, at this setting, all the engine's gauges were indicating above the red-line markings so the engine could not last long; perhaps only a few minutes. Machado unfeathered each dead engine in turn, and attempted a restart. At 3,000 feet, he ordered his crew to put on their life jackets and took over the controls. Gin wiggled into his jacket but Machado concentrated on keeping the airplane steady and, attempting more restarts, was unable to find his.

At 1,000 feet, he ordered the crew to prepare for ditching. Olsen then tapped out a final SOS and clamped down his Morse code key. A single long dash was now being heard by anxious radiomen aboard dozens of ships and shore stations across the vast Central and Western Pacific. The listening radiomen knew that the signal would soon end so they quickly jotted bearing information from their RDF (radio direction finder) receivers. This frenetic activity was being done aboard many ships and shore stations from Hawaii to Japan. The hurriedly prepared estimated position provided by Machado's crew may have been inaccurate so direction finding bearings could become important. Bearings from three or more receiving stations could be combined and "triangulated."

After Olsen was satisfied that he had done all he could, he sat down on the deck behind Gin and braced himself for impact while in dozens of ship and shore radio rooms, radiomen waited in silence. They didn't have long to wait. Suddenly there was silence. The tone ended. Tiger N90433 was down! The radioman aboard the Advocate removed his headset, wiped sweat from his forehead and wrote in his log: "Flying Tiger flight 433 believed to be down at time 0646."

Ventresca had given up his struggle with the cargo and had wedged himself against a bulkhead as far aft as he could. Hightower left the jump seat and took the radio operator's position that Olsen had just left and swung the seat around to face the tail. They waited for the inevitable.

The two pilots in the front seats tightened their seat belts and braced their feet on the rudder pedals. At 500 feet, they could make out the pattern of sea swells on the dimly moonlit sea. Machado took over the controls and banked left to parallel them. In a last-minute, nothing-to lose effort, Gin unfeathered number three engine and was working throttle and mixture control for a restart when the DC-4, nose high, its single good engine screaming at absolute maximum power, ripped into the Pacific.

There was a banging jolt and a pause. Just as the first flicker of optimism that wanted to say, that wasn't so bad and I'm still alive, came the final, sickening, slamming impact. After the strained howling of number four engine, the wind noise and the shouted commands, there was utter silence and darkness. Almost immediately they were waist deep in water. The impact had breached the fuselage and it was flooding fast.

Cold sea water around his lower body brought Machado back to consciousness. His head ached and he could feel a welt across his forehead where he had

The ill-fated Douglas C-54A N90433 at Manchester Ringway on May 29 1955 four months before the accident   *photo RuthAS*

slammed into the instrument panel. To his right, he could hear and dimly see Gin grunting and struggling, and he realized that the cargo, loosened by Ventresca in his attempt to jettison it, had slammed forward on impact, trapping Gin and Hightower under heavy crates.

Reaching down into the rising water, Machado released his seat belt and bent down out of his seat to help Gin. By tugging alternately at the man and the crates, he was able to get him loose and then, working together, the two men freed Hightower. The doorway to the cargo compartment, where Ventresca was, was a broken, impassable, jumble of wooden crates. Olsen had released the plastic astrodome in the plane's top, and one by one the four men, in the nose section, crawled out. Gin and Hightower could feel the cool aluminium of the fuselage on their bare feet, having lost their shoes and socks in the struggle with the crates.

It was like riding the back of a dying whale. In the moonlight, the empty sea stretched all around them and a slow swell sloshed over the horizontal stabilizer and onto the wings. Machado carefully made his way back along the top of the fuselage until he was above the cargo door. He laid on his belly and reached down but the door handle was out of reach. He banged on the top of the door with his fist and yelled. "Ventresca! Hey, Dom! Dom! Open the door and get out fast! She's sinking!"

From beneath the shiny aluminium, they could hear Ventresca's voice. He sounded calmer and steadier than any of them were. "I can't see, Tony. Which way do I go?" "Here, Dom, here!" Machado was still hammering with his clenched fist when the DC-4 slipped from beneath them, Ventresca still aboard, and was gone. Four men were now alone in the sea.

And yet, in a way, they were not alone. A score of ships' bows had turned toward them and high in the air, from where they had just fallen, the noses of a half-dozen planes turned toward their position. The air above them, although they could not hear it, buzzed and crackled with search and rescue orders. The long, electronic fingers of radar groped for them through the darkness.

The human beings closest to the Flying Tiger crew were the men aboard the Steel Advocate. All that night she closed on the Tiger crew's position at the rate of one mile every three minutes, men on watch aboard the ship discussed the chances of rescue, and they wondered if the steam turbines, running at full power, could endure.

The word quickly spread from a mate, with some knowledge of aviation, that the chances of a successful night ditching with only one of the four engines turning, were not good. There would probably not have been enough time to launch life rafts. Even if they survived the impact, searchers would probably only have five tiny, dark heads to search for across the immensity of the ocean. Despite the pessimism, there was determination. All sailors live with the spectre of disaster at sea and they can readily put themselves in the places of the shipwrecked and desperate.

At dawn, the Steel Advocate's blunt bow, plunging through the sea at full speed, was still over a hundred miles away, but now, with daylight, the air search had a chance. Before dawn, from Midway Island, Johnston Island, Oahu and Wake Island, Navy, Air Force, and Coast Guard planes took-off and were converging on the crash position.

All things considered, it was not such a bad night for the men in the water. After the shock of the crash began to wear off, a kind of instinctive, blood-deep delight in their survival dulled even their sorrow at the loss of Ventresca. Through the long night hours they bobbed and couched in a circle, facing each other at arm's length, laughing and joking at the ridiculousness of their situation. All were experienced airmen and all knew the magnitude of the effort that was being made to find them. The tropic sea, once they were used to it, was warm and not rough, and the air was clear and visibility good in the moonlight. Not once did any the four doubt that rescue would come with daylight.

Tony Machado had reason to be more anxious than the others. He had no life jacket. All through the night he treaded water, taking care to use just enough energy to keep his head out, and no more – but even working as easily as possible, there were times when he had to rest, wrapping arms and legs around one or

another of the other men whose jacket would support them both. Fortunately, Machado was only 40 years old and was in robust physical condition.

As the eastern sky began to lighten, and the four tiny human faces peered up hopefully out of that vast waste of water, it seemed that the faith in the search and rescue net which had kept up their spirits during the night would be justified. Over the rustle of the wavelets lapping around them, they heard the familiar and unmistakable hum of an aircraft's engines. The sound grew louder then faded, built again, and faded again as the plane flew a standard search pattern. The wind broke and twisted the mutter of the exhaust sounds and the sounds of the spinning propellers.

They didn't see the first plane but the second, some thirty minutes later, with the sun just breaking the horizon, was clearly visible. It was flying at about 1,500 feet and was obviously on a search mission. But it flew steadily on until it disappeared in the west, passing perhaps two miles north of the swimming men. The four survivors waved and splashed and could not help shouting but then the sound of the engines died out and then there was only the slapping of the waves and the breathy whisper of the sea breeze. Machado, Gin, Olsen and Hightower told each other there would be plenty of others and one would certainly see them before too long, they were sure of it.

Then, in a single, heartbreaking moment, it became desperately urgent that they be right. Cruising 50 feet or so away and just below the surface, a group of sharks spotted the poor distressed airmen that would be their prey. To the sharks the men showed up nicely against the sky. A ten-foot blue shark sighted the flash of bare, white feet, then eight dangling, waving human legs. The beast heard the splashing of the men and planed upward to investigate.

The dorsal fin broke the surface perhaps 20 feet from the little knot of men. Warren Gin, who couldn't swim a stroke, saw it first and shouted a warning. The four airmen twisted to face the new danger, feeling their mouths go dry and their heartbeats increase as the shark circled. Frantically, they tried to remember all they had ever learned about sharks. Machado said that splashing and shouting would frighten them off, but Gin had heard that they attacked anything wounded or in distress, and wouldn't splashing be a sign of distress?

The shark seemed to be in no hurry. Patiently, curiously it circled, sometimes so close they could almost touch him, sometimes farther out. Now the men's attention was divided between the circling beast and the sky which could hold deliverance.

At mid-morning, a dark-blue navy Lockheed P2V Neptune patrol plane swept overhead, so low that they could read the Navy markings on its wings and tail, but it continued unswervingly on course, and a few minutes later two more fins joined the patient circler. The crew began to pray.

The sharks edged in closer and began to snap at their feet and legs as the planes continued to fly by, unseeing. Hope began to fade.

It was no fault of the rescuers in the air that day that they came so close but never saw the Flying Tiger crew in the vastness of the shifting, wind ruffled, sun-flecked sea over which they were flying. At some three miles every minute, the four dark heads, only inches across, were so tiny that a scanner could miss them if he blinked or sneezed or turned aside for a one second gulp of coffee.

In mid-afternoon, with Gin and Olsen already bleeding in several places from shark bites and from the tearing, sandpaper-like skin of the sharks' hides brushing by them, the men saw the smudge of a surface ship on the northern horizon. It was the Steel Advocate! But, after a few minutes, she turned and was gone. The big freighter, steering straight and navigating accurately, had arrived in the vicinity of the crash at noon. Now, with every available man on look-out duty, she was executing a search pattern in the form of an expanding square, calculated so that scanners with high-powered binoculars could sight a man in the water two and a half miles on either side. All afternoon she steamed slowly on her search pattern, her men hoping and determined but afraid that they would find nothing.

Dick Rausch, the navigator on the Steel Advocate, checked his position with an observation of the sun at noon, and then at twilight confirmed it with a five-star fix. As darkness fell, the vessel reduced speed to five knots and began to sweep the surface methodically with a 36-inch searchlight mounted on the bow. All available crewmembers stayed next to the searchlight throughout the night even skipping the evening meal. Huge amounts of coffee kept them awake.

As their second night began, the Tiger crew, hungry, thirsty, wounded, exhausted, chilled by now even in the 80-degree water, and still under sporadic attacks by half a dozen sharks, made up their minds to help themselves. They began an impossible 500 mile swim toward Johnston Island. Feebly, they paddled to the southeast, periodically resting and praying. Occasionally, a man would scream in pain as a shark clamped down on his foot or leg. The others would come splashing and shouting to his aid. The shark would back off and the little foursome, trailing more blood, and weaker, would resume their crippled crawl toward land.

At some moment in the timeless nightmare of darkness, a shark killed Warren Gin. The others heard him groan and turned again to help, but his blood darkened the moonlit sea around him, and in a few seconds he was dead. Tony Machado lifted his smarting eyes to the remote stars and offered a prayer for this man who only hours ago had been his partner in the near miracle of flight. Then, sorrowfully, yet gratefully, Machado slipped the life jacket off his friend's body and shrugged himself into it. In the next second Gin was gone.

Now there were three. Machado, Olsen and Hightower resumed their hopeless marathon toward Johnson Island while the Steel Advocate, somewhere over the horizon, swung her searchlight back and forth across the Pacific. Other ships and planes crisscrossed and groped, and the air pulsed with radio and radar waves desperately searching as the men in the water fought to live in an almost hopeless battle against sharks and the sea.

During the night the sea swells built until the three survivors were, at one moment, on a high peak in the full light of the moon, and a moment later in a dark, watery valley from which they could see nothing. The Steel Advocate rolled and wallowed and her lookouts knew that if a swell shadowed the men as the light swept past, they would miss seeing them.

By daylight of the second day, the three men knew that if rescue did not come before darkness fell again, it would be too late. The sharks were still with them, and they were losing strength to fight them off. A dozen planes flew past that morning, most of them commercial airliners that had diverted to fly through the search area with the faint hope that they would see them, but all were too high and none of them saw the three flyspecks on the horizon-to-horizon sea.

A little after noon, a shout went up aboard the Steel Advocate! A lookout had sighted wreckage! The ship hove-to, grappling hooks were lowered, and a 20 x 30-inch aluminium and plywood hatch cover was recovered. It was part of the Flying Tiger DC-4! This find narrowed the search area to a few square miles. The Steel Advocate's radio now opened up on the emergency frequency letting all search ship and planes know that they were very close to where the big Tiger DC-4 went down.

The search ships' speakers crackled with the code message transmitting the latitude and longitude of the find. In chart rooms of perhaps a dozen ships the navigators feverishly plotted that position. When plotted, the ships' captains ordered course changes to zero-in on that place in the vast Pacific where three desperate men were clinging to life. All search ships and planes within 200 miles turned and headed at full speed toward the now smaller search area. The searchers knew that they were in a race against the sun and that it would be this afternoon or it would be never.

Now, in the lonely world a few inches above the sea's surface, little waves slapped and choked the men and the sharks glided by snapping and tearing flesh. Sometime after noon, another man lost the race. Richard Olsen, starved, exhausted, and drained of half his blood, quietly turned his face to the broiling sun and

died. Machado and Hightower paddled feebly on with the sharks still circling, nipping, and menacing them.

Suddenly there was hope. In the early afternoon, the two men, through burning, hollow eyes made out a ship in the distance. With renewed strength they began swimming toward it but after a few minutes, it turned away. Four or five times it changed course, now toward, now away. Machado and Hightower were nearing the end. Machado had one final prayer: "God," he said, "If it is Your will that I should die or if I should keep swimming, let me know." When the next swell lifted him, he could see the ship clearly for the first time. The huge bow was only 100 yards away. The ships engines were in reverse to slow her. She was backing down and coming straight for them, "On as true a course", Machado said later, "as if God Himself were at the helm."

One of the very weary lookouts aboard the Steel Advocate had seen them! A lifeboat was put over the side, with Dick Rausch in command. Its engine failed a few yards from the ship, but the men broke out the oars, and in a few minutes Machado looked out of burning, salt-caked eyes to see human faces above him. He felt himself being hauled into the boat, and could only gasp, "My buddy, my buddy... Over there."

Rausch then maneuvered the boat alongside Hightower, and two men grabbed him and got his chest and shoulders over the gunwale. Then they froze in horror! A ten-foot shark had Hightower's left leg in his mouth and would not let go. Rausch leaped over the seats rushing from his position at the tiller to where the struggling men were trying to wrest Hightower from the jaws of the shark. Carefully aiming his .38 revolver, he emptied it into the fish's head. The shark's jaws opened and it slid downward in a cloud of blood and the men pulled Hightower into the boat.

Tony Machado, on the final edge of consciousness, looked straight up into the tropic sky and said very softly, "Thank you, God".

N90911 at Wake Island in 1947, N90433's unreached destination　　*photo Flying Tigers Club Archives*

STEEL ADVOCATE, SHIP'S LOG.

7/25/55: At approximately 1318 on September 25, sighted and rescued Captain A. J. Machado and copilot R.C. Hightower who were floating in life jackets, the only survivors of the crash of Flying Tiger Line's DC-4, N90433. This plane, having left Honolulu at 0013 September 24, was on an IFR Flight Plan to Wake Island. At 0633 an emergency was declared to Wake ARTC, advising of loss of power in three engines and an inability to return to Honolulu. Of the remaining three crew members, one went down with the aircraft and two died in the water.

The above story was published in Saga Magazine in 1964 and was edited by Captain Dwight Small

REMEMBERING CAPTAIN TONY MACHADO

Dwight Small

Tony Machado

I'm one of the few remaining ex-Tigers that can be connected in any way to the crash of the DC-4, N90433. My connection is meagre indeed but I did fly with Captain Tony Machado later, nearly 15 years later. I had at least one trip with him in late 1968 or 1969 when I was his first officer on a DC-8. We didn't talk about the crash but that incident was never far from my mind when we were together in the cockpit. I also had the same FAA Aviation Medical Examiner (AME) for 25 years as did Bob Hightower, the co-pilot on the DC-4. The AME we shared was Dr. Reich whom had a practice on Pill Hill in Oakland, CA. Dr. Reich became a bit forgetful in his later years so he told me many times about the first time that Bob Hightower came in for an FAA Physical. When Dr. Reich first saw Hightower's terribly scarred body he, of course, asked what happened and was told about the crash and the multiple shark attacks.

I believe Tony Machado was about 55 years old when I flew with him. I remember taking note of his robust physical stature and thought that perhaps his good, strong physical bearing might have been one of the reasons that he survived the ditching and the time in the ocean. The chat around the crew rooms at that time was that, after that crash, Tony often went to Mass when he had an opportunity on trips. I know of no other crew member that went to church when on Tiger trips.

I also remember having a beer with him, or maybe a couple, at the Old Plaza (crew hotel) Hotel bar in Tachikawa, Japan. That was the only experience I had with him outside of the cockpit. I remember that he was rather pleasant, quiet and gentlemanly, a man of few words. Even when I had a beer or two with him he didn't open up about his life, his thoughts or opinions and wasn't a guy to talk about the crash. He was the same way in the cockpit. (I also remember that I enjoyed that trip.)

5

Remembering The Curtiss C-46

Guy Van Herbruggen

As an aviation enthusiast, you cannot resist the sight of a C-46. It only raises interest and curiosity. Key in the development of the Flying Tiger Line in the 1950s, it is a massive plane, much larger than the Douglas C-47, with about twice the payload thanks to its trademark 'double-bubble' fuselage.

The Curtiss-Wright C-46 Commando was a transport aircraft originally derived from a commercial high-altitude airliner design. It was instead used as a military transport during World War II by the United States Army Air Forces (USAAF) as well as the U.S. Navy/Marine Corps under the designation R5C. Known to the men who flew them as the Whale, or the Curtiss Calamity, the C-46 served a similar role as its counterpart, the Douglas C-47 Skytrain, but was not as extensively produced.

Official US Army poster

The hour of glory for the Curtiss C-46 Commando clearly came during its operations in the China-Burma-India theatre (CBI) and the Far East. The Commando was a workhorse in flying over The Hump (as the Himalaya Mountains were nicknamed by Allied airmen), transporting desperately-needed supplies to troops in China from bases in India and Burma. A variety of transports were employed in the campaign, but only the C-46 was able to handle the wide range of adverse conditions encountered by the USAAF.

Back to China in 1943, Bob Prescott participated to the Hump airlift over Burma; his love of freedom combined with his past as a Flying Tiger led him to join China National Airways Corporation (CNAC) – the subsidiary of Pan Am that worked for the Air Transport Command. At the controls of the C-46, Bob Prescott made over 300 flights before returning to the United States at the end of 1944.

The Hump airlift is remembered with unpredictable and violent weather, heavy cargo loads, high mountain terrain, and poorly-equipped and frequently-flooded airfields, along with a host of engineering and maintenance nightmares due to a shortage of trained air and ground personnel. After a series of mechanical gremlins were resolved, the C-46 proved its worth in the airlift operation. It could carry more cargo and higher than other Allied twin-engine transport aircraft in the theatre, including light artillery, fuel, ammunition, parts of aircraft and even livestock. Its powerful engines enabled it to climb satisfactorily with heavy loads, and stay aloft on one engine if not overloaded, though "war emergency" load limits of up to 40,000 lbs often erased any safety margins. Nevertheless, after the troublesome Curtiss-Electric pitch mechanism on the propellers was removed, the C-46 continued to be employed in the CBI and over wide areas of southern China throughout the war years.

The C-46's huge cargo capacity (twice that of the C-47), large cargo doors, powerful engines and long range also made it ideal for the vast distances of the Pacific island campaign. In particular, the U.S. Marines found the aircraft (known as the R5C) useful in their amphibious Pacific operations, flying supplies in and wounded soldiers out of numerous and hastily-built island landing strips.

After World War 2, a few surplus C-46 aircraft were briefly used in their original role as passenger airliners, but the glut of surplus Douglas C-47s dominated the marketplace; the C-46 was soon relegated to cargo duty.

Flying Tigers C-46F at Burbank early 1950s

photos Flying Tigers Club Archives

Washing the preservative paint off one of the C-46's that Prescott bought from government stores after World War II

In 1949, the Flying Tiger Line expanded its business model to become a scheduled carrier and started operating Cargo Route 100 from Los Angeles to New York. Having flown the C-46 with his companions over the Hump, Bob Prescott knew the plane's capacity and performance well. Its 200 mile-an-hour speed, 13,000 lbs of cargo capacity and 900-mile range were going to make it the Queen of the Flying Tigers fleet. He leased a fleet of 25 from the USAF to supplement its fleet of Douglas C-47 and C-54 and he was able to put them in good use with the US as the airlift of men and material across the Pacific to Korea began to use all available long-range cargo aircraft. Most of these C-46s were purchased outright within a very few years.

On June 25, 1950, following a series of clashes along the border, North Korea invaded South Korea and the United States quickly reacted; just a few days later C-46s of the Flying Tiger Line disembarked the first reinforcements in Korea. The Korean War airlift had begun.

Together with Slick Airways, The Flying Tiger Line was the largest civil operator of the C-46 in the early 1950s, with up to 42 machines on strength at one time or another, either owned, leased or sub-leased.

With the exception of N4860V (a C-46A), all Flying Tigers C-46s were C-46Fs, the cargo version, equipped with single cargo doors on both sides of the fuselage and square-cut wingtips. Built in Buffalo NY, they were equipped by powerful Curtiss-Wright R2800-75 of 2,000 hp each.

In 1953, a JATO (jet-assisted take-off) solution was installed and tested on a Flying Tiger C-46F to provide extra power for take-off and emergencies. The small jet engine ran on gasoline and was only 82 inches long and 25 inches in maximum diameter, adding about a 10 percent kick to the total take-off power a single engine on the C-46.

N67979 sustains level flight relying on the power of its JATO jet engine, with props stopped and feathered

photo Bill Watson / Flying Tigers Club Archives

An eyelid, recessed and open in this image, can close when the engine is not in use, covering the intake scoop and eliminating drag

photo Flying Tigers Club Archives

With the introduction of the Douglas DC-6 in 1955 and the significant order of L-1049Hs in September 1955, the Flying Tiger Line's C-46s started to see a rapid reduction in the fleet from 23 in 1956 to only two in 1959. These two were gone by 1962.

From a safety perspective, like every other major type in long service and operation, accidents and incidents occurred, but with no fatalities at Flying Tigers – luck or experience accumulated during the Hump days perhaps. In total, only three aircraft are known to be written off. The first was lost on July 30, 1950,

N67960 came to rest in the backyard of a family residing adjacent to Stapleton Field, Denver, CO. Cause of accident due to its gross weight of 48,268 lbs. being too great to enable it the climb out of mile-high Stapleton Field

photo The Air Line Pilots Association

N4862V was written off at Cape Perry in Canada's Northwest Territories during the construction of the DEW Line; remains are seen here shortly after the accident

photo Flying Tigers Club Archives

The remains of N9995F located about five miles south of the town of Kugaaruk, Nunavut (formerly Pelly Bay) in September 2011. Note the fading Flying Tigers colors on the nose section

photo Jason Pineau

when N67960 crashed on take-off from Stapleton International Airport due to performance problems; both pilots and both passengers survived. On March 18, 1956, N9995F crashed at Pelly Bay, Canada after the left wing struck rising terrain at 1000 feet while on a nighttime VFR approach. The aircraft was still visible in September 2011, wearing a fading Flying Tigers livery. Lastly, N4862V was written off at Cape Perry in Canada's Northwest Territories – unfortunately no details are available.

Although the number of active C-46s around the world gradually began to dwindle, they continued to operate in remote locations, and could be seen in service in Canada, Alaska, Africa and South America. In the late 1970s and early 1980s, Canadian airline Lamb Air operated several from their bases in Thompson and Churchill, Manitoba. One of the largest C-46 operators was Air Manitoba, whose fleet of aircraft featured gaudy color schemes for individual aircraft. In the 1990s, these aircraft were diverted to other owner/operators.

Between 1993 and 1995, Relief Air Transport operated three Canadian-registered C-46s on Operation Lifeline Sudan from Lokichoggio, Kenya. These aircraft also transported humanitarian supplies to Goma (Congo) and Mogadishu from their base in Nairobi. The best-known operator of recent years is Buffalo Airways with two C-46s, primarily used in Canada's Arctic. Their aircraft have been featured on the television show Ice Pilots.

On April 21 1955, N67992 suffered an engine failure on take-off at Corral Harbor, Canada, ran into snow bank and was repaired

photos Flying Tigers Club Archives

MONKEY CHARTER ON A C-46

Dick Feuerherm

In the late 1950s, I remember good old Mike Melnick calling me up on a Saturday afternoon, and asking me if I could come in to give them a hand working a "C-46 Charter". No mention of "Monkeys". Of course, I told him I would be there as soon as possible. When I got there, I clocked in, Mike grabbed me by the arm almost lifting me off my feet, dragged me out to the C-46, and before we were 100 feet from the aircraft, I could smell something pretty bad. At first, I thought it was the usual smell from the city dump that was near the south end of the airport, but no, it was the monkeys. I think old Tommy Nichols was there, and tough Tony DePalma. Even Lennie Tursi, who made sure he had secured the job of driving the fork lift. As the loading progressed, the smell was almost unbearable, so we hurried to get the C-46 loaded.

One day, after one of those monkey charters, my wife wouldn't let me in the house when I got home unless I took off all my clothes and headed for the shower. I'm sure all of us Old Tigers have had a hand or two working these monkey charters. That's got to be the one job that either makes you or breaks you.

Paid well, 80.90 cents per hour, and we made a lot of money in those days anyway because we all worked at least 18, and sometimes 24 hours a day. I can still remember the old maintenance storage room in the hangar that had all the shelves still set up in it, and on several of the shelves it had somebody sleeping on old Tiger blankets with a note hanging on the end of the shelf that said, wake me up at 0300, or whenever they were supposed to hit the next charter. And boy didn't we have fun in those days. I wouldn't trade those days, friends and co-workers for anything in this world.

Former Flying Tigers C-46s into the Twenty First Century

Michael S. Prophet

1. CANADIAN NORTHERN C-46S

One of the C-46Fs used by Flying Tigers survives today and still earns its keep, flying freight in Canada's northern frontier.

This particular example was built by the Curtiss-Wright Buffalo (NY) plant as a model C-46F-1-CU, USAAF construction number 22556 and serial number 44-78733, and delivered in August 1945. It served with the USAAF out of Boeing Field in Seattle until September 1947, when the Flying Tiger Line leased it from 1950 until 1957 with civil registration N1258N. That same year she was purchased by Wings Inc. and leased to Wien Alaska Airlines. Wings Inc. sold her to FA Conner in May 1969. A year later, in September 1970, she appeared in full two-tone green-and-white Shamrock Air Lines livery including company titles. During the 1970s she served several cargo operators, such as Plymouth Leasing Co, Ortner Air Services, Trans Continental Airlines and Atkins Aviation as N519AC. In April 1986 she travelled northbound, joining Air Manitoba, the last big C-46 operator as C-GTPO based out of Winnipeg, receiving a flash grey/bare metal scheme including a two-tone blue and red cheat line. In 1993 they streamlined into an all turbo-prop HS-748 operator, so four of the Commandos were sold; three went to Kenya to fly on the United Nations relief contract in to the Sudan.

A fifth C-46, C-GTPO, remained in Canada; in October 1989, she developed engine trouble on take-off, overran the runway at Pickle Lake airstrip in northwest Ontario, and left behind ever since. Joe McBryan, president of Buffalo Airways, had a soft spot for C-GTPO and decided to repair the stricken bird. He sent a crew from Winnipeg who repaired the landing gear, propeller and engines. She was ferried to Seattle for refurbishment, and joined the Buffalo's fleet during 1994.

C-FAVO and ex-Flying Tigers C-GTPO parked in Yellowknife next to the maintenance hangar   *photo Michael S. Prophet*

She was sold off to First Nations Transportation Inc (FNT) in August 2004 as a freighter flying out of Gimli Manitoba (famous for the July 1983 deadstick landing by an Air Canada Boeing 767 after fuel exhaustion), still in her basic Buffalo colours in a fleet of Douglas DC-3s and C-46s. Together with sister company SASCO Ltd, operating as First Nations Trucking, FNT served many remote communities in Manitoba and northwest Ontario with intermodal truck-air service. FNT was shut down by the Canadian CAA in June 2009 and C-GTPO was left behind, unloved once more!

In 2010 Buffalo Airways came to the rescue once more, and brought her back to Yellowknife. Since December 2017 she has remained a fully-operational freighter from its Yellowknife hub. As a passionate aviation photographer and journalist, I visited Canada numerous times in search of these unique workhorses and in June 1998, I travelled to Yellowknife via Edmonton to track down the green Buffalo fleet, which at the time included Douglas DC-3s, DC-4s, C-46s and Canadair

CL-215 water-bombers. During my visit, the friendly folks at Buffalo Airways granted myself and a fellow traveller full ramp access for our photoshoot. Whilst photographing on the ramp, I bumped into Jim Smith, Buffalo's chief pilot. I explained my photographic pursuit of the old propliner, which was the main reason why I was there. Jim then told me that he was scheduled to make a supply flight to the BHP diamond mine at Koala near the Lac de Gras lake, 300 km northeast of Yellowknife, and I was welcome to ride along in the C-46. Thrilled by his generous offer, I gladly accepted and quickly checked my camera gear and inventory of film.

C-46F registered C-GTPO parked in Yellowknife, ready for loading

When I arrived at the loading ramp, she was almost ready for departure. 14,000 lbs of supplies, ranging from soft drinks to explosive detonators, had been loaded. Co-pilot Mark Cary was on the wing tending the refueling and checking the engines' oil quantity. The C-46's enormous cargo compartment was packed. Jim Smith gave me the OK sign to make my way up to the cockpit, but first I had to climb over the cargo. With several bruises and cuts on my hands and knees, I entered the cockpit. Jim and Mark followed quickly and settled in for lengthy preflight checks. Both Pratt and Whitney

R-2800 radials engines were fired up effortlessly and were running smoothly. Air traffic control cleared us to runway 27 for a northeasterly departure. Brakes were released and the heavily-laden Commando began its taxi to the runway holding point. After the required engine run ups, we were cleared for takeoff.

Cockpit of C-46F C-GTPO   photos Michael S. Prophet

Captain Smith opened up the throttles and slowly we gathered speed. The C-46's distinctive engine noise during take-off was evident. At 2,300 rpm (37-inch engine manifold pressure), we slowly lifted off and established a 500 feet-per-minute climb rate. We made a gradual right turn towards 010 degrees and the engines were set to METO power – Maximum Continuous Except Takeoff – at 2,000 rpm and 33-inch pressure. Leaving Yellowknife city limits, we started our climb towards our cruising altitude of 5,500 feet. With a speed of 150 knots, Jim and Mark settled in for the one hour flight to the Koala landing strip. Down below, the barren tundra looked most unappealing. Scattered with hundreds of little lakes, some still with an icy crust, it seemed endless. It was a familiar area for the crew, who were enjoying a late breakfast.

Jim had flown these northern skies for quite a long time. He pointed out the Koala landing strip in the far distance but I could not yet see it. Power was reduced and we began our long and slow descent. Air traffic control issued a warning for local weather conditions indicating gusty crosswinds up to 30 knots. Due to its size and wartime reputation, the C-46 is widely-feared for some unforgiving handling characteristics. During the Southeast Asia airlift, more than 700 machines were lost out of a production run of about 3,500. Jim preferred the C-46 by a wide margin; for all its aerodynamic quirks, it enjoyed superior single-engine performance.

With landing gear firmly locked down and the flaps set for landing, we began our final approach. Power was added and the note of the engines rose. Looking out

In-flight picture of engine #2　　　　photo Michael S. Prophet

the side windows, our shadow racing across the ground came closer and closer, expanding in size. With both hands firmly on the control wheel, Jim set the throttle levers to a 10-inch manifold pressure differential to help counter the crosswind. Both engines were roaring as we crossed the threshold, and Jim settled the old lady firmly on the strip. Power was chopped and we slowly transitioned to taxi speed, made our way to a desolate loading platform and shut down engines.

Mark opened up the big cargo door and a chilling breeze entered the cabin. Several trucks and a forklift began unloading. Due to the strict mines policy, I was prohibited from taking any pictures. On our return flight, Mark piloted the C-46. After a full runway backtrack and a short takeoff run, we climbed to 8,500 feet for the trip back to base, with an indicated airspeed of 175 knots. About 90 miles from Yellowknife, we began our descent with a sink rate of 400 feet per minute. After a righthand circuit we landed back on runway 27 and taxied to the maintenance ramp. I thanked both Jim and Mark for an unforgettable flight, which I will treasure all my life.

2. BOLIVIAN C-46S

In June of 2010, I travelled back to Bolivia, accompanied with some aviation enthusiasts for the third time, visiting the Canedo family, who were living in Cochabamba. We had become close friends with both father and sons of the Canedo family who were all pilots, the last Bolivian operators of pure piston engine propliners. At that time, Lineas Aereas Canedo (LAC) operated an immaculate Douglas C-117D Super Dakota, and the world's only passenger configured Curtiss C-46D Commando.

We arrived at the beautiful city of Cochabamba, the city of Eternal Spring, as the Bolivians call it. We stayed at the Gran Ambassador Hotel downtown Cochabamba and the first couple of days we adjusted to the crisp cool air at an altitude of 2,558 metres (8,392 feet). The main reason for our trip was to charter the immaculate 1944 vintage C-46D CP-973, fresh out of restoration. We decided to fly over the rugged Bolivian Andes and land at the world's highest commercial airport, La Paz El Alto international, which sits at an elevation of 4,061 metres (13,323 feet).

The history of aviation in Bolivia is long and varied, and made use of numerous surplus US piston engine transports such as the Douglas DC-3, Douglas DC-6, Convair 440, Martin 404 and of course the trusty C-46 Commando. Most if not all were used on dangerous meat-hauling flights to and from La Paz. Due to lack of roads, freshly-slaughtered meat from the farmers in the Beni (lowland country) had to be flown up to La Paz over the rocky Andean mountain peaks and often in marginal weather. The C-46 was a favorite on these routes, with its sturdy design, large cabin, and powerful Pratt & Whitney R-2000 radial engines for good high-altitude performance; it was the flagship of most operators at La Paz.

Several ex-Flying Tigers C-46s ended up in Bolivia, still flying cargo up until the very late 1980s. Our 1944 vintage CP-973 was converted to an all-passenger configuration and flew with C-46 Parts Inc as N32227.

After our adventurous flight to La Paz, we were trying to catch our breath on the dry weed-covered airport ramps. That's where I noticed another C-46 which used to belong to the Flying Tiger Line. Against the skyline of shabby Bolivian-style apartments, I noticed ex-North East Bolivian Airways C-46 CP-1319, built as a model C-46F-1-CU and delivered to the United States Army Air Force back in July 1945 with serial number 44-78605. The following year she was sold to the China National Aviation Corporation (CNAC) with civilian registration N8374C. In December 1949 she was sold to Taiwan's Civil Air Transport. Reregistered to N4863V, she was purchased by the Flying Tiger Line in 1952. In February 1955 she was sold to Zantop Air Transport and leased back to the Flying Tiger Line. Eventually she ended up in the Zantop fleet proper, then reregistered N617Z and subleased to Universal Airlines in 1966. She was sold to Span East Airlines in 1970 as N600SE and further leased to Ortner Air Service and Plymouth Leasing Company in 1973. She was withdrawn from use (wfu) and stored at Detroit Willow Run airport in 1976. According to the register, she was sold to Air Procace with Bolivian registration CP-1308, but it's unclear if she actually left the US due to a repositions notation on record. She was officially sold to Bolivia to Transportes Aereos Bolivar (TAB) as CP-1319 during November that same year. During the 1990s she flew with Camba Transportes Aereos and was also known as '100% Camba'. During my first visit to Bolivia, I logged her with Camba at Santa Cruz airport, then in 2005 as NEBA at El Alto La Paz, and reported for sale.

Her flying career did not end well; on Saturday April 21, 2012 she crashed after take-off from Santa Cruz Viru Viru airport. All three crew members were killed and a single passenger survived. Operating a cargo flight to Cobija, the aircraft developed engine trouble after take-off and the pilot radioed that they were returning to the airport. The airplane was on short final to runway 16 when it pulled up sharply. Control was lost and the aircraft fell off to the right, impacting terrain about 200 m from the northern end of runway 16. Thus ended the long and diverse career of one an early Flying Tigers machine.

AVIC C-46F CP-1280 formerly N1801M with the Flying Tiger Line between 1950 and 1952 seen at Cochabamba Bolivia in 1994 still wearing a basic Flying Tigers livery   photo Chris Mak

C-46F CP-1319 formerly N4863V with the Flying Tiger Line between 1952 and 1955 seen at La Paz, Bolivia in 2010   photo Michael S. Prophet

6

My Dad On A Flying Tigers Refugee Flight

Helena Herceg Burke, Membership Director, Flying Tigers Club

I was hired on November 11, 1980 as a Records Retrieval Clerk based in LAX/HDQ. My employee number was 38698. By July 1989, I had already logged nine years at Flying Tigers and working the greatest job ever in OpsCon (Operations Control) on the 3rd floor of Hi Tiger. We were getting ready to turn over the proverbial keys to Federal Express and all a little melancholy about the transition, knowing that the best thing we've ever known was coming to an end.

I came home to my parent's house one evening to tell them about the transition to the new company when my dad announced, so nonchalantly, "You know, I came to this country on a Flying Tigers refugee flight."

"What?" I answered in disbelief. Seriously, this was the first time my father ever mentioned this. In all my years at Tigers, all my stories about this great company, the incredible people, the jumpseat experiences, he mentioned this to me as we were getting ready to turn out the lights.

He told me he had a picture of their aircraft when they landed in Gander, Canada. He had to find that photograph, which he did; an old 2 x 3 inch print, which I immediately had duplicated, blown up and framed. One of my most prized possessions. I realized that I had somehow always been destined to become a Tiger, as it was part of me, even before I was born.

Fast forward 29 years to the era of literally everything being online, and I found the passenger manifest with my dad's name on it! Flying Tiger flight 8412-23, October 23, 1956, departed from Munich, Germany. The flight made several fuel stops including in the Azores and in Gander, Canada, where my father took the picture, then on to New York. Kresimir J. Herceg was name #13 on the manifest of a total of 72 passengers (imagine the tight fit!) and 70 bags (many people literally arriving with the clothes on their backs).

My father was born in Croatia, then Yugoslavia, and was a soldier during World War II. He spent time as a prisoner of war in Stalag 17B, a prisoner camp located in Austria. After the German defeat, he was released and given a one-way bus ticket to Zagreb. Soon after the war, Yugoslavia fell under the control of the Communist Party and my father started desperately to seek a way out. He ultimately ended up back in Austria. He was able to move to the United States as a war refugee aboard Flying Tigers via his work with the Catholic relief organization Carita, and lived in Los Angeles for the remainder of his life.

Flying Tiger Line C-54B N95414 in Gander October 1956

photo Kresimir Herceg

Super H N6912C on approach for landing

N45516 in Anchorage, April 1972

photos Jacques Guillem

7

Sleek And Powerful Constellations

Charles Kennedy

In January 1953, the Flying Tiger Line intended to lease a Lockheed L-049 Constellation from Intercontinental Airlines for use on its military contract flights, but the aircraft was destroyed in a training accident prior to delivery. With Lockheed next door at Burbank, in September 1955, it was natural for Flying Tigers to became one of the first companies to place an order for the new L-1049H Super Connie convertible model. Ten machines were ordered at a total cost of $28,000,000 ($262 million in 2019), with a follow-up order for an additional two more shortly afterwards.

The Flying Tiger Line had been granted U.S. Airfreight Route No. 100 by the CAB on July 29, 1949, coming into effect on August 12, to fly scheduled domestic freight services from Boston, Hartford/Springfield and New York, to Chicago, Detroit, Los Angeles and San Francisco, with many intermediate points. The first L-1049H was rolled down the Burbank taxiway from Lockheed to Tigers on February 1, 1957. By the end of June, all ten of Flying Tiger's initial order for L-1049Hs had been delivered, and two leased aircraft had been leased.

N38936 is engulfed by flames on January 22, 1953 after a gear-up landing in Burbank on a training flight

photo Los Angeles Examiner / Flying Tigers Club Archives

Connie L-049 N38936 being prepared for Flying Tigers

photo Flying Tigers Club Archives

The Connie flew Flying Tigers' main scheduled transcontinental cargo services, including six times weekly non-stop New York to Burbank, six times weekly Detroit to San Francisco, and five times weekly Cleveland to Burbank via Detroit, under Super Daybreaker brand. Some trips called at Chicago (Midway) with connecting flights flown by C-46s.

During their first year of operations, the L-1049Hs began flying charters for MATS across the Pacific from Travis AFB and other points in California to Wake Island, Honolulu, Tokyo, Okinawa and Manila.

Tourist and student charters across the Atlantic included West Germany and the United Kingdom for travel agents and tour operators. This business was a 1950s staple for Flying Tigers; additional transatlantic flying included Jamaican emigrant charters on behalf of BOAC from Montego Bay to London, and British emigrant charters from London to Canada.

From 1957 until the introduction of the Canadair CL-44 propjets in mid-1962, the L-1049Hs were the mainstay of Flying Tigers' operations. On top of the flying detailed above, additional stops at Minneapolis St. Paul (once weekly) and Binghamton (six times weekly) were added on the return legs from San Francisco, and by mid-1960, a six times weekly service to Seattle and Portland (Oregon) was added as an extension of the New York to San Francisco route.

In July 1962, CL-44s took over five of the 19 weekly services on the New York - Burbank – San Francisco route; the remaining 12 weekly flights continuing to be flown by the Connies. Charter flights continued to be made throughout the Pacific as far as New Zealand, and the Atlantic regions during this period.

In 1961, Flying Tiger offered its lowest-ever summer charter passenger rates at just over £35 return (£765 in 2019) from London to New York on their 118-seater L-1049Hs. This rate was applicable for closed groups chartering the whole of the aircraft and originating in Europe only. Needless to say, many clubs and other organizations took advantage of this low fare to the USA in the summer of 1961 and succeeding summers, with a passenger charter flight scheduled at least once a day from New York to a European city such as London, Paris, Manchester, Brussels, Glasgow (Prestwick) or Amsterdam during the peak summer season from May to September. By 1964, the North Atlantic group charter business had been built up to two flights daily from the USA to Europe with the L-1049Hs, in spite of the rise in rates charged to £45 (low season; £895 in 2019) or £57 (high season; £1,135 in 2019) return.

Welcoming crowd of employees, families and friends in Burbank for the first CL-44 N451T on June 2, 1961

photo Conley, Flying Tigers Club Archives

The Big Reach campaign ad used in newspapers in all Constellation cities and adjacent areas served by The Flying Tiger Line

Flying Tigers Club Archives

Although CL-44s had taken most of the scheduled US transcontinental freight flights and MATS charters from 1962 onwards (by March 1963, the number of CL-44 flights on scheduled transcontinental freight services equalled the number of L-1049H flights), Flying Tigers continued to operate a large number of L-1049Hs until the late 1960s, purchasing or leasing nine further aircraft in addition to their original 12 during the period from May 1958 to May 1964.

The last MATS/MAC overseas contract flights with piston propulsion such as the L-1049H took place in June 1963, after which the use of turbine-powered planes was mandated by the Pentagon for the carriage of its personnel. Super Connies, however, could still be used on the domestic Quicktrans military cargo charters for the Navy until the end of 1965, the aircraft bearing Quicktrans titling in small letters on the rear fuselage. During the latter part of 1963, several CL-44s were taken off the scheduled network, and, in the winter of 1963-64, the Super Connies were again flying the bulk of Flying Tiger's scheduled cargo services.

In 1964, the L-1049Hs flew New York to Los Angeles (instead of Burbank) via Detroit and Chicago, and Boston to Seattle via Hartford/ Springfield, Cleveland, Los Angeles, San Francisco and Portland daily. In mid-summer 1964, the CL-44s started returning to more of the scheduled services, again sharing the transcontinental schedules with the L-1049Hs. Philadelphia was added to the Boston to Chicago westbound and Seattle to New York eastbound daily Connie schedules from January 1965.

From October 31, 1965, CL-44s replaced Connies on routes west of Chicago, but the Connies continued to operate ten times weekly from New York to Chicago via Philadelphia, Cleveland or Detroit, five times weekly from New York to Binghamton, of which three flights weekly continued to Detroit. The New York to Binghamton service changed to a Hartford/ Springfield - Binghamton service from January 1966 on the westbound schedule for a few months, but by April 1966, the L-1049H schedule had been reduced to five times weekly New York to Detroit (via Binghamton outbound and Cleveland on the return), and five times weekly New York to Chicago. The L-1049H continued in use on these two routes until the late spring of 1967, when CL-44s took over on these routes as well.

In June 1966, seven L-1049Hs were transferred to a subsidiary company, Flying Tiger Air Services, to

Connie taking off from Burbank in February 1959 *photo Flying Tigers Club Archives*

Super H N6913C being loaded *photo Flying Tigers Club Archives*

Super H N6916C in March 1966

Super H N6924C of Flying Tiger Air Services operated between 1966 and 1967 flying Far East inter island flights for the US Government. N6924C was named 'City of Manila'

photos Jacques Guillem

operate charters in Southeast Asia during 1966-67. By the end of 1967, however, all but one of the remaining L-1049Hs (a total of ten), had been retired, flown to Kingman Arizona for storage. One L-1049H remained in use for charter work in the Far East until the middle of 1968, when that, too, was retired, superseded by the CL-44s and then stretched DC-8 freighters.

During its service with the Flying Tiger Line, the 1049H set numerous records. The aircraft had been successively modified and updated until they could carry a payload of up to 45,000 lbs, either cargo or 120 passengers, though the record for a civil L-1049H must surely be the 144 American Field Service scholars who were uplifted from Christchurch, New Zealand in Flying Tiger's N6922C on August 19, 1962. In March 1962, Flying Tigers carried one of the heaviest single objects ever to be flown in a L-1049H, a 26-foot ship's tail shaft weighing 34,000 lbs from Newark to Hong Kong. 30 engineers and labourers took eight hours to unload it using a special platform, with an 18-ton truck filled with stones, secured to the nose of the aircraft for ballast.

The high cruising speed and reliability of the turbine-powered CL-44 (a 40% improvement on operating costs), and ease of loading and unloading thanks to its swing-tail (a 62,000 lb palletized payload could be loaded in an hour, compared to three to five hours to bulk load 46,000 lbs into an L-1049H) meant the Connie was ultimately consigned to the history books. However, for a decade, the Lockheed Super Constellation represented the cutting edge of technology and productivity, and with its devastating good looks, put the Flying Tiger Line at the front of the pack.

Super H N6916C withdrawn from use at Kingman, AZ in 1968

photo Jacques Guillem

8

Aardvark On The Loose

Pat Bliss

All too soon, we had to board the waiting big silver Flying Tiger Line triple-tailed Constellation aircraft. It had departed from Sydney, Australia with a fuel stop in the Fiji Islands 16 flying hours earlier. It would soon depart for San Francisco and on to our home base in Los Angeles, California. There had been a fuel stop and crew change here in Honolulu.

On this wonderful warm and tropical morning in the Hawaiian Islands, we had to say, "Aloha" and bring to an end, our perfect Waikiki Beach layover. There was a fresh and very experienced three-man Tiger crew in the cockpit, eager to fly the last leg homeward bound, after their rest time, following a flight from the Orient.

We were very comfortably seated in B compartment located directly behind the cockpit and the galley. My pilot husband and I had the compartment all to ourselves this day. Aft of our compartment, was the main passenger cabin. On this trip it had been converted for a freight load bound for San Francisco, with a manifest listing unknown to us at that time.

We were a little tan, a little tired, very spoiled, and quite happy to be enjoying one of the advantages of airline life: a free flight home.

As the sleek airliner began the climb out to reach the requested flying altitude, we were watching

Stewardess Patti Bliss

beautiful Waikiki Beach and famous old Diamondhead disappear beneath the left wing. We took one last loving look at a sight very close to our hearts.

It was a beautiful day to begin a flight across the breath-taking blue Pacific. A few billowing white clouds hung low over the islands. The pilots would describe this day as CAVU, Clear and visibility unlimited.

In a short time, the seatbelt sign flickered off and I decided to serve the crew some hot Kona coffee from the forward galley. In those days, cockpit doors were never required to be locked and besides, that particular door had always seemed to be so light weight,

photo The 6 Watson Bros./Flying Tigers Club Archives

Jack and Patti Bliss   *photo Flying Tiger Line Pilots Association*

it appeared almost flimsy to us. The crew would be served first, then I would offer a cup to my deadheading husband (as off duty crew members were referred to in the lexicon of the airlines). Being an ex-stewardess forced to end my career because of the marriage rule in the 1950s, it was perfectly appropriate to assist in the galley and give the second officer a break from that duty on this freighter flight. In fact, it was welcomed!

I opened the cockpit door and offered the trio of tanned, smiling and thirsty pilots the hot delicious Kona coffee – a special Island treat. The second officer, known as a bit of a clown said, "My sweet Patti Lou, how many times do I have to remind you! I take sugar, sugar?" My memory was not that bad, but I had not seen him or flown with him in seven years! But it did get a laugh from all of them in the front office.

I walked back and poured another cup of coffee for my pilot and myself and we settled back into the big soft leather seats to enjoy our wonderful and smooth flight across the Pacific Ocean to our home in California. It would be an all-daylight flight heading eastbound and it would last most of the day.

I sat there and imagined this beautiful aircraft as our very own private airplane today, enjoying the empty compartment that we shared all to ourselves. It was fun! As were all of our good airline friends and adventures and the interesting people we met, and the

exciting sights that we were so privileged to visit on our trips around the world with the airline.

Halfway along our route, after passing the PNR (point of no return) everyone had lunch. The food always seemed to be outstanding when it was prepared and loaded in Honolulu. There would be fresh papaya and sweet pineapple slices and exotic fruit drinks and other island dishes, then delicious macadamia nut pie or ice cream and so much more to fill each island tray. A day in flight was always enjoyable when your destination was to or from the Hawaiian Islands.

Our airplane kept humming along, a lovely uneventful flight. Within a few hours, we had passed the Farallon Islands and we were soon coming up on San Francisco. No fog delay today, CAVU all the way. Great!

Then it happened. I almost choked. "Look out! Oh no! What is this?" I thought we were alone here!

Something is loose! It's awful! Something horrible, a chilling sight moving right there so very close to my husband's elbow. It was trying to slide down the aisle. I wanted to scream. Was it a huge cobra snake making its slimy way down the aisle? Was it the wily trunk of an elephant? It looked like it. It must have broken loose from a container in the aft cabin. It was scary and big and looked wild-eyed as it slowly made its way along the aisle, so close to my husband! But we could not see all of it yet! Now it started to fill the whole wide aisle and a sickening odor penetrated.

Time had passed so quickly and we had begun letting down for the final approach to the airport and the most critical part of our landing before touchdown. I dropped my magazine and climbed over my husband's knees as fast as I could move. I yelled out, "I'll get to the cockpit, and try to hold the door, before it breaks through and tangles with the controls!" I left my poor brave husband to fend for himself. Just as I slammed the cockpit door, I could see that he had grabbed some loose ropes that had probably secured it in the main cabin before it broke loose, in the vain effort of trying to tie it down.

Both pilots were very busy monitoring our approach, critical airspeed and decreasing altitude of

Flying Tigers Club Archives

the big aircraft for our landing. It was definitely not the time to announce that something, big, bad, and terribly menacing was about to crash through the cockpit door. I held very tightly to the locked cockpit door with both of my arms. Then, suddenly, I was aware of that thankful sound of the landing gear hitting the runway. It seemed to take forever!

As we slowly taxied to the hangar, I tried to peek around the door I had locked to see if the monster had now trapped my husband down on the floor in the aisle or much worse! But I could see he was furiously trying to tie the ropes around something that I had never laid eyes on before!

I took a quick look out onto the tarmac as we slowed to a stop. There, below us, I saw five very hearty men wearing heavy long gloves all the way up to their elbows. I quickly surmised all were awaiting our arrival with it onboard.

The second officer had opened the large cargo entrance to the aircraft and the five big men scrambled onboard, as the pilots closed down the cockpit. I pulled my hapless husband far back from all of the commotion in the aisle, thinking, Well, maybe I helped save our airplane from catastrophe, or maybe not, but I certainly left my poor brave husband all alone back there to valiantly fight it off. Not a good thing!

A curious group of onlookers had already gathered. Along with the amazed crew and ground crew workers and the two very relieved deadheads from compartment B, there were local news photographers and some very alert zoo keepers.

Our rascal passenger had travelled all the way from the Australian outback. It had flown over 7,000 weary air miles to become the latest, very newsworthy VIP to arrive at San Francisco International airport. It turned out to be a single Giant Aardvark with a very long threatening, ugly and powerful snoot. This odd-looking creature was a big beautiful and priceless specimen for the excited zookeepers witnessing its arrival with their big eyes and big smiles – very different from our harrowing meeting with it in the aisle of the plane and our immediate reaction!

Next time you visit the zoo, please take a good look at it yourself. He had travelled a very long distance. And I feel certain he is much more content now that he has been grounded. And maybe, he is even a little lovable, after all?

I do know we will always remember the VIP from the Outback, Down Under, and our shocking encounter onboard the Connie. We have shared many laughs about our strange flying companion, and I did learn that Aardvark is much more than the first word in the dictionary.

We continued our almost uneventful flight on down along the California coastline to the final destination. And I did know for certain, that my wonderful deadheading husband, whom I had locked into harm's way, was my hero that day, AS ALWAYS!

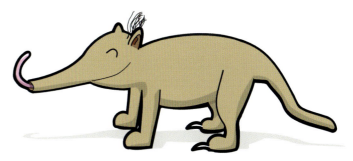

Here is IT! A great flying companion or what!

Super H N6911C, the first aircraft to be lost in 1962

photo Flying Tigers Club Archives

9

1962 – Year Of The Tiger

Guy Van Herbruggen

1962 was the Year of the Tiger in the traditional Chinese calendar, and at its inception, Robert W. Prescott announced that it was going to be a great year for the Tigers, but by its end it turned out to be a historically bad year, with the loss of four Lockheed Constellations and a temporary loss of the military contract for a few months. With the exception of the first accident on Adak Island, the Tigers Constellation losses of 1962 were high profile tragedies, taking 158 souls in the process, including the worst-ever accident of an L-1049 Constellation with 107 fatalities when, on 16 March, N6921C was lost in the Pacific Ocean between Guam and Angeles City.

The 1962 Connie accidents are listed in chronological order. Official final accident reports have been used as the prime source of information together with newspapers and other miscellaneous web sites or press mentions. All dates and times are Greenwich Mean Time (GMT) unless specified.

MARCH 15, 1962 - N6911C ADAK ISLAND NAS, AK

N6911C was operating Flying Tiger Line flight 7816/14, a Military Air Transport Service (MATS) cargo flight from Travis AFB to Okinawa-Kadena AFB with refueling stops at Cold Bay and Adak in Alaska, and Misawa in Japan. The crew consisted of Captain Morgan W. Hughes (in command), Captain Thomas M. Mitchell, First Officer Wayne W. Lowe, Flight Engineer Henry Guttman, Flight Engineer James M. Johnstone, Navigator Michael E. Green, and Navigator Kenneth Drusch.

The flight departed Travis AFB on March 14 at 2100 with a gross weight of 142,050 pounds (just 50 pounds below the maximum allowable takeoff gross weight). Buffeting developed on climbout due to an open hydraulic reservoir access door. Captain Hughes decided to return, and make an overweight landing (max landing weight was 119,975 pounds) rather dump fuel. Captain

Mitchell, flying from the left seat, made the landing at 2132. The access door was closed, a satisfactory overweight landing inspection was conducted and the aircraft departed Travis again at 2230, landing at Cold Bay at 0805 on March 15 after an uneventful flight.

The leg from Cold Bay departed at 0919 and the enroute portion of the leg to Adak Naval Air Station (NAS) was also uneventful, with First Officer Lowe flying the aircraft from the left seat and Hughes acting as copilot in the right seat. Instrument conditions prevailed at Adak when N6911C contacted Adak Approach

Captain Morgan W. Hughes
photo Flying Tiger Line
Pilots Association

Control at 1137 and a Ground Controlled Approach (GCA) was started. Soon after reporting at 8,000 feet, the flight was cleared for a runway 23 straight-in approach. The landing gear was extended and locked and the flaps extended 60 percent.

During the approach, the GCA controller warned the crew on seven occasions that they were below the glide slope and finally advised them to execute a missed approach. At about the same time Captain Hughes advised GCA, "Roger, we have the field in sight, thank you 911" and the approach was continued, visually.

Copilot Lowe asked Captain Hughes for 80 percent flaps but Hughes did not comply. Near the approach end of the runway, Hughes remarked to Lowe, "You are too low," and Lowe added power as Captain Hughes pulled back on the yoke. Almost concurrently the right landing gear struck rocks short of the runway.

Initial contact was at a point approximately 328 feet from the threshold lights and four feet below the runway elevation. The second contact was with the right inboard tire on a rock approximately eight feet forward of initial impact. The aircraft then struck an embankment at the runway threshold approximately four feet below the runway elevation, and the main gear separated. As the aircraft continued forward it veered to the right, leaving the runway at the 1,000-foot marker. The right wing was torn off while the rest continued forward until coming to a halt on a heading of approximately 30 degrees, at a point approximately 2,000 feet from the approach end of the runway.

Fire erupted following the separation of the main gear and continued after the aircraft had stopped. Six of the seven crew members evacuated the burning wreckage without serious injury but working Flight Engineer Johnstone was trapped in the cockpit area. Two crash and rescue trucks were at the scene within an estimated 30 seconds after the crash. The crews extinguished the visible fire within about 10 minutes. However, fire quickly broke out again and, fed by acetone and oxygen in the cargo, became uncontrollable. Continuing attempts to free the imprisoned flight engineer were futile and he died in the fire.

Following the investigation, the Civil Aeronautics Board (CAB) reported as probable cause that the pilots misjudged distance and altitude during the final approach for landing.

MARCH 15, 1962 – N6921C BETWEEN GUAM-AGANA NAS TO ANGELES CITY - CLARK AIR BASE

On the same day as the tragedy at Adak, N6921C Flying Tiger Line flight 739/14 was operating

Super H N6921C at London Airport

MATS' Military passengers board a night departure of a Super H Connie at Travis Air Force Base   photos Flying Tigers Club Archives

on a MATS cargo flight from Travis AFB in California to Saigon, with four refueling stops scheduled at Honolulu, Wake Island, Guam and Clark AFB. It departed Travis AFB at 0545 on March 14 with 96 military passengers aboard, mainly electronics and communications specialists. Their orders were to relieve soldiers in Saigon who had been training South Vietnamese troops to fight Viet Cong guerrillas. Also on board were three members of the Vietnamese military and a multiple crew of 11 under the command of Captain Gregory P. Thomas. Other crew members were First Officer Robert J. Wish, Second Officer Robbie J. Gayzaway, Flight Engineer George M. Nau, Flight Engineer Clayton E. McClellan, Navigator William T. Kennedy, Navigator Grady R. Burt, Jr., and Stewardesses Shirley Bolo, Diane Hernandez, Joyce Osland, and Joan Lambrose.

The aircraft arrived in Honolulu at 1744 after a routine flight of about 12 hours. After some minor

First Officer Robert J. Wish
photo Flying Tiger Line
Pilots Association

maintenance works on the engines, the aircraft departed from Honolulu at 2040 with a small delay of 30 minutes because of complaints by the stewardesses concerning inadequate crew rest facilities aboard N6921C that were subsequently addressed.

The aircraft arrived at Wake Island at 0354 on March 15. Minor maintenance was again required and the aircraft was then serviced. The four stewardesses were replaced at Wake Island by Patricia Wassum, Hildegarde Muller, Barbara Wamsley, and Christel Reiter.

The aircraft and departed for Guam at 0515 and arrived in Guam at 1114 after a routine flight of approximately six hours. During the ground time of 1 hour and 33 minutes, the aircraft was serviced. There were no mechanical discrepancies reported and no maintenance was required. Preparations for the next leg of the flight were completed by the crew in a routine manner. This included filing an Instrument Flight Rules (IFR) flight plan to Clark AFB in the Philippines. The estimated time en route for this flight was 6 hours and 19 minutes. Available inflight weather information did not indicate anything exceptional at the planned cruising altitude.

The aircraft departed Guam at 1257. Shortly after takeoff, radar contact with the aircraft was established by Guam Air Route Traffic Control Center. Approximately 28 minutes after departure, the flight contacted Guam again and requested a change in cruising altitude from 10,000 feet to 18,000 feet. No reason was given on the altitude change request. Authorization was given to climb to 18,000 feet.

At 14:22 the flight contacted Guam and reported being at position 13°40° North and 140°00° East at 14:16, cruising at 18,000 feet above the clouds, and estimated position 14°00' North, 135°00' East at 1530. It further estimated Clark AFB at 1916 and stated that it had eight hours and 12 minutes of fuel remaining. This was the last radio transmission received from N6921C. No indication of any difficulty was given in this or any of the previous messages.

At 1539 Guam attempted to contact N6921C to obtain its overdue 1530 position report. Despite numerous attempts, radio contact could not be established. At 1600, Guam Center declared the flight to be in uncertainty phase status. At 1633 the flight was placed in alert phase status, and at 1943 its status was changed again, to distress phase. Continuous attempts by all stations and aircraft in the area to contact the flight were unsuccessful.

Search and rescue operations were instituted at 1943 by the Joint Rescue Coordination Center, Agana NAS, Guam, in conjunction with Clark AFB. At 2227, the aircraft's fuel exhaustion time, Flight 739/14 was officially declared lost. The aircraft was not seen or heard from again.

At 2105, on March 15, a message was received by Mackay Radio in Manila from the SS T. L. Lenzen, a supertanker owned by Standard Oil of California, under Liberian registration, and manned by an Italian crew. The message stated that at 1530 (90 minutes past midnight, local time, on March 16) she had sighted a midair explosion from her position at 13°44' North and 134°49' East, and had searched the area for approximately five and a half hours. Unable to contact US Navy radio stations at Manila or Guam prior to this time, she then assumed the explosion must have been the result of military or naval exercises and resumed her original course.

It was established, upon interrogation of five of the crew members, that shipboard lookouts had observed a midair explosion at the approximate position and time when N6921C was expected to reach 14°00' North and 135°00' East. It was recalled that a vapor trail, or some phenomenon resembling a vapor trail, was first observed overhead and slightly to the north of the tanker and moving in an east to west direction. The Lenzen was cruising on a heading of 077° at this time. As this vapour trail passed behind a cloud, there occurred an explosion which was described by the witnesses as intensely luminous, with a white nucleus surrounded by a reddish-orange periphery with radial lines of identically colored light. The explosion occurred in two pulses lasting between two and three seconds and from it two flaming objects of unequal brightness and size apparently fell, at disparate speeds, into the sea. During the last ten seconds of the fall of the slower of the two objects, a small bright target was observed on the ship's radar bearing 270°, range 17 miles.

The captain of the Lenzen stated that he arrived on desk in time to observe the fall of the slower object for approximately ten seconds before it disappeared from view. He estimated its position in reference to a star and ordered the ship's course reversed and, after aligning the heading of the vessel with the star, found his heading to be 270° - the same as the bearing of the target previously seen on the radar. The captain reported that the weather at the time. "Moonlight, clear atmosphere, 1/4 covered sky by small cumulus evenly distributed." No signals or unusual sightings were reported.

The subsequent search, one of the most extensive ever conducted in aviation history at that time, covered 144,000 square miles and utilized 1,300 people, 48 aircraft, and 8 surface vessels. A total of 377 air sorties were flown which involved over 3,417 flying hours. Despite the thoroughness of the search, nothing was found which could conceivably be linked to the missing aircraft or its occupants.

Secretary of the Army Elvis Stahr told newspapers, "We have not given up hope that it will be found and that those aboard are safe," and that, "a maximum effort" was being made. After four

MY FATHER GEORGE MICHAEL NAU

Catherine Nau

In this photo from 1958, I was seven years old. I full-heartedly loved any opportunity there was to be with my father, even if it was only for a photo or sitting on one of his shoes when he came through the door right from work. Once, he let me sit on his knee while he rubbed his scratchy five o'clock shadow on my cheek; I laughed and laughed.

George Michael Nau in front of his home in Pacoima, CA with Catherine Nau on his left and her younger sister on his right

photo Catherine Nau

But then there were a few times when he was frustrated with me. When the nurse at my elementary school called home because I had a 102° temperature, I waited for someone to come and get me. Surprisingly, it was my father. On the way home, he walked about fifteen feet in front of me and did not say a word. He had his one-piece white (but greasy) mechanic jumpsuit on which led me to believe that he was home working. I knew I must have interrupted him and I felt bad about it.

Another time, all four of us kids were wading in the ocean with my father standing in the centre of us while the waves splashed in our faces. My three siblings were holding onto our father for support. But when I tried to join in with them, my father shook his arm and lifted it so high that I couldn't reach it. I then felt afraid because my feet couldn't touch the bottom and I didn't know how to swim.

Then, our whole family was getting ready to drive to the outdoors drive-in to see a movie but, I was the last one of my siblings out the front door. My father was frustrated with me since I had not tied my robe belt. He tried to instruct me, but I just couldn't understand. He said I couldn't get in the car until I learned how to tie my belt.

Little did I know then that those were some of the only memories of my father that I would run over and over in my mind for more than fifty-seven years. In addition, the smell of airplane fuel and mechanic's tools always brings my memories to life.

I dedicated my whole life to search for answers regarding my father, George Michael Nau, and the other 106 who disappeared on N6921C that fateful day of March 16, 1962 over the Pacific.

Sincerely

Catherine Nau, nau62@n6921c.com

days of searching, Major General Theodore R. Milton of the 13th Air Force told newspapers that although the chance of finding survivors was doubtful, every effort would be made, "as long as there is any hope at all." After eight days, the search, which was at the time one of the largest to ever take place in the Pacific, was called off.

A complete review of the aircraft maintenance records was conducted, previous flight crew were interviewed, flight line and ramp areas of the en route airports used by N6921C were examined, but nothing was found to explain the midair explosion witnessed by the crew members of the tanker SS Lenzen. Not a single shred of debris from the plane was ever found.

A summation of all relevant factors tends to indicate that the aircraft was destroyed in flight. However, due to the lack of any substantiating evidence the Civil Aeronautics Board (CAB) was unable to state with any degree of certainty the exact fate of N6921C.

Both flight 739/14 (N6921C) and flight 7816/14 (N6911C) were Military Air Transport Service (MATS) and destroyed on the same day. This led both airline officials and the media to offer suggestions of sabotage and conspiracy.

The Flying Tiger Line released a statement outlining some possible reasons for the two occurrences, including sabotage of either or both aircraft, and kidnapping of Flight 739 and its passengers. The airline also said that these were merely "wild guesses" and that there was no evidence to support either theory.

Frank Lynott, executive vice president of operations, said that experts considered it impossible for explosions to occur on the Super Constellation in the course of normal operation. Additionally, he claimed that there was nothing powerful enough aboard the aircraft to completely blow it apart, and that, "Something violent must have happened."

To date, this remains the worst aviation accident involving the Lockheed Constellation series.

23 SEPTEMBER 1962 – N6923C
WEST OF SHANNON, IRELAND

Flying Tiger Line flight 923/23, operated by aircraft N6923C, was a MATS flight from McGuire AFB, New Jersey, to Rhein Main Airport, Frankfurt with a schedule and flight crew change and refueling stop at Gander, Newfoundland.

Prior to departure from Newark to pick up passengers at McGuire AFB, preliminary flight planning for the Atlantic crossing was acccomplished by dispatch personnel and the flight plan was checked by the navigator. The aircraft departed McGuire AFB at 1145 and the flight to Gander was routine.

The crew from Gander to Frankfurt consisted of Captain John D. Murray, First Officer Robert W. Parker, Flight Engineer James E. Garrett, Jr., Navigator Samuel T. Nicholson, and stewardesses Elizabeth A. Sims, Carol Ann Gould, Ruth Mudd, and Jacqueline L. Brotman. There were 68 passengers on board the airplane, mostly American paratroopers on their way to their unit in Germany, and some women and a mother with two children.

During the ground time in Gander, the aircraft was serviced. There was no entries of any significance in the aircraft's logbook and weather information was reviewed by the crew. Preparations for the next leg of the flight were completed and the flight departed from Gander at 1709 with the same 68 passengers and 8 crew aboard. Captain Murray occupied the left pilot seat, and Copilot Parker the right pilot seat.

The flight was given an instrument clearance to Frankfurt to maintain FL110 (Flight Level 110, or

Super H N6923C photo Aviation Photo News via J. Ryan

11,000 feet). The en route flying time was estimated as 9 hours and 22 minutes. Takeoff and climbout were described as normal, and regular radio communications reported navigation progress of the aircraft. Due to light icing, at 1851 the flight requested to climb to FL130. It was approved and at 1900 the flight reported reaching FL130. At this new altitude, the flight again encountered light icing and Murray requested FL210. This was approved by Gander control center and at 2010 the flight reached FL210.

Within a few minutes after reaching this altitude, and, according to navigator, approximately eight minutes past the precomputed ETP (Equal Time Point), a fire warning occurred on the number three engine, and this propeller was feathered. While in the process of engine shutdown, Stewardess Sims came to the cockpit and reported a fire in the number three engine. Captain Murray then instructed the flight engineer to check the engines visually. The engine check was accomplished from the passenger compartment.

At 20:19, Parker called Gander Radio, reported the failure of number three engine, and requested permission to descend to FL90, the highest altitude which could be maintained on three engines at the computed aircraft weight. Gander approved descent to FLO90 and asked if the flight needed escort. The flight replied, "Standby."

According to Murray, about six or seven minutes after the number three engine fire warning and shortly after the flight engineer returned to the cockpit from examining the fire in the No. 3 engine, the number one engine oversped and was shut down and its propeller feathered immediately. Subsequent attempts to restart this engine were unsuccessful. Maximum Except Takeoff (METO) power was then established on engines two and four in order to maintain a minimum rate of descent. The flight engineer checked the aircraft performance charts and determined that at the computed weight of the aircraft, it would be impossible to fly higher than 5,000 feet.

At approximately 2025, Parker called Gander Radio and reported the propellers for engines one and three were feathered, and requested flight level 50 and an escort.

Gander asked N6923C if it was returning to Gander or proceeding to Shannon. The flight replied, "Proceeding to Shannon." The flight called Shannon at 2039 for weather conditions at Keflavik, but due to the poor conditions that were relayed, Keflavik was dropped as a possible diversion point.

At this point the procedures for ditching were reviewed and the senior stewardess was called to the cockpit and briefed. Murray was about to speak on the PA system switch to inform the passengers of events, but the senior stewardess was "Doing such a fine job of briefing them," he decided not to interfere. During this time Parker was in constant radio contact with Shannon and Gander.

At 20:45, FT923 requested sea conditions from Gander, relayed and communicated back by a DC-7 eastbound flight, callsign Riddle 18H.

For the next 30 minutes, many radio communications were established with Gander, Shannon (that declared an alert). Two other aircraft relayed messages, MATS 33146 and Riddle 18H.

At approximately 2115, a fire warning on engine number two engine occurred. Murray reduced power; the fire warning light went out and the alarm bell stopped ringing. He then reapplied power to approximately one or two inches of manifold pressure less than METO power. At this time he had the passengers don their lifevests and altered course for Ocean Station Vessel Juliett which was 480 nautical miles away. Again a fire warning for number two engine was experienced, power was further reduced, and the warning stopped. Power was then increased to slightly less than the previous power setting and Parker called Shannon to inform them that the flight would be unable to maintain FL50.

Upon reaching FL30, altitude was maintained at approximately 150 knots IAS, with METO power on engine number four, and reduced power on engine number two.

In the meantime, preparation continue to prepare for ditching, reassuring passengers, explaining ditching procedures and brace positions, collecting any sharp objects, shoes and boots, ensuring passengers had their lifejackets on and preparing emergency liferaft.

Respectively at 2154 and 2157, MATS 33146 and Riddle 18H were in visual contact with N6923C. At approximately this time engine number two failed; however, its propeller was not feathered. Murray then turned on the PA system and announced, "Ladies and gentlemen, this is the captain speaking. We are going to ditch." A ditching heeding of 265° magnetic was then decided. Directional control of the aircraft was difficult with METO power on the outboard engine number four, and the aircraft was turned to the left in order to obtain the heading of 265°. As N6923C was lined up on a heading of 265°, Murray reduced power on the remaining engine so that lateral control could be maintained. Flaps were used throughout the approach to the water with the selection of first 60 percent, then 80 percent, and finally 100 percent.

Everyone was in position prior to ditching, stewardesses assuming strategic positions near emergency exits and doors. Cabin lights were turned down so that passengers might accustom their eyes to darkness.

Just prior to impact, landing lights were switched on and power on engine number four was cut. The intention was to land just past the top of a swell. Moments before impact, the nose of the aircraft was raised to parallel the face of the approaching swell.

There was only one deceleration but due to the severity of it, several triple seats failed at impact. After initial impact, there were no skips or subsequent impacts. In near darkness and with only a handful of flashlights, evacuation immediately started. Survivors reported that the left wing of N6923C had separated during the ditching.

When the last passengers left the aircraft that water inside was at least waist deep. Five 25-man liferafts (one in the cabin, two in each wing compartment) were aboard but only the cabin 25-man liferaft was ever used, the other ones not seen by survivors during the evacuation. A total of 51 souls including Murray, Nicholson and Stewardess Gould swam to the raft. Being over capacity, the raft took on water and survivors had to hold the heads of others out of the water. N6923C sank within a few minutes later in the Atlantic Ocean.

The water was cold – about 10° C – and covered with white caps with swells up to 20 feet high. Both MATS 33146 and Riddle 18H continued to circle above the crash scene for approximately six hours until Swiss deep-sea freighter MS Celerina arrived to rescue the survivors. The freighter was on the way from Canada to Antwerp and was asked to sail to the scene of the accident only a few minutes after the ditching. The recovery of the survivors took about an hour due to the high waves. Of the 51 people in the liferaft, 48 survived. Two people died on the raft, another shortly after the rescue on the freighter. Survivors were later transferred to the Canadian aircraft carrier Bonaventure.

A total of 28 people (23 passengers and five crew members) lost their lives in the accident, 18 of them remained missing.

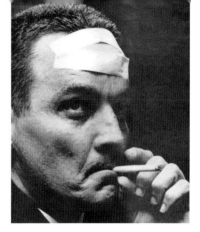

Captain John D. Murray hit his head on the control panel and was bleeding to the extent that he could hardly see

photo flyingtiger923.com

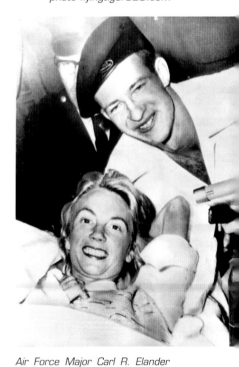

Air Force Major Carl R. Elander of West Point, NY, and his wife, Lois, both of whom survived the N6921C ditching in the Atlantic, are shown here after being landed by helicopter at Shannon airport, Ireland on September 27, 1962

photo Flying Tigers Club Archives

The reason for the malfunction of engine number one was determined by the investigation to be that the flight engineer had inadvertently switched off its supply of fuel as well as lubricating and hydraulic oil. One to two minutes without oil resulted in this engine suffering major damage, which also explained why it could not be restarted. In addition, it was reported that a variety of safety routines during flight and ditching were not performed correctly. The final report also found that the liferaft's lighting system was inadequate and that lifejackets should be equipped with automatic lights in future.

14 DECEMBER 1962 – N6913C
WEST OF HOLLYWOOD-LOCKHEED AIR TERMINAL, CA

Flying Tiger Line flight 183/13, operated by aircraft N6913C, was a cargo flight originating in Boston, Massachusetts, on December 13, with stops scheduled at Windsor Locks and Chicago, destination Burbank.

Captain Karl C. Rader, First Officer David L. Crapo, and Flight Engineer Jack W. Grey assumed flight crew duties on the final leg. Two non-revenue passengers also boarded at Chicago, John A. Olson, husband of Flying Tigers employee Janet Olson and Mrs. Violet Blazek, Flying Tigers field administrator.

Local newspaper clipping with pictures of the flight crew, from left to right, Captain Karl C. Rader, First Officer David L. Crapo, and Flight Engineer Jack W. Grey　　　*Flying Tigers Club Archives*

The aircraft departed O'Hare at 1508 after receiving an IFR clearance to Burbank. The flight plan indicated an estimated time en route of seven hours.

At 2149, approximately ten minutes northeast of Palmdale, the flight contacted the Los Angeles station of ARINC (Aeronautical Radio Inc) and requested they advise FTL that existing weather conditions at Burbank were below minimums and that the flight was proceeding to Los Angeles (LAX) for landing. After reporting over the Palmdale VOR at 11,000 feet at 2159, the flight received a special Burbank weather observation from the Center indicating, "... sky partially obscured, five hundred overcast, one-half mile visibility with fog."

N6913C acknowledged this transmission by reading back the message, then stated that they would like to make an approach at Burbank. At 2205 the flight was contacted by ARINC and provided with the 2200 Burbank weather: partial obscuration, estimated five hundred overcast, one mile fog and smoke, temperate five two, dewpoint five one, wind north one, altimeter thirty fifteen, runway zero seven visual range one and three quarters miles, fog, eight tenths, tower visibility one half mile. Flight 183 acknowledged this transmission and stated, "We're going to shoot an approach at Burbank and then if we miss we'll go over to LA." The ILS approach minima at Burbank was 300 feet ceiling and ¾ mile visibility.

The flight was cleared to descend to 8,000 feet, and at 2205 control was transferred from the Centre to Burbank Approach Control. Normal radar vectoring services were provided, and subsequently the flight requested to be vectored close in for its ILS approach. The flight continued its descent in visual flight conditions, as reported by the pilot, to 3,500 feet on headings of 145 and 090 degrees. A turn to the ILS localizer course of 076 degrees was commenced at a point one and a half miles northwest of the ILS outer marker. At 2210, the approach controller advised N6913C that they were intercepting the localizer course 1/2 mile west of the outer marker, and cleared the flight for an ILS approach to runway 7 with instructions to, "Report the outer marker to Burbank Tower on 118.7."

The last contact with N6913C, at 2211:55, was the flight acknowledgment of its radar-observed position two miles from the approach end of runway 7. The approach controller stated that the flight, as viewed on his radar scope, appeared to be on the localizer course throughout the approach up to this point. Approximately 20 seconds later the aircraft crashed into a residential/industrial area, approximately one mile from the approach end of runway 7. The local electric utility company experienced a massive power interruption at 2215:15 in what was later determined to be the area of the accident as the approach controller lost video on his radar scope at this time.

The aircraft initially contacted ground obstacles located 7,696 feet from the approach end of runway 7. This position is approximately 1/2 mile east of the ILS middle marker and on the extended centreline. The aircraft first brushed the top of a 24-foot high tree, then struck a billboard 22 feet high parallel to the aircraft's course. The signboard received slash marks from the propeller of engine number one. The right wing struck a 65-foot high utility pole at this point. It was determined that the aircraft was on a heading of about 075 degrees magnetic, in a nose-level attitude, and with a left bank angle of approximately 19 degrees. It proceeded for a distance of approximately 700 feet, crashing into several small houses, before it struck and passed through a brick factory building. The rear fuselage section separated from the aircraft and had almost completed a 360-degree swing-around before coming to rest right side up, approximately 280 feet beyond the factory building. Five dwellings, one factory building, and a workshop were destroyed by impact and fire. Three other houses and one factory were damaged and several powerlines were severed.

All aboard were killed and three local residents on the ground also perished, Miss Cathleen Roche, Jose Chavez Jr and Mrs Doris Malouin.

The forward section of the aircraft was destroyed by impact and fire while the rear fuselage structure remained essentially intact. All four engines and propeller assemblies separated from the aircraft during its disintegration and were recovered in the wreckage area. Based on the propeller blade angles, governor settings, and measured propeller slash marks, an airspeed of 139 knots at impact was established. The main landing gear and the nose gear were in transit to the retract position at the time of impact. The wing flaps were symmetrically extended to 60 percent.

Witnesses on the ground were interviewed, a complete examination of the other aircraft components and systems was conducted, maintenance and operational records were examined, the ILS system was checked, and a flight test was conducted to duplicate the approach of N6913C.

A complete post-mortem examination of all persons fatally injured in the accident was conducted; evidence of possible inflight incapacitation of the captain was first discovered. While only a portion of the captain's heart was recovered, pathological examination revealed evidence of severe pre-existing coronary artery disease.

In view of the weather situation and the rapid, high speed descent to intercept the ILS, it is highly unlikely that the captain would have permitted the co-pilot to make this approach. The first officer would be expected to perform the normal duties of a co-pilot while the captain was the handling pilot.

The voice transmission emanating from N6913C during the approach were identified as those of the captain, yet radio communications are normally the responsibility of the co-pilot. However, it was stated by associates of the captain that he frequently would handle the radio communications while flying the aircraft.

As evidenced by the findings and all testimony presented at the public hearing by expert medical witnesses, Rader – with gear down and flying the ILS approach in a particularly stressful moment – suffered a heart attack resulting in a sudden complete or partial incapacitation. It was the only logical explanation for the sudden deviation below the glidepath of N6913C.

The landing gear of N6913C was determined to have been in transit to the up position at the time of impact. The time involved from the last voice contact from the flight to the time of the accident was 20 seconds. Thus, incapacitation of the captain immediately after the last radio contact would leave the co-pilot only a minimal amount of time to identify the situation, take whatever action necessary to recover control of the aircraft, and then attempt to fly the aircraft out of a precarious position, The CAB believed that the co-pilot ultimately recognized the situation, applied engine power and initiated landing gear retraction. However, the rate of sink was not arrested in time and the aircraft continued its descent into the ground obstacles.

Compounding the severity of the situation, it is likely that Captain Rader fell forward onto the controls, limiting aft movement of the control column to the extent that the aircraft could not be rapidly rotated to a positive climb attitude. Further, because of a low fog bank condition with the relatively good visibility above,

PILOT'S HEART FAILED, CAUSED L.A. CRASH

N6913C's first contact with the ground was a propeller slicing through a billboard

The rear section separated from the rest of the aircraft

The scene of devastation in the aftermath of the crash

One of N6913C's vertical stabilisers

all photos Flying Tigers Club Archives

it is believed that the co-pilot Crapo would not be monitoring the captain's approach as closely as he would in an IFR situation. Therefore, following the rapid deviation from glide slope it is probable that N6913C entered the fog bank before Crapo could fully assume control of the aircraft and then transition to instrument flight conditions.

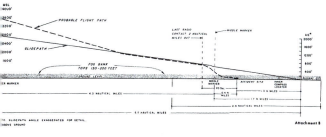

Based on the test flight data and witness observations, a flight profile of N6913C was developed

CAB file No. 1-0035 released on January 2, 1964

WE LOST AN AIRPLANE LAST NIGHT

Captain Starr Thompson

Karl Rader was the captain on N6913C. I was supposed to be deadheading on it with my crew, but I called the company and talked them out of putting me on there. But I missed my connection to go from cargo terminal to the passenger terminal at O'Hare as it took me three and a half hours to get a cab. So, I missed the flight and I called Jim Ossello in crew scheduling and told him. He said, "Well, go on back over to the cargo terminal and deadhead home on 13C and I'll round up a crew in Newark and pax them over to Detroit to bring your flight back." I said, "Jim, I think I have a better idea." "Yeah, what's that?" "I brought in 19C, it's going out

Captain Starr Thompson at the FTLPA reunion in Reno, May 1994

photo Eliot Shulman/ Flying Tiger Line Pilots Association

of O'Hare, Cleveland, Newark, and if you rerouted through Detroit, he could taxi in, drop us off, taxi out, go on across the lake and we won't lose twenty minutes." "Great idea, consider it done."

There was a lot of people trying to deadhead home for the holidays, bearing in mind this was December 14th. And so that's what we did and I thought normal, saved airfare for all those kids getting over there, because I told him, I said "You know, I like flying my own trips?" I bailed his ass out a number of times. Anyway the next day morning Phil Rossmore (?) alerted me for my flight back to Burbank. And he said "By the way we lost an airplane last night." I wanted to know all the particulars – who was it, where was it, and so forth. It turned out it was 13C, the one they wanted me to deadhead home on. And I thought, Holy God, if I did what the company had asked, I was supposed to be dead now. Well that made my mind up to quit drinking. And so we flew the trip home and I was an hour late getting off the ground, the company never said anything to me about it. I was so upset with all the news and so many friends.

FLIGHT ATTENDANT CAROL ANN GOULD HANSEN

Robin Burkey Pestarino, Senior Flight Attendant

Stewardess Carol Ann Gould after the accident in 1962

photo author's collection

There were 76 men, women and children on board – 48 lived, 28 died. There was only one usable life raft available – the one Navigator Sam Nicholson got out through the aft cabin door and lost in the wind. Sam swam after it, retrieved it, brought it back to the aircraft upside down. The safety lights, emergency kit were unreachable as they were underwater. The ocean waves were between 10 and 12 feet high with swells reaching up to 35 feet. Gale-force winds drove the raft 22 miles from the crash site in just six hours.

The plane sank in ten minutes. A Swiss freighter, the Celerina, changed course to get to the last known heading of the plane when it crashed, but they were six hours away. A Tiger freighter, captained by Joseph Lewis, heard the mayday call, knowing it was a sister ship. Lewis found the ditching site and circled for five hours to direct rescue efforts and drop spotting flares. Life expectancy in the North Atlantic is 45 minutes; for most of that, one is hypothermic. The life raft, made to hold 25 men each weighing 200 pounds, was occupied by 51.

Captain Lewis and his crew had to leave the scene as they were getting low on fuel. The *Celerina* was on her way, and just an hour later, plucked the survivors out of the ocean while the Canadian aircraft carrier *Bonaventure* delivered medical supplies and badly needed provisions. The *Bonaventure* opened its modern hospital facility for those passengers who needed it. 17 passengers were airlifted to Ireland.

The officers of flight 923 were Captain John Murray, First Office Robert W. Parker, Flight Engineer James Garrett, and Navigator Sam Nicholson. The flight attendants were Carol Ann Gould Hansen, newlywed Betty Sims on her last flight, Jacqueline Brotman, Ruth Mudd.

Carol has recounted this harrowing event several times, graciously telling the story to the Flying Tiger Line Pilots Association several years ago. She wasn't part of the original crew but filled in for another flight attendant. She briefed her passengers in her section so well that they all survived. She had them follow her from the plane but lost sight of the raft in the 35-foot swells. Then she saw a light and swam to it. As the raft light was under water, the CAB investigators wanted to know, "What light?" She insisted there was a light, and that was the only way she knew where the raft was.

As it turned out, the captain returned to the cockpit to get his flashlight. He was the last to leave the aircraft and the last person the raft. It was reported that the passengers on board the raft weren't going to let him board as it was crowed already. One saw his epaulets and they let him board with his flashlight to signal for help. This was the only visible light on the raft. Carol will tell you that she saw a light on the raft before the captain boarded, and the only explanation to her is that God showed her the way.

Carol was a regular 'Molly Brown' in the raft, signing songs, giving as much first aid as she could. When the captain ordered, "Bail, bail if you want to live!", Carol showed the passengers how to help as the raft was taking on water. Many credited Carol for keeping their spirits up until they were rescued.

Carol is the last surviving crew member of Flying Tigers 923 and works as an international tour guide. She is not afraid of flying, amazingly enough. She and her husband were walking down a New York street when a car went out of control, hitting and killing her husband, missing her. She has openly wondered why she is still alive but concedes that God must have a plan for her. She very may be right.

10

In With A Bang, Out With A Whimper

Captain George Gewehr (FTL, FDX)

1962 was moving along, but then there was another Tiger flight lost. It was a ditching in the North Atlantic on September 23. It was a Constellation with 68 U.S. Army passengers plus some civilian government people, and a crew of eight, led by John Murray.

The airplane lost three engines with one running. It ditched at night in a very high wind and high seas. There is one crew member still alive, a stewardess by the name of Carol Hansen. She and the navigator Sam Nicholson were heroes who saved lives. Sam was able to launch the only 25 man life raft, which ended up holding 48 people.

The accident was a great shock to us at Tigers. The company had already lost two airplanes in recent months; now this. The Year of the Tiger wasn't looking good. The company lost its military contract for a few months until the powers that be decided we could operate again.

I've always wondered what the west coast operations were doing to handle this calamity. The company seemed to weather the storm and I continued to fly the North Atlantic, with a few hiccups. One was a trip I had with a heavy crew – three pilots, two flight engineers, one navigator, and four stewardesses. We stayed together for the entire trip.

The trip started by taxiing over to the Newark passenger terminal, picking up a load of Greek-American tourists going to the island of Rhodes in their ancestral homeland. They boarded full of expectation of an adventure. We took off and headed for Gander in Newfoundland, our first stop for fuel and service. Everything went well until we arrived over Gander with the weather fogged in. The captain decided to fly to our alternate field at Harmon Air Base in Stephenville, Newfoundland.

The base is gone but the airport is operated by the Newfoundland government and the local authorities.

We landed with no problems and offloaded our passengers while we refueled. Captain Bliss was planning to fly direct to Shannon from Stephenville.

The startup was OK but after the engines were running, the engineer said the number four generator wasn't working. He said he couldn't isolate it, because in those days it wasn't possible (nowadays with jet engines and modern equipment you can do this). The captain asked him what he wanted to do.

Since we didn't carry a spare generator, the engineer suggested he and the other engineer remove the generator and place a pad cover over it using a spare parts kit in the rear belly compartment. The captain agreed to remove it and bolt the cap cover over the generator drive. I was instructed by Captain Bliss to go inside with the passengers to the terminal and explain to them what we were doing, and that they should not worry about it as it wasn't anything serious, which they seemed to accept.

Both engineers had been mechanics before becoming flight engineers so it was possible for them to do the job. They borrowed some coveralls from the Air Force staff, plus a work stand. The job was accomplished in reasonable

Captain Jack Bliss in the early 1970s

photo Flying Tigers Club Archives

Captain Lew Cason

Flying Tiger Line Pilots Association

time. The passengers were loaded back onboard, and we started up and taxied out.

The second captain, Lew Cason, was flying the airplane now and I was in the copilot's seat. We made the takeoff, but after becoming airborne the engineer called out, "Engine number four power loss."

I had retracted the gear just as he called it out. Since we had left in the late afternoon the temperature was fairly warm. Because of this and our heavy weight we weren't climbing very well. Captain Bliss had been setting in the jump seat on takeoff. Now he was hunched over next to the engineer looking at the engine analyser. We hadn't feathered the engine yet, so it was still producing power.

The tower called us and asked me what our altitude was; I replied, 300 feet. They instructed us to climb immediately to 2,000 feet and turn left to a southerly heading. The reason for this was the hills on our left which were on our departure route and above us. I told them, we are climbing immediately – at 100 feet a minute. We stayed over the water of the bay next to the airport which gave us an unobstructed flightpath. I turned to look out my window at the number four engine on the right side.

What I saw was a very large amount of oil spraying out of the cowl flaps. I turned back to them both and yelled, "The number four engine is spitting oil!" For more effect, and louder, "Look at number four engine through the crew door window!" Captain Bliss looked through the prism window in the door and exclaimed, "Oh shit, we got a problem." In the meantime departure control was also asking us if we have a problem. Captain Bliss had taken over from the other captain, and told me not to say anything; we will get back to them.

The engineer feathered the engine and secured it. Captain Bliss instructed me, "Tell them we are continuing to Gander". We continued to climb at a slow rate but finally reached an altitude to ask for a clearance to Gander. The weather was now clear in Gander and would present no problem landing. The engineer asked if we were going to dump fuel. The captain replied in the negative – "I don't trust the dump valves." The engineer

replied that we would be over our maximum landing weight. Captain Bliss said, "They can make an overweight inspection in Gander. We'll have plenty of time there." He was right about that. We weren't going anywhere with the engine like that. We asked for a visual approach which was approved. The captain made a good landing and taxied to the gate.

After we parked the airplane, the passengers were very upset, to say the least. This is when it got a bit nasty. They felt they had been lied to about the number four engine with its problem. Remember I had gone into the terminal at Stephenville with them to allay any

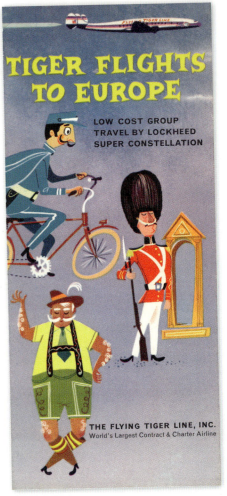

Tiger Flights to Europe brochure
Flying Tigers Club Archives

worry – it would be all OK. Then on takeoff the same engine spits oil out of it. The two problems were not related but you couldn't tell them this, and they wouldn't believe us anyway. As they exited the airplane, some of the women passengers spat on the stewardess at the door. I never learned how the company got blankets and pillows for our passengers to sleep in the terminal but they did. We went to the hotel and spent the rest of the night a bit subdued. We were all tired so it was not a late night for sure.

The next day our chief pilot Oakley Smith brought us another airplane from Newark. We finally left late in the afternoon for Shannon. The crossing to Shannon was actually a fairly smooth flight. We arrived in

A tourist group flown by Flying Tigers to Europe

Shannon in the late morning after which the passengers seemed to have mellowed their feelings a bit. They all went to the duty free store with interest. The airplane was serviced and we left for Greece, arriving in Rhodes in the afternoon.

There was a large crowd at the airport to greet our passengers, who had a change of heart for their behavior towards the cabin crew. When they exited the airplane, they gave the captain a collection of money to distribute. This was well received by the girls so everyone was in a good mood when we left.

After a short time on the ground in Rhodes, we took off for Prestwick in Scotland. The airplane was empty and the cabin crew plus myself with one of the engineers proceeded to stretch out in the seats for a nap. The seating was a three and three across configuration, with a single aisle. The problem with a long trip is after a while you start feeling like a weathered tree or a strand of wheat. You have to keep hydrated but back then it was hard. We didn't carry enough water or juice as we did later.

We flew across the Alps, across the channel and into Prestwick. We loaded passengers on board and took off, heading west to Gander. That leg was the first time I saw icebergs. We were at a fairly low altitude, around 10,000 feet, on a clear day with sun rising behind us which made them easy to see. What impressed me most were the small lakes in the middle of them; the water had a crisp blue colour. Of course now you can see this on a travel show on your television at any time but at the time it was something I'd never seen before.

The landing in Gander was uneventful, and servicing of the airplane was conducted in a timely manner; we were in and out within two hours. We headed for New York's Idlewild Airport, which is now John F. Kennedy International. The arrival at JFK went smoothly, and with the passengers deplaned we ferried over to Newark airport. After all of the things which took place on this trip I was surprised on how short it was. We left on the 10th in the morning and arrived back in Newark on the 13th in the late afternoon. We flew over 15,000 miles in three nights including a reasonably dramatic emergency and ship change.

Piper Colt To CL-44

H. Paul Rebscher

I hired on at Flying Tigers as an air freight salesman at O'Hare field in February 1964, and the following year, 1965, was the company's 20th anniversary. The Chicago employees had a small celebration at a local restaurant and invited local politicians and airport managers.

My good friend Chet Majewski was an elected member of the Chicago sanitary district, an important position, so I invited him. In Chicago being Polish or Irish was a very deal. He showed up at the restaurant along with others. Everyone had short speeches on the history of Tigers at O'Hare and Midway.

I began taking flying lessons in the hope of "catching on" as a crew member. Most carriers were buying new aircraft and the need for pilots was increasing.

To pay for flying lessons, I took a part time job at night loading 7-Up trucks from seven in the morning until ten at night. I already had my foot in the door by flying a desk at the airline which was a big help. As I progressed through private, commercial, instrument and multi-engine licences, I would upgrade my application with the company.

The call came in 1967, so I flew out to LAX for an interview with John Holmes and started class in 1967 training on Canadair CL-44!

Captain John L. Holmes
photo Flying Tiger Line Pilots Association

CL-44 turnaround in Portland, Spring 1966

photo Flying Tigers Club Archives

Return To Blanca Peak: a son's search for his father

Mark Hunt

He was born Thomas Duane Hunt of Los Angeles, California and he was my father. He was hired by the Flying Tiger Line on April 19, 1965 and he was flying as first officer on December 15, 1965 when his Lockheed L-1049H Super Constellation registered N6914C struck the southwest face of Blanca Peak (13,849 feet high) located about 22 nautical miles northeast out on the 039-degree radial from the Alamosa, Colorado VOR at 0130 hrs PST.

Super H N6914C being loaded with freight
photo Flying Tigers Club Archives

There were three crew members aboard and we lost all of them that night. The captain was Everett D. 'Pete' Reed and the second officer was Brian M. Ferris. The crew was performing a scheduled domestic cargo service from Los Angeles to Chicago. While cruising at the assigned altitude of 13,000 by night, in low cloud and snow, the crew apparently became disoriented and failed to turn to Airway V-210 outbound heading to Alamosa VORTAC according to the flight plan for an undetermined reason.

Given that our time together was cut short when I was but a year and a half old, what I know about him is what I've been told. Sure my grandmother, his mother (before she passed) shared with me. As well as my aunt, his only sister and my mother have shared with me as well. But I have always had an interest in what others could tell me about my father, their memories of time spent with him.

Thomas Duane Hunt was N6914C first officer on December 15, 1965
photo Mark Hunt

In my search I found a gentleman by the name of Larry who was friends with my father. I told him that we lived in Orange County, California and he said he would be happy to meet with me and talk. In fact, as luck would have it, he was delivering a King Air to John Wayne Airport. (At the time, Larry was a corporate pilot as well as buying and selling corporate aircraft.) He offered to show us the plane and I thought, what a perfect place to talk. He, my wife and I climbed aboard. Up in the cockpit, he in the left seat and I in the right, he began to share. They both had a common passion, the love of flying. He said they were both competitive. My dad got his license, followed by Larry. Larry got his instrument rating and then so would my dad. Next was checked out on a twin, and so on and so on. He valued their friendship and was sad that he was gone.

My maternal grandfather was a private pilot and said that he had gone up with my father on a number of

Mark with Debbie near one of the vertical stabilisers

photos May 29, 1989 - Mark Hunt

Mark shares a moment of levity with his fellow climbers

Small fuselage titles from underneath the cockpit windows

occasions. He said that my father was an attentive pilot, critical of his flying and always seeking to better himself. Grandpa said one time, they were doing touch and goes. As my father landed the plane, Grandpa thought it was good but my father thought the landing too firm. Up and around they would go again until my father felt it was right. This young man in his twenties demanded professionalism of himself.

I had told myself, one day, I would make that climb to see and be at my father's final resting place. That time was coming.

A couple more years had passed when I was introduced to two brothers that grew up below the crash site and had made the climb numerous times to the wreckage. In fact, it was their father that led the rescue attempt on the night of the crash. They told me and my wife that they would be happy to guide us up to the wreckage and we coordinated the whole trip and timing with them over the phone.

To say this was a special journey would just not be saying enough. Our little car was packed with camping gear, food and the hiking boots we bought and broke in for our climb. We camped along the way – Grand Canyon, Mesa Verde – and then drove into their town and parked in front of their home. We were welcomed inside and the conversation we exchanged was as if between long lost friends not new acquaintances.

The weather was perfect and it was all falling into place. We would climb the next day. We asked where the nearest KOA (Kampgrounds Of America) site was so we could get a camping site. Our hosts would have nothing of the sort and said we would be staying the night with them.

The next day, we woke, their gracious wives made the four of us lunches for the climb, and we all squeezed into the front seat of a pickup truck and began to drive. It seemed both fitting and special that the day this was happening on Memorial Day.

We drove up the mountain to about 7,500 feet, got out of the truck and began our hike. Up through the green trees, through a stand of Aspens, passing two old miner's cabins along the way as we made our way up. Near the top, the terrain changed to what they call scree, loose rock. The Civil Aviation Board accident report states that the aircraft struck the mountain at 13,849 feet above sea level, 150 feet below the summit.

At the base of the scree is a plaque in memoriam and lists all three of the crew. We walked amongst the wreckage, located three of the four Curtiss-Wright turbo compound engines, and found little wheels from the toy Mustang cars that were part of her cargo. I took some time just sitting on the steep slope near pieces of the plane and reflected. That moment was so many things to me that would be hard for me to put into words. Closure is a popular word for times like these, but I'm never completely closing that door. I'll always welcome a ray of light that is my father into wherever I am.

Anyone that tells me that they knew my father and care to share those memories with me, they have my ear. But given that the crash is now over a half a century ago, I know those moments are becoming rarer. But thankfully they are not gone. I was recently introduced to a fine man by the name of George Gewehr, who both knew and flew with my father. This gracious man shared his memories as well as introduced me to and amazing group of Flying Tigers that still gather each year. There I met two more pilots that knew my father.

For me it's nice knowing that even though his time on earth was short – he was only 25 years old – there were many that were and are grateful to have known him.

As a footnote, one time, while I was still in the Navy, I called my mother and we talked. She said, you've been halfway around the world, what have you liked? I told her that even though I enjoyed Europe, it's the Caribbean that I would always return to. The phone line went silent. She went on to say that she had not told me but that my father was already planning to start a charter company down in the Caribbean. I was given some Super 8 movies of which one shows him and my uncle in the Caribbean. Maybe Aruba, I don't recall.

Even though he didn't have years to mold me, I am my father's son.

Boeing 707-349C N322F

photo The Boeing Company / Flying Tigers Club Archives

13

The Pole Cat – A Wild 'Can Do' Tale

It was 7 o'clock in the evening and outside rain fell steadily as two men signed a paper which finally set in motion one of the most remarkable feats of aviation. The date was November 9, 1965. Across the table, facing each other, were Fred Benninger, executive vice-president of The Flying Tiger Line, and Harrison Finch, an 18,000-hour captain of Trans World Airlines, now on leave as president of Geo Atmos Explorations, Inc.

Finch and his associate, Fred Austin, another TWA captain (and formerly TWA's chief pilot) had been meeting almost constantly with Bob Prescott, Flying Tigers president, Benninger and Ed Pinke, FTL's vice-president of operations. For two years, Austin and Finch had been trying to appropriate an aircraft which would launch them on what Lowell Thomas, Sr., explorer, writer and newscaster called, "the last great exploration, this side of space, by conventional aircraft." Now, with the Rockwell-Standard Corp. of Pittsburgh as sponsor of the $250,000 project, they had succeeded in getting the Flying Tiger Line to lease them a brand-new Boeing 707-349C for a flight which would take them around the world, including over both poles.

AVIATION 'FIRST'

In all the long history of aerial exploration, nobody had succeeded in doing this. Austin and Finch had contacted company after company in an effort to make this historic exploration. Time and again, as they seemed on the verge of success, they would hit a hurdle of one kind or another. Now the paper was signed. All that remained was to fly the flight.

And with what time remained, that seemed a task even more formidable than Austin and Finch's quest to find a sponsor and a plane. For they wanted to leave on November 14, just five days hence, and the airplane

– the Pole Cat as it was later named – which they had obtained was even now still flying from Tokyo to the United States on a regular MATS sortie. Five days in which to put together one of the most ambitious projects ever attempted by airmen. Five days for a job which normally might take five months, or even a year of preparation.

POLE CAT PREPARATION

Suffice to say that what the Tigers did in one week in November 1965 may very likely have set an all-time record in getting a big job done quickly. Jim McLachlan, vice-president of maintenance and engineering, was sitting in his office one day when the phone rang and Fred Benninger, executive vice-president, began talking. The Tigers, said Benninger, had a chance to take on a contract with one of their newly delivered Boeing 707-349C Intercontinentals, flying it around the world in about 50 hours, over both the North and South Poles. They'd be well paid. The only thing was that the airplane would have to be modified to take on extra fuel tanks holding about 4,000 gallons, have some scientific research instruments installed, and accommodate about 20 or 30 passengers.

'WHEN?' IS THE QUESTION

"When do we do this?", McLachlan wanted to know. Benninger said he thought if we did it, we'd know in a month or so. Then the big question: "Can we do it?" There was a moment of silence and then the reply: "Yes, we can do it!"

And there the great project rested until the week of November 8. In the meantime, Vice-President of Operations Ed Pinke, McLachlan, Chuck Steeves, manager of engineering and quality control, and John Dewey, manager of maintenance, decided to do a little pre-planning, just in case this crazy thing actually came off.

At this point, the two men who had been dreaming of this flight for several years - Fred Austin and

Harrison Finch, two veteran TWA captains, hadn't got an official sponsor. Although eventually they were to get Rockwell Standard Corporation to finance it, there were literally a million details for them to iron out when they did get backing. In fact, Austin and Finch hadn't even been able to get an airplane up to this point but they had at least intrigued the Tigers, the best prospect they'd had to date.

TIGERS BRIEFED

The operations and maintenance executives conferring with the TWA captains and got a briefing on what modifications would be required for the Boeing. For one thing, huge 2,000-gallon fuel tanks – two of them – would have to be installed in the main cabin to extend the aircraft range on certain flight legs. For another, considerable scientific instrumentation to be installed in the forward cabin would require special electrical circuitry, since it could not be operated off the existing aircraft power.

With this knowledge in hand, Chuck Steeves, the Tiger engineering manager, called on the Boeing factory for help in getting schematic drawings for the tank and electrical installations. This did not involve a lot of investment in time or money in case the flight didn't go, but if it did, they'd be far ahead of starting from scratch.

Steeves praised Don Nordstrom, Boeing engineering supervisor, and John Clark, Boeing fuel systems engineer, for co-ordinating the challenges on the fuel tank installations, both in the preplanning stage and later overseeing the operation when the tanks were fitted into the main cabin and fuel lines were hooked up. Additionally, the Tiger electrical department built up wire bundles of circuits to provide power to the scientific instrument installations.

FORESIGHT PAID OFF

This foresight and willingness to take a chance on the flight was a key to success in the remarkable job that followed when word finally came down the line that the flight was on. With this planning in the works, the Tiger operations, engineering and maintenance forces carried on their regular work of servicing and flying the Tiger fleet and worried no more about what was happening "up front" while Bob Prescott, Benninger and Pinke were negotiating with the TWA captains Austin and Finch.

By this time, early November, Austin and Finch thought they had a chance of finally getting an airplane – the Tiger Boeing. They now, finally, had the interest of a sponsor, the big Rockwell Standard Manufacturing Corp., headed by another pioneer, Col Willard Rockwell.

In Benninger's mind, the flight was off and on since he hadn't seen any money. And then it happened. Austin and Finch got the backing they needed. Now they could talk to Benninger in the terms he understood best: cash on the barrelhead. A substantial down payment was requested and submitted.

Now Prescott and Benninger had to produce the airplane. It was a tough decision. The Tiger Boeing, which the airline had received in September, was busy shuttling across the Pacific flying on the Tiger's Military Airlift Command (MAC) contract. To make the polar flight, it would have to be diverted and modified.

On the afternoon of November 9, Benninger got his down payment. At that very moment, N322F, the Tiger Boeing 707, was enroute from Tokyo to Burbank for maintenance. Benninger called Pinke and told him to get the Boeing ready by November 14. The alert was quickly passed on to McLachlan, Steeves and Dewey, who silently congratulated themselves on the preliminary work that already had been done – the schematic drawings, the wire bundles. It would save a lot of time and now time was the most valuable thing around.

At 8:30 a.m., November 10, N322F hit the ramp at Burbank. It had 381.2 hours on it and was due for its 400-hour check. Quickly, maintenance crews under General Flight Line Foreman Lou Melzer got to work on the ship.

The sheet metal crews under Foreman Willie Skaggs were studying the modifications they'd have to make in the cabin, while in radio, Foreman Angie Elizondo was looking over the problems of communication which would result from the installation of special power packages, together with Foreman John Whitelaw of Electronics and his men. Steeves and Dewey were rapidly assessing the work they and their men would have to do now to get 322F ready to fly, not in a week, not in a month, not in two months which would be a normal requirement in most airline shops - but in two or three days!

TIME IS SHORT

Austin and Finch had to be airborne on the polar flight by Sunday, November 14, and it was now 8:30 a.m., November 10. As John Dewey was to say later: "There's nothing we can't do if we have enough time, equipment and people. This time we didn't have very much time!"

And the things to do? Well, first of all they had to install the two 2,000 gallon additional fuel tanks which they'd never even seen and wouldn't until the next day, November 11. Skaggs and his sheet metal men had to build a huge drain pan 42 feet long and nine and one-half feet wide with four-inch-high sides, all riveted and sealed, to hold the fuel tanks.

They had to install fore-and-aft bulkheads in the main cabin, a job never before done on a Boeing, and install six crew bunks up forward and 25 passenger seats in the rear with galley and lavatory. They had to install plumbing to service the fuel tanks. They had to install scientific equipment with proper circuitry such as the following: Litton inertial guidance system, Collins H. F. radio system, Edo Loren "C" system, two Douglas time-lapse cameras, a NASA radiometer, a laser altimeter by Litton, two pieces of New York University cosmic ray equipment, a 20-2 sample for the US Weather bureau, life rafts, 10 walkaround 02 bottles, fire extinguishers for overhead racks and air outlets for the passenger compartment, flight recorders and accelerometers from Lockheed – and this all had to be in and working by no later than noon of November 13 so Captain Jack Martin, system chief pilot, could take 322F up on the one and only test hop to make to be sure everything was working!

AND THAT'S NOT ALL

As if this were not enough, on Saturday morning as the aircraft was rushed to final readiness for its test flight, three additional pieces of NASA recorder equipment arrived, about which the Tiger crews had no advance warning. When 322F, the Pole Cat as the aircraft had now been named, got ready for final take-off on Sunday morning, Nov. 14, mechanics were still rushing completion of the installation of this equipment. One small but not minor detail remained to be taken care of in all this rush of work – the FAA approval of all the work done. And they got it.

NEVER BEEN DONE

The tank installation was the big one. For one thing, said Engineer Dale Fogel, it had never been done before in a commercial aircraft. Made of a special rubber-nylon material, the tanks were manufactured by Air Logistics of Pasadena, and were primarily designed to provide emergency fuel on battlefronts. Each holding 2,000 gallons, they could be transported on pallets in military aircraft to a battlefront and used for fueling tanks and other military vehicles.

The plumbing to feed fuel from the extra tanks into the aircraft centre section tanks and thence into the engines was routed down through the air conditioning equipment bay in the main cabin. Fuel lines ran the length of the extra tanks to permit filling them from the usual wing and wing box tanks. Additionally, other lines ran the length of the top of the tanks to vent fumes.

From the air conditioning bay, a cut was made through the fuselage into the center section tanks so the fuel could flow through lines into these permanent tanks. These had to be carefully engineered and sealed to prevent any pressurization leak in the aircraft. Other such cuts also had to be made in the fuselage for some of the scientific equipment in the belly such as the laser and camera installations. Again, care had to be exercised to insure full retention of pressurization.

Bob Bennett, electronics engineer, said one of the knottiest problems was to provide power for all the varying systems in the aircraft. There had to be

The huge rubber/nylon fuel cells, each holding 2,000 gallons of fuel, installed to provide extra-long-range capability. Flight captains gather to look over some final papers. Left to right are Bob Buck, TWA; Jack Martin, FTL system chief pilot, Harrison Finch and Fred Austin of TWA, who served as flight captains with Martin in command

Inside the main cabin   photos Flying Tigers Club Archives

special DC for some of the scientific equipment. Two large batteries had to be installed for the Litton inertial navigation package to ensure that it would run from two hours before take-off to final completion of the polar crossing without one-tenth of a second of power interruption. Thus continuous power had to be insured for 75 hours, which would more than cover the flight time assuming all went well.

All of the special electrical systems had to be separated from the normal electrical system of the aircraft and everything added had to work independently so there would be no effect on either the aircraft instruments or navigation equipment.

ELECTRICAL CONVERSION

To accomplish this, installations were made to draw power off the normal aircraft supply and then convert it into the separate systems. The aircraft had 115-volt, 400-cycle systems and this had to be converted to 115 volts and 60 cycles for the scientific installations.

The conversion was accomplished by borrowing a 900-pound converter from Douglas Aircraft. Then to tie-in the Collins telegraphic system, a redesign of the rack and routing cables from the forward baggage racks through the floor to the instrument deck in the cockpit had to be accomplished.

But wait – there were other problems, too. Bob Oppegard, senior engineer, recalled that observer seats had to be installed so that experts following the scientific instruments could operate and check them. And since the Tigers had no chance to see the instruments before they arrived on Thursday, Nov. 11, two days before flight time, they had to figure out how to accomplish such installations literally at the last moment. It took some fast and fancy footwork by all concerned to get this seemingly little job done quickly and right. All electrical devices in the fuel tank area had to be deactivated so there would be no danger of a spark and ignition of any vagrant fuel fumes.

PARALLEL RUNNING – FLIGHT PLANNING

As for planning the flight, Captain Jack Martin, system chief pilot for Flying Tigers was sitting at home when at 8:15 on the evening of Nov. 9 when he got a telephone call from Vice-President Ed Pinke. "I need to see you in my office at 10 a.m., tomorrow. The round-the-world flight is on for this weekend and you're the captain in command."

From then on, through November 10-11-12-13, Jack Martin got little sleep. Neither did Pinke, Vice-President Jim McLachlan of maintenance and engineering, Chuck Steeves, director of engineering and all the rest of a Tiger crew who, Austin and Finch said later, performed what seemed an impossible task. "I met Austin that next morning (November 10)," Martin recalled, "and he outlined the plan of flight. Then I asked Ernie Hickman (FTL's chief navigator) to lay out a flight plan. Gene Olson, who was then in San Francisco on a Boeing training program, was assigned as flight engineer for FTL although we couldn't reach Gene at the time and he never learned until Friday, the 12th, what was up for him. Hickman laid the preliminary figures on the time of the legs, based on the flight route that Austin and Finch wanted to follow, and came up with the figures on fuel consumption."

CAPTAIN BUCK ARRIVES

"On the 12th, Captain Bob Buck of TWA (one of the world's foremost weather pilots and himself the captain of many experimental weather flights) arrived. I'd known Bob over the years but hadn't seen him in some time and I was delighted to sit down with him and talk over flight deck problems. I told him I wanted Ernie to come along as navigator and he agreed that this was necessary, so I called Ernie at home the night of the 12th and told him to get ready – he was going, too! When our Boeing arrived here, it had just 381.2 hours of time on it. It was the ship the company had acquired at the end of September and the latest Boeing version of the intercontinental jet. On the 12th, we didn't even have the big fuel cells in the cabin yet here we were scheduling a take-off from Burbank for 8 a.m., Sunday morning, the

14th. The boys got the tanks in later in the day on the 12th. We were going to have just one test hop to see that everything was right before take-off Sunday. It got to be noon of the 13th and still we weren't ready for the test flight. We were really sweating this one out. Then shortly before 3 p.m., it looked like we were ready and at 3:25 p.m., Bob Buck and myself took the Boeing off the Lockheed field at Burbank. We had just a little more than two hours of time in which to test it all out. We had to be back in Burbank by 6 p.m., because of the restrictions there against landing after that hour with a jet."

INSTALL 9-G TIE-DOWNS

And just to be sure that all was shipshape, all tie-downs were geared to withstand a 9G pull, which is normal in Tiger installations, instead of the 3G tie-downs which might have sufficed. Noon Saturday of November 13 came and passed and the Pole Cat was still getting a going over on the ground like ants working on a molehill. Men had been working 16 to 18 hours at a stretch because in addition to all the special modifications that had to be accomplished, the Pole Cat was still getting the required 400-hour check. Since this was the first operation that Tiger crews had ever pulled on the Boeing, the first time they had ever seen the airplane, the job was not made easier. All wheels were replaced to obviate any possible trouble in this area, and in all, 900 man-hours of work in the routine check were put in during the hectic period from the morning of November 10 to the morning of November 14, in addition to the special modifications previously described.

If this sounds as though all of maintenance and engineering had been turned over to the Pole Cat project, it was only partly true. The Tigers still had an airline to run and maintenance was still doing the regular jobs expected of it to keep the other 26 Tiger ships in the air. And yet there were still other jobs to be done to get the Pole Cat airborne.

FERRY GROUND GEAR

Ground equipment was being ferried to Palm Springs from San Francisco and Burbank so that everything would be shipshape in the desert capital, from which the Pole Cat was to depart officially as part of the International Aeroclassic being staged there. Two truckloads of personnel and equipment were put down in Palm Springs, an air starter and electrical power unit from San Francisco, engine stands and all that might be needed to insure an on-time departure. The air starter was a piece of foresight that won't be forgotten. A starter borrowed from another carrier broke down. Had not the Tiger equipment been on hand, a problem embarrassing to say the least – like getting the engines started – would have confronted the crews there.

TIME RUNNING OUT

Now it was getting on into Saturday afternoon. Captain Martin was muttering to himself and taking quick glances at his watch with appropriate remarks. Time was running out for that all-important test hop. The aircraft had to be flown and back on the ground by 6 p.m. to meet an airport restriction at Burbank prohibiting jet operations after 6 p.m., because of noise. "We've got to get this thing up," exclaimed Martin. "If those tanks don't work, there isn't any flight!" Finally at 1518 Saturday – 3:18 p.m. – Martin got his clearance and the Pole Cat rolled down the Lockheed runway.

"We headed for Phoenix and then back to Burbank, using 16,000 pounds of fuel from the fuselage tanks. Everything went like clockwork." When Martin landed, a big smile told waiting crews of the job they'd done. "Worked like a charm," Martin reported. Weary men shook their heads in relief.

"The boys had done a terrific job of getting those tanks installed and working in less than 24 hours time. There were no leaks and it was obvious that the fuel could be successfully transferred from the fuselage tanks. But when we landed, we still had 10,000 pounds of fuel in those tanks and what we didn't know was whether the tanks would empty completely. In other words, we didn't really know then whether we could use all the fuel out of those tanks and it was certainly apparent from our flight plan that on some legs, we were going to need all of that fuel to make it! In fact, it wasn't until we were enroute to

Honolulu out of Palm Springs that we found out the tanks would empty completely.

Some of the hangar crews had been almost around the clock since Wednesday, a 24-hour-a-day job, and many more had been going at it 16 to 18 hours a day, doing in three days a job that should have taken 60 to 90 days at most shops. They had put in 2,000 man hours since Wednesday morning, representing the work of approximately 110 men. And they had also put in 7,578 pounds of additional equipment, such as the tanks and scientific gear.

Martin remembers "We went home that night of the 13th and got some sleep because in the next four days, we weren't going to get much."

WINDOW REPLACED

Everything was ready, almost. There was distortion in one camera. Apparently, it resulted from a temperature change. A window was replaced and that

The maintenance crew, from left to right, Fred Stunkel, Charley Pryor, Isadore Holtz, John Munoz, Bob McNally, Bob Prescott, Al Cormier and unknown   *Anderson Photography, Flying Tigers Club Archives*

Scientific test equipment which was placed aboard the aircraft to research factors in aerial navigation, polar effects, solar and cosmic radiation, cloud photography, measurement of the jet stream, air sampling and laser determination of air density

photo Flying Tigers Club Archives

solved it. Saturday night and early Sunday morning the final work touches were applied. Vice-President Pinke had set the departure for Palm Springs for 8 a.m., Sunday, November 14, which came and passed. The passengers were on board, the crew on hand. All was in readiness and now came the ridiculous clincher. One technician was missing. Frantic calls finally routed him out of bed. He'd overslept! A rush trip got him to the field.

"On Sunday morning, the 14th, everything was OK as far as we could determine, so with Bob Buck in the left seat and me in the right, we took off for Palm Springs with 11 other crew members, nine scientists and 18 official observers and press." Martin continued

So it was 9:42 a.m. on that Sunday morning, with the rain pouring down, the Pole Cat lifted off the runway for Palm Springs and her historic trip. A few hours later, to the applause of the Aeroclassic crews at Palm Springs, she took off again, still in the rain, and

headed for Honolulu and the official start of her flight around the world. She was to fly over the North and South Poles in record-breaking time of 62 hours, 27 minutes from take-off to touchdown in Honolulu and a flying time of 51 hours, 27 minutes, covering 26,500 miles- the first time that man had ever flown around the world over both poles.

SCIENTIFIC GEAR

Riding behind Martin and Buck in the cabin was 5,000 pounds of scientific instrumentation to measure solar and cosmic radiation, take air samples for spores and micrometeorites, accomplish laser determination of air density, and photograph clouds to furnish correlations of meteorological satellites now in orbit. For, in addition to seeking to be the first to circle the globe over both poles, Austin and Finch and their sponsor, Rockwell-Standard, were also seeking scientific data from instrumentation supplied by Litton Industries, Collins Radio, Lear-Siegler Corp., Weems Corp., and the U.S. Weather Bureau.

FORTY ABOARD

Cockpit crew was headed by Captain Jack Martin, Flying Tigers System chief pilot; Captain Fred L. Austin of TWA; Captain Harrison Finch of TWA; Captain Robert N. Buck of TWA, International Division; and Captain James R. Gannett, Boeing senior engineering test pilot best known for co-piloting the Boeing 707 prototype that zoomed low and performed two perfect barrel rolls over a Seafair crowd in 1955 with flamboyant test pilot Alvin "Tex" Johnston.

Three Flights engineers were onboard; Eugene Olson of Flying Tigers, and Dino Valazza and James M. Jones of TWA. They were joined by a similar number of navigators; Ernie A. Hickman of Flying Tigers, John Larsen, formerly TWA & now consultant of Weems Corp, and Lauran DeGroot of Lear-Siegler.

Goodwin Lyon of Geo Atmos Explorations was also part of the crew for the Flight Operations side, together with John Demuth of Collins Radio.

Among the 40 aboard was a scientific team headed by Dr. Serge A. Korff and William Sandie of

Flying Tigers' flight crew aboard the Pole Cat were (left to right) Gene Olson, flight engineer; Ernie Hickman, chief navigator; and Captain Jack Martin, FTL system chief pilot

New York University; Capt. N. A. Lieurance USN (Ret) of the Weather Bureau; Dr. Donald Goedeke of Douglas Aircraft Co (space research division); Walter B. Gartner of Serendipity Inc; and William King of NASA.

Also on board were various observers and executives including Flying Tiger's president, Bob Prescott; Col. Willard F. Rockwell, 77-year-old chairman of the board of Rockwell-Standard and key sponsor for the flight; Edward J. Williams, VP of Rockwell-Standard Corp; Col. Bernt Balchen, pioneer aerial explorer of the Antarctic and the pilot who flew Admiral Byrd over the South Pole in 1929; Dr. Randolph Lovelace, noted medical authority on aviation; Edward C. Sweeney, president of the National Aeronautics Association (NAA) and Bart Locanthi, official flight timer of the NAA (for this flight if successful was to go into the record books as "official"); Lowell Thomas, Jr.; John DuBois and Earl D. Johnson, all three of the Explorers Club.

Also, aboard were Clete Roberts, famed Los Angeles TV newscaster; Wayne W. Parrish, publisher of American Aviation and probably the world's most traveled air traveller at that time; Don Moser and J. R. Eyerman of Life magazine; Joseph Longo of Geo Atmos Explorations; Father Anderson Bakewell of the Holy Trinity Church, Washington, D.C.; William Schulte, former FAA & Chairman of the International AeroClassic; and Melvin B. McKinney, VP of the Union Bank of Los Angeles.

Final handshake before the Burbank take-off on November 14 under the Pole Cat's nose. Left to right, Lowell Thomas, Jr., whose father made history by flying on the first round-the-world flight many years ago; publisher Wayne Parrish of American Aviation; Captain Bob Buck of TWA; and Bill Wilks of the American Aviation staff at Los Angeles
photos Flying Tigers Club Archives

PALM SPRINGS TAKE-OFF

The Palm Springs departure had been written into the flight plan because of the International Aero Classic being held there. Austin and Finch had wanted to make this the unofficial start of the flight.

"Shortly after noon," Martin continued, "we lifted the Pole Cat out of Palm Springs and headed for Honolulu, with me in the left seat and Buck flying co-pilot. Honolulu was to be the official start and finish of the flight. Except for a couple hours, we were on instruments

The Flying Tigers' Pole Cat as it lifted off Palm Springs airport on a rainy Sunday shortly afternoon on November 14

photo UPI, Flying Tigers Club Archives

and running into 150-knot headwinds. When we landed in Honolulu, it was raining and dark just as it had been in Palm Springs and Burbank and you began to wonder where the sun was. Jim Gannett, Boeing's senior test pilot on transport aircraft, set her down in Honolulu with Buck in the right seat. We refueled and now came the most critical part of the whole flight. The heavy rain was leaving some pretty big puddles on the airport runway. When you hit those on take-off, it is like hitting the brakes and we had aboard the heaviest gross weight of the flight, 332,610 pounds, of which 186,072 pounds was fuel - some 27,855 gallons. Because it was relatively cold at Honolulu, the fuel was heavier than if it had been warm. The fuel weighed out at 6.68 pounds per gallon.

ENOUGH RUNWAY?

"We were doubtful about that take-off but we couldn't get too much tower information. However, Pan American had a Boeing there on a training flight and we asked the pilot for a check on water conditions. He said he'd taken off, holding her down as long as possible, which would be much less in our case because of that heavy load, but he thought we could make it. So we taxied out and started her rolling. There was a 13,000 foot runway stretching out in front of us and we needed all but 1,500 feet of it before we got her airborne. It was dark at the time, a little before 10 p.m. local time, and we were to fly now in the dark most of the time until we had left Lisbon and were approaching the Brazilian coast. Our first stop was London and en route, we'd cross the North Pole. We hit the pole at 39,000 feet. It was dark and we could see nothing, but a fix Ernie Hickman made by celestial navigation showed we'd crossed within three miles of it. On to London, the flight was routine, but the landing in London was far from that.

LONG RUNWAY CLOSED

"We'd filed for Stansted airport, which had the only 10,000 foot runway available in London and which we needed for full fuel tanks. Heathrow had been the original destination but the long runway was closed for repairs and although we asked the British Air Ministry for permission to use it, they declined. When we left the North Pole, weather reports said Stansted was going down and when we crossed the Scottish border, we were advised of a 100-foot ceiling at Stanstead, and ice fog. I hoped we could change our destination to Paris, but Austin and Finch had decided on London, so we went into Heathrow and damned if they didn't put us down on the shortest runway there. It was no problem but we couldn't take on full tanks. Buck landed the aircraft. I was in the right seat. Now we had to revise the flight plan for a refueling at Lisbon, since we couldn't make our next original destination of Buenos Aires non-stop. This was to cost us just about five hours of elapsed time and one and one-half hours of flying time. If it had not been for this diversion, we would have made the entire flight almost exactly on schedule, even possibly a little better than our flight plan."

Upon arrival at Heathrow on the evening of November 15, Flying Tiger's President Robert W. Prescott left the flight to return home due to the heartbreaking news that the company Lear Jet, leased from Paul Kelly Flying Service, had crashed at Palm Springs following take-off on a flight to Burbank. Six persons were aboard including Peter E. Prescott, Bob's only son. The group aboard the Lear Jet had been visiting in Palm Springs and had attended the take-off of Pole Cat.

REPLACED FAN

"London also gave us the first and only mechanical we had in the entire flight," Martin continued, "And this was only minor. We had to change a gasper fan which circulated air in the main cabin where the extra fuel tanks had been installed to prevent any accumulation of fumes. We'd had this fan on continuously and it had just burned out. It was quickly replaced and after that, we'd alternate its operation and had no more trouble with it. Buck took over the left seat out of London and I was in the right seat. They gave us a 9,000-foot runway for take-off and the Pole Cat lifted out of there with a gross weight of 273,300 pounds. A funny little thing happened then. When we took off, as we learned later, the London airport authorities cited the flight for noise abatement! I landed the Pole Cat at Lisbon with Buck in the right seat and now the funniest thing of the whole flight occurred, although for those involved, it wasn't much fun. I'd gone to Customs for clearance, while Buck, Gannett, Hickman and John Larsen, our other navigator, had gone to the tower to file a flight plan. The weather office was on the fourth floor and when I got there, none of them were in sight.

STUCK IN ELEVATOR

"What we found out was that they were all stuck in an elevator in the basement! And it was 55 minutes before we could get them out. Clete Roberts, the TV commentator, heard about it, grabbed a cameraman and went down to take a picture because in Lisbon, those elevators are not in closed shafts like ours but are open cages. It was a funny sight when we arrived to see these fellows trapped in there like animals and Clete started to have the photographer take a picture when Buck yelled out: 'Knock off that silly picture-taking business and get us out of here!' We finally got them free and walked upstairs to the weather bureau. Gannett took her out of Lisbon with Buck in the right seat. We were grossing 329,733 pounds and our fuel density now was 6.62 pounds per gallon, so we were a little lighter than Honolulu for this long leg. I climbed in the bunk and went to sleep. I'd had about an hour and a half of sleep up to this point and I really doused the lights. Below Rio, I got back in the left seat to see the most beautiful summer weather you could imagine. It was routine into Buenos Aires, where I landed the Pole Cat with Buck in the right seat."

BEYOND POLE, HASH MARKS

"Now we ran into another little complication. The Argentine weather bureau could give us the weather to the South Pole but beyond, the chart was a lot of hash marks. I asked them what that meant and they said they didn't have any weather forecast beyond the pole. And this was to be the most critical leg of the flight time-wise, due to fuel. We grossed out at 324,333 pounds with our fuel density now down to 6.42 pounds per gallon. Since our mileage was based on pounds of fuel instead of gallons because an airplane engine knows only weight, not quantity, we knew we were going to have to stretch it as far as possible. Also, if there were any complications, the only place we could land if we had to was McMurdo Sound, which is on the continent of Antarctica about 40-45 minutes beyond the pole toward New Zealand and Christchurch, our next destination. And the weather at McMurdo was zero-zero, so actually there was no place to land. There is a 12,000-foot runway strip at the Pole, but the elevation is 9,100 feet and it's an ice strip, so you couldn't really picture yourself putting the Pole Cat down there! The weather was good all the way to Antarctica until we saw our first icebergs and then we got cloud cover."

LUCK STILL GOOD

"But our luck held. Forty miles from the South Pole, we streaked out into beautiful clear weather without a cloud in the sky. The visibility was unlimited. We saw the South Pole weather station. We had a little navigational problem because you had to follow sunlines but the weather station saw our contrails in the sky and called us, telling us to alter our course by 10-15 degrees and we'd pass exactly over the pole. We crossed the pole with Buck flying her. "The weather station wanted us to buzz 'em but at 37,000 feet, that was out of the question and also, we had to really watch our fuel. We told him we would make a 270-degree circle over the station. I'd taken her over at this time so we re-crossed the pole. Our radio contact with the station was excellent and we were advised that the weather was beautiful to Christchurch, which was a nice piece of news. It was dark when we landed at Christchurch with Gannett putting her down and myself in the right seat. I had a thrill about an hour and a half out of Christchurch. The Collins Radio man aboard, John Demuth, asked me if I'd like to talk to my wife in Woodland Hills, California. At the time I said not now – let's wait until we have a better look at our flight plan. When we were an hour and a half out of Christchurch, I said let's go ahead. I now was convinced for the first time that our flight would be a success. We'd just about passed all the trouble and we had enough fuel to reach New Zealand. So Demuth got in contact with his base at Cedar Rapids, Iowa, where they had a hot line to California, and in a moment I was talking with my wife. It was 11:15 p.m. her time. I told her I was sure we had it in the bag now. She called Joyce Hickman and Gene Olson's wife and they had a little celebration over the phone."

COMFORTABLE FLIGHT

Wayne Parrish, noted aviation writer and publisher, was one of the press aboard the Pole Cat. He noted, "Surprisingly enough for such a long trip, it was relatively comfortable and free of fatigue throughout. Six-abreast tourist seats were in the rear. Collapsible fuel tanks occupied the main cabin; but when the extra fuel was used up, the deflated tanks were fine for stretching

WHAT HAPPENED TO THE POLE CAT?

Once stripped of the equipment put aboard Flying Tigers Boeing 707-349C N322F (msn/ln 18975/445), she was returned to standard configuration and put back onto Pacific flying for MAC. The aircraft was leased in full FTL colors to KLM between May and August 1967 for Amsterdam-USA cargo flights to replace a KLM DC-8 destroyed in a hangar fire Amsterdam. She was leased again to KLM between July and August 1968. On August 30, 1968, N322F was purchased by London Gatwick-based charter carrier Caledonian Airlines and registered G-AWTG. In 1969, Caledonian merged with British United Airways (BUA). On April 11, 1971, the aircraft broke a non-stop point-to-point speed record between Gatwick and Singapore. The aircraft was re-registered G-BDCN when Caledonian and BUA created their new corporate entity British Caledonian in 1975.

In October 1977, the aircraft was purchased by TAAG Angola (Transportes Aéreos Angolanos) and registered D2-TAC, serving European, African and South American destinations from Luanda. In 1980, the aircraft was re-registered D2-TOB and D2-TOI. Its career ended on February 8, 1988 with a hard landing in Luanda. Beyond economical repair, the aircraft was removed from service, placed in storage and scrapped in 1989.

D2-TOI of TAAG at Paris CDG on May 9, 1981

photo Jacques Guillem

Captain Jack Martin gets a special welcome from the Tiger Girls

And then a homecoming welcome from his son, Robert, and daughter, Leslie   photos Flying Tigers Club Archives

out on, with sleeping bags. A galley provided hot meals. There was always plenty of coffee and soft drinks. As the flying was mainly north-south and not on the disruptive east-west pattern, eating was maintained on a normal schedule. Those on board were either working as crew members or monitoring scientific instruments or talking or snoozing. There was no stress or strain, no upset tempers. A surprising amount of the flight was made in darkness. Leaving Honolulu after dark, the next stop was the following night in London, with time zones clicking off like computers. The only semblance to one full day was an hour and a half of red glow indicating where the sun was shining far below the horizon. It was not until we

The entire Pole Cate crew and passenger group were welcomed in New York's Waldorf Astoria Grand Ballroom at a special Explorers Club dinner to commemorate the historic flight

photo Delmar Watson / Flying Tigers Club Archives

reached the South Atlantic area that we experienced daylight, and by the time we reached New Zealand it was dark again. Strange as it may seem, only two stops were made in daylight. One was in Buenos Aires at noontime in fine spring sunshine. The other was on the return to Honolulu about noon on the final day."

EIGHT WORLD RECORDS SET BY THE POLE CAT

Captain Jack Martin, pilot in command of the Pole Cat, received word from Ed Sweeney, president of the National Aeronautic Association, that eight records were being certified to the Fédération Aéronautique Internationale, Paris, which officially promulgates all world aviation records.

Prefacing his listing of the records, Sweeney told Martin that the Pole Cat was the first jet ever to cross Antarctica; that it flew higher over both poles than any other aircraft; and that it carried the largest number of personnel ever transported over the poles. He also said that from the altitude of 37,000 feet at which the Pole Cat crossed the South Pole, mountains east of the route southbound were studied which never had been observed before.

Here are the eight records certified to Martin as the commander:

- Round the world over both poles in 62 hours, 27 minutes, 35 seconds; 26,230 statute miles; average speed 415 mph.
- Honolulu to London over the North Pole, 13 hours, 54 minutes; 7,413 statute miles, average speed 520 mph.
- London-Buenos Aires, 16 hours, 41 minutes including ground time at Lisbon; 6,928 statute miles, average speed 416 mph.
- London-Lisbon, 2 hours, 19 minutes; 958 statute miles, average speed 414 mph.
- Lisbon-Buenos Aires, 11 hours, 56 minutes; 5,957 statute miles; average speed 497 mph.
- Buenos Aires-Christchurch, 14 hours, 17 minutes; 7,035 miles; average speed 431 mph.
- Christchurch-Honolulu, 9 hours, 1 minute; 4,861 statute miles; average speed 539 mph.
- Pole-to-Pole, 34 hours, 36 minutes; average speed 357 mph.
- Fix over the North Pole within three miles of exact pole, determined by celestial navigation.
- Fix over the South Pole, exact pole crossing, determined by celestial navigation and visual observation.

These records were the second official round-the-world records by air. The only previous official record was the flight by Max Conrad in 1961, which required 8 days, 18 hours, 36 minutes covering 25,946.5 miles. All other flights, such as those by Wiley Post, Howard Hughes, the Army, Graf Zeppelin, Bill Odom and the military B-50 and B-52 flights were unofficial. The first unofficial round-the-world flight was in 1924 by the Army.

CUTS FUEL CONSUMPTION

Martin continues, "Enroute to Christchurch from the pole, we'd climbed up to 41,000 feet. This enabled us to cut our rate of fuel consumption down from 3,700 pounds per engine to 2,100 pounds, thus greatly improving our cruising capability. Out of Christchurch, Gannett took the Pole Cat off an 8,400-foot runway with a gross weight of 285,333 pounds, which was our regular normal fuel load with no emergency fuel tank backup. This was the only time since the start of the flight, except for the London-Lisbon leg, that we could fly without using the extra fuel tanks. "Now we hit the first real weather of the flight. There were terrific thunderstorms above Samoa, standing up to 60-65,000 feet. We were cruising at 33,000 and worked our way around them. To make up time, we stepped our cruising speed up to Mach .82 from Mach .80. After a while, the weather cleared at daylight and sunshine greeted us when we landed at Honolulu with Austin flying and me in the right seat. We refueled at Honolulu and headed home. I was flying with Finch in the right seat and we rode into Burbank routine but in the rain, just as we'd left!"

TRIBUTE TO SKILL

Eight world speed records were set by the Pole Cat with 40 men aboard, flying around the world in slightly more than 60 hours without one miscalculation or adverse incident. It might well be called the "perfect flight," so free of trouble was its record. The entire flight was a tribute not alone to flying and navigational skill, the skill of aircraft manufacturer and design but also to the tireless work and skill of Tiger crews – such as putting together in five days a flight which normally might require five months of preparation. Not a spare part of the replacement equipment placed aboard was used and as Captain Martin said when he landed at Burbank at the conclusion of the great flight: "She's as ready to fly now as when she started." And she was. Ten hours later, she had been completely stripped of the modifications put aboard and was back in standard configuration, ready to take up her task again on the long Pacific flights for MAC.

Based on Tigereview of Nov-Dec 1965 and Jan-Feb 1966, and edited by Guy Van Herbruggen

IN MEMORIAM...
CAPTAIN JACK L. MARTIN

Captain Jack Martin joined Flying Tigers on September 30, 1950. He served as a Training Command pilot during World War II, stationed both in New Mexico and Arizona. Later he served as an instructor for the University of Southern California's Flight School at Santa Maria, before joining Tigers. In 1961, he became an instructor pilot for the airline. Later he became check pilot, and in 1965 he was promoted to assistant chief pilot. In 1968, he became director of flying for Tigers, a position he held when poor health caused him to give up flying in June, 1968.

Captain Martin died suddenly February 16, 1970. "Jack was a loyal Tiger and a good friend," said Bob Prescott. "We'll certainly miss him." Art Seymour, senior director of Flight Operations added "He was an outstanding pilot and a wonderful friend."

Captain Jack Martin in 1965
photo Flying Tigers Club Archives

14

Tiger Girls

John F. Dickson and Guy Van Herbruggen

Bob Prescott knew the power of imagery for public relation purposes. Many photos exist of Bob with celebrities, politicians, military brass and other distinguished people on the ramp with the unusual freight that FTL often transported by air.

Prescott cutting the 10th anniversary birthday of the company in Burbank with a Tiger Girl   photo Flying Tigers Club Archives

Captain Tommy Haywood with a Tiger Girl inside C-54G Skymaster N90911   photo Bill R. Watson / Flying Tigers Club Archives

The company's motto, Anything, Anywhere, Anytime was important to Prescott and he wanted to make sure that the public's eye was caught during any promotional efforts.

Always the practical humorist, Prescott came up with the idea of a Miss Tiger costume for various public relations shots. It was a tight one-piece tiger-striped bathing suit, complete with cute matching ears and a tail. Through the 1950's and into the early 1960's celebrities, models, and company employees were asked to don the outfit for promotional photos in and outside of aircraft, or with unusual cargo that might be on the ramp ready for shipment. Various Miss Tigers were also seen as greeters at corporate functions and parties over the years.

Pat Kelly (now Rayburn) worked in Sales and Promotion in a Quonset hut beside the Tigers ramp at Burbank Airport between 1955 and 1960. One day in 1958, Prescott approached her with the idea of donning a Tiger Girl costume for a photo shoot with some unusual cargo being shipped that day. As was typical for the era, women jumped at the chance and Pat was able to play the role of Miss Tiger several times before leaving the company to fly for Alitalia

photo Flying Tigers Club Archives

Captain Dick Rossi with a Tiger Girl

photo The 6 Watson Bros / Flying Tigers Club Archives

Loading a C-46 freighter with a Tiger Girl

photo Mort J. Donoghub, Flying Tigers Club Archives

Bob and the Tiger Girls
photo Delmar Watson / Flying Tigers Club Archives

Tiger Girls at the door of a CL-44 photo Flying Tigers Club Archives

MISS FLYING TIGERS

The popularity of the beauty pageants in the US prompted airlines and other organizations to establish similar contests in the 1950s and beyond. Some were fairly significant like the Miss Flying Tigers and the Miss Credit Union where contestants from different chapters were reviewed during a ceremony at restaurants or hotels to win the crown. Unlike the Tiger Girls, beauty pageants were still popular in the late 1970s.

One of the early Miss Flying Tigers
photo Flying Tigers Club Archives

Kathy Smith participated in May 1979 to the Miss Interline beauty pageants and represented the Flying Tiger Line
photo Kathy Smith

15

Lost, Almost, At Sea

Captain Dwight Small

The alert came at 0330 local time. I first heard the thumping of tundra boots in the barracks hallway as ops agent Ralph Gallagher made his way from door to door alerting the five of us that we would fly Flight 7316-18 from Cold Bay, Alaska to Tachikawa AFB, Japan. The date was May 19th, 1966.

The agent approached my door, made three sharp raps and called out, "She'll be on the ground in 30 minutes, pickup's in 45." I acknowledged, rolled out of bed, gathered my shaving gear and headed for the communal bath and shower facilities. Although I had been flying the CL-44 within the U.S. for several months and had been with Flying Tigers for a year, this would be only my second flight to Japan.

Less than an hour later, we were in Operations, a corrugated steel building at the edge of the small parking apron. The driver delivered us close to the front door. He was being considerate because it was usually cold and often extremely windy at this remote outpost on the southwestern tip of the Alaskan peninsula. We unloaded our bags and placed them under the nose of the big CL-44. I took note of the N-number; we would be flying N124SW, an airplane Flying Tigers recently got in a lease/swap deal with Seaboard World Airlines.

Inside Operations, we were handed a thick folder containing faxed copies of weather charts, wind charts, pressure charts, sea-state charts, NOTAMS, destination and alternate forecasts, and other information pertinent

photo Jacques Guillem Collection

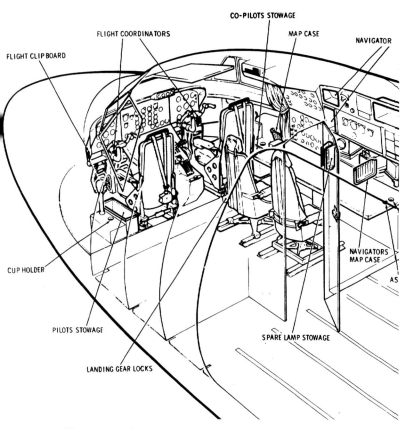

FLIGHT CLIPBOARD
FLIGHT COORDINATORS
CO-PILOTS STOWAGE
MAP CASE
NAVIGATOR
CUP HOLDER
NAVIGATORS MAP CASE
AS
PILOTS STOWAGE
SPARE LAMP STOWAGE
LANDING GEAR LOCKS

The cockpit of the CL-44 showing crew member stations

author's collection

to our flight. I first checked the destination and alternate forecasts and they were good, but Shemya AFB, at the tip of the Aleutians Island chain, was marginal, with strong winds and fog. Significantly, there was a deep low-pressure area centered over the Kamchatka Peninsula and a high- pressure area over the Western Pacific Ocean east of Japan. All looked good and there were no troubling maintenance items.

We were to have two navigators on this flight. One was about to complete his initial route qualification, and the other was his check airman. Since the student navigator had considerable previous experience and nearing the end of his qualification program, it was planned that he would do the navigating. The navigators asked for the wind chart and the 500mb chart. They said that the flight plan, prepared at our planning office

in Los Angeles, was unusually long with very strong head winds after crossing 160 degrees east longitude.

The captain became a bit uneasy when he overheard the navigators discussing the slim fuel margin; after giving the navigators time to look things over, he asked Marv, the check navigator, if he was satisfied with the flight plan and was "happy" with the fuel load. The Check Navigator chuckled and said, "I've never been happy with a fuel load so why should today be any different."

We were always fuel critical on this route. The Company had bid the Air Force contract to transport 62,000 pounds of freight, leaving little room for extra fuel. As we gathered up our gear and headed for the airplane, the flight engineer met us with the fuel drip-stick readings, confirming that the airplane had been properly fueled.

As we stepped into the predawn darkness, a blast of cold air hit us. It will be much warmer in Japan I thought, much warmer, and the beer at Amy's Bar will be a fine reward. Our flight plan time was estimated to be 9 hours and 22 minutes, long enough to work up a mighty thirst.

The cockpit was warm. Canadair, the builders of the CL-44, had incorporated electric cockpit heaters for ground heating. Even some later airplanes such as the DC-8 didn't have that luxury. We ran the checklist and I tuned in Cold Bay Radio on 126.7 Mhz. for our ATC clearance. We were cleared, the voice said, to "Tachikawa Airbase via fifty-five north, one seven zero west, flight-planned route. Maintain one-six thousand." After I read the clearance back to him he told us to contact Cold Bay Radio when airborne with our off-blocks time.

It was a rather long taxi to the end of runway 14 but soon we were soon lined up in position for departure. The captain called, "Max power." The engineer advanced the power levers and, when set, and after checking the TGTs and torque gauges, announced, "Power's up!" I felt a comforting surge as each of the four big Rolls-Royce Tyne turboprop engines spooled up and began delivering 5,730 HP to the 16-foot four-bladed de Havilland propellers. Even though we were at maximum takeoff weight, the big '44 became airborne well before the end of that long runway – the strong south wind and the cold temperature shortened our takeoff roll.

We made a left turnout over the bay and headed northwest toward the VOR. "Ninety-five one," the captain ordered. "Flaps 5", he called. When we rolled out of the turn the captain called for climb power: "Eighty-eight three." His next command was for the climb checklist. We were on our way! A minute later, as we passed over the VOR, the navigator said, "After the VOR, fly heading 260."

The next two hours were routine. When we were about to pass abeam of Shemya, I tuned in the SYA Tacan on the shadow frequency of 109.00 to get the distance from Shemya. Tacans were designed for military use and offered no azimuth information to civil airplanes. To get azimuth information I tuned in the SYA radio beacon (ADF) on 221 kilohertz. When we were exactly abeam, I noted a magnetic bearing of 165 degrees and the DME showed 62 miles. This would be the only solid position fix we would have for the next several hours. Just after passing abeam of Shemya I tuned in the Volmet weather broadcast on 8903 KHz

CL-44 above the ocean as depicted in a postcard

Flying Tigers Club Archives

and learned that the Shemya winds, just as forecast, were very strong and were blowing from the south, directly across the only runway. Any emergency requiring a landing at Shemya would have to be dire indeed.

About 30-45 minutes after passing SYA, the navigator passed a tape forward with a new heading. It was customary, at that time, for the navigator to write the desired heading on a bit of masking tape. The pilots would stick the tape to the instrument panel near the captain's slaved compass and then set the heading cursor to the new heading.

I was a bit surprised when the new heading was 258 degrees. On my previous and only other trip on this route, the navigator, a respected veteran named Sam Nicholson, told me that once beyond Shemya, the heading should never be greater than 242 degrees. I struggled as to whether or not I should challenge the navigator but decided to wait to see if he might recheck his work and give us a correction. If Sam Nicholson's warning was correct, this heading would put us 93 miles right of course each hour! He was working feverishly so I rationalized that it was only a matter of time until he would find an error.

To my discredit I allowed us to stay on this heading for more than an hour. When I finally decided I must do something about it, the check navigator entered the cockpit. He had been in a bunk and was rubbing sleep from his eyes. I soon heard lots of busy and animated chatter and commotion as the check navigator took the seat at the nav station. Within a minute or two, the check navigator passed a tape forward with a new heading of 198 degrees. Could this be real, I wondered? He wants a 60 degree left turn? I quickly set the new heading and, as the big '44 rolled into the turn, the captain opened his eyes and asked, "What's going on?"

The check navigator popped out of his seat but tried not to show too much alarm as he told the captain that there had been a serious mistake. He said that we were perhaps as much as 150 miles right of track and that we might be very close to over-flying the Soviet Kamchatka Peninsula. There was a solid cloud cover so we couldn't be sure.

He said that, because it was near sunrise at our position, LORAN signals were unusable. Also, the sun was not yet visible and there was no moon, so there was no possibility of getting a celestial fix. All that was available was dead reckoning and that they, the navigators, had made a 27 degree heading error. There is, and was at that time, a huge Soviet submarine base near the southern tip of Kamchatka at Petropavlovsk. It would have been very serious indeed to find ourselves near there!

We flew that heading for 30 minutes, long enough to be fairly certain that we were out of Soviet airspace. We kept a watch to our right for interceptor contrails but we saw none. The navigator then gave us a heading to "Intercept our course about 200 miles down track." The captain was definitely upset and was asking for information faster than the two navigators could provide answers. The engineer got involved, refining his fuel remaining figures to the best accuracy possible. We all knew that this course deviation would have a serious impact on our fuel remaining at destination but we didn't know as yet how serious it might be.

The check navigator was desperately trying to get a LORAN fix. The sun was now just above the horizon and was nearly directly behind us ("on the tail" as the navigators say). The check navigator had taken charge completely and called an order to the student: "Quick, see if you can get a speed line." When the sun, or other celestial body, is directly ahead or behind, ground speed information can be determined with a sextant but no left or right of course information can be obtained.

The student shuffled through the Air Almanac, made some calculations, put the sextant into the sextant port and soon gave the information to the check navigator. At this point the captain was surprisingly calm. Apparently, the captain had decided to give the navigators space and time. He was obviously very concerned and must have been pondering the possibilities, but he sat quietly for perhaps 15 minutes. He had great faith in the veteran check navigator who he knew well and had flown with many times in the previous 15 years. He figured

First Officer Dwight Small

it would be only a short time until he would get things sorted out.

Finally, navigation was able to get a LORAN position that was deemed reliable. That, along with the speed line the student got from the sun, gave the check navigator confidence that he now knew where we were. He came forward and said that we'd lost 48 minutes and that we should probably be planning to land at Misawa AFB on the northeast coast of Honshu, Japan. The captain didn't answer him but was clearly digesting the information as he puffed on his pipe. It seemed that the situation may have stabilized and that, in the worst case, we might be making a fuel stop at Misawa, AFB. The navigator soon told us we were now back on track as he gave us a heading of 234 degrees.

About an hour later the navigator again came forward. He was obviously troubled. He said that we now had headwinds of 140 knots and that, "If the winds continue like this we can't make landfall!" This announcement hit like a ton of bricks. He further explained that, according to our flight plan, we weren't supposed to encounter these winds for two more hours. He said that, since we had hit these winds early, the whole weather system may have shifted north and that the winds may diminish when we got to the area where we should have encountered them but, he said, "I can't be sure of that."

This was more than the captain could take. He asked loudly, "What the hell should I do, turn this thing around and head for Shemya?" I had been monitoring Shemya's weather and there was currently a 40 knot crosswind with fog and low visibility. Shemya was not an option! The now-crestfallen navigator said that we couldn't make it to Shemya with any reserves so if we got there and couldn't land we would have zero options. With that information, the captain bounded out of his seat and said, "Show me the chart, we've gotta figure out what the hell we're gonna do."

The next two hours were gut wrenching for all of us but the navigators, feeling responsible, were desperate. Our ground speed was down to 210 knots. Below us the sea surface, when visible was a frothy, white-streaked cauldron. The thought of ditching under such conditions was terrifying. All of us were busy consulting cruise charts, long range cruise options and wind/altitude trade-off tables. We discussed shutting down two engines and descending, as the navy sometimes does in its P-3 Orions, to extend endurance. Hopefully, we thought, we might find more friendly winds at perhaps 5,000 feet. Because we had no performance charts for doing this, that idea was rejected, but we were desperate.

We studied the ditching manual and we were ready if it came to that. One suggestion that got a lot of consideration was taking up a heading of true south and plan to ditch 500 miles east of Tokyo. The navigators, working with the engineer, kept refining the estimated time and position for dry tanks. For more than an hour, their best about 50 miles short of landfall. It was during this hour that the captain wrestled with whether or not to turn south for a certain ditching. Maritime information in the weather folder estimated the sea swells to be between two and five feet in the area 500 miles east of Tokyo while the swells off the northeast coast of Honshu were forecast to be between 14 and 22 feet.

We all gave our opinion, and mine was that, under no circumstances should we take a chance on having to ditch in the heavy seas off the northeast coast of Japan. I remember thinking of my two toddlers back home. It appeared to me that we could stay on track for perhaps 30 more minutes before turning south and that we should probably do so if the winds didn't abate. The captain listened to every suggestion. He liked mine but, when the 30 minutes were up and conditions had only improved marginally, he made the decision. With his pipe clenched in his fist, he jabbed his right hand forward and said, "Press on!" For better or for worse, the decision was made. We all accepted it without question and, for some reason, I felt better.

About 20 minutes later, the nav, now talking over the interphone, announced that the ground speed was up to 240 knots. Minutes later he said we were doing 280 knots and that we could overhead Misawa with 15 minutes of fuel remaining. As we continued, the winds dropped off even more until our ground speed was 325 knots. Eventually, as we neared top of descent, the winds became light and variable and we had a ground speed equal to our TAS of 350 knots.

Surprisingly, we had made it all the way to Tachikawa, 30 miles west of Tokyo. We didn't have a lot of fuel remaining but had enough to make a last minute diversion to nearby Yokota, AFB if that became necessary. The normal flight time for the PACD-RJTC (Cold Bay, Alaska to Tachikawa, AFB, Japan) leg for that time of year was 9 hours and 18 minutes. This day it took 10 hours and 42 minutes.

We landed somewhere around noon local time. As we signed in at the New Plaza Hotel, the captain said, "Let's have a beer." Four of the five of us were soon across the street in Amy's Bar. We sat quietly at first but slowly opened up and began to discuss our experience. Personally, I remember being very thankful. Our lives had, for a few hours, hung in balance. The outcome could have been very different.

At one point the captain said, "In 25 years of flying, I've never had a day like this." As I said, there were only four of us at the bar. The trainee navigator didn't show up. The captain had made a point of inviting him but perhaps he was too embarrassed. I never saw him again. He left the Company, whether he resigned or was asked to leave, I don't know.

16

Black series for the CL-44

Captain Thomas E. Constable

Coming in to land
photo Flying Tigers Club Archives

On March 22 1966, we took-off from Naval Air Station (NAS) Alameda to Norfolk NAS on a Navy Quick-Trans Navy charter, hauling freight in a CL-44. Quick-Trans was designed to provide specialised airlift service with rapid reaction to Navy needs. Ahead of us was another CL-44 crew also going to Norfolk NAS. I was on the last two legs of my check-out as a flight engineer. Checking me was Joe Revegno. The captain was Arnie Bredon and the first officer was Scott Brown.

The crew in the CL-44 ahead of us to Norfolk was captain Carl Prentiss, first officer Jim Prescott and second officer was my classmate Ernie Belanger.

When they arrived, they had a hard landing and the left wing had sheared off. The aircraft – registered N453T – rolled upside down and slid down the center line of the runway. Ernie, hanging upside down, later commented that looking out the center window, it was right on the center line all the way until it stopped.

We arrived the next morning and as we landed and rolled out we saw a wing off to the left and then we saw a very disturbing sight, the CL-44 upside down with the landing gear sticking straight up in the air. What a horrible sight to behold! Luckily all six-man crew walked out of the wreck unharmed.

The next morning, we took off for the return trip to Alameda NAS. All went well until we were approaching the runway. Scott Brown the copilot was flying the approach and as we were about 50 feet in the air above the runway, he pulled the power levers to idle, something

N453T upside down after its landing accident
photo CL44.com archive

you don't want to do in a CL-44. We dropped like a stone toward the runway, because the elevators are controlled by flying tabs that are moved by airflow and move the elevators. Well since he pulled the propellers back to idle, they flatten out, driving less airflow aft, with less lift over the wing and no airflow over the flying tabs which control the elevators. The elevators sagged down which gave us a pitch down attitude, and we headed for the runway. The quick-thinking captain jammed the power levers forward to the firewall and he pulled back on the yoke.

We hit the runway very hard and bounced back into the air. I immediately thought of the other crash in Norfolk. Joe, my check second officer, was standing behind me to the floor and he was knocked to the floor. All the lights on my panel came on.

We were hanging in the air only by those big sixteen foot props with only 110 knots of forward airspeed, and we were running out of runway. The captain wisely decided not to try to put it back down,

Second officer Tom Constable is deputised as a cruise pilot on a transpacific CL-44 with an inoperative autopilot

so he took it around and did another approach and we landed safely.

We taxied in and parked. We inspected the damage and it was considerable. The two inboard engines and nacelles were bent down and the cowlings were wrinkled and torn. The landing gear struts and bogies had metal shaved when they bottomed-out as we hit.

There was an FAA investigation that delayed my graduation as a flight engineer for several days. Our captain's quick reaction on this Quick-Trans flight saved our lives. What a great pilot. After the investigation the FAA found certain prior things that ended first officer Scott Brown's Flying Tiger Line career.

In the Alameda NAS crash-landing, the FAA investigation revealed that first officer Jim Prescott was flying the approach to runway 10 to land. He was too high on the glide slope and the resulting 2000 feet-per-minute descent resulted in them being unable to arrest the vertical speed and came down hard on the left main gear and nose wheels. The aircraft started to disintegrate immediately as the left wing separated. It appeared that at the time of the accident, Jim did not have a multi-engine rating and only had a total of 18 hours in the CL-44.

PLANE LIMPS TO LANDING WITH TWO OF ITS FOUR ENGINES OUT

A Flying Tiger Line CL-44 with a full load of cargo out of Saigon made a "routine" emergency landing on two engines at Portland's International Airport about 3 p.m. on Wednesday, February 9, 1966. Captain William Hoey, of Wauna WA (who had a brother, Jim Hoey, in business at Portland) brought the propjet in while emergency vehicles stood by. Captain Hoey told The Oregonian he began to lose oil from the outboard jet engine on the right wing soon after taking off from Cold Bay, in the Aleutian Islands after a refuelling stop.

"The engine would still have operated, but I feathered the propeller to prevent possible damage," he explained. "The weather was too bad to return to Cold Bay, so I continued on course to San Francisco. After about an hour on three engines, I got a warning light indicating trouble in the gear box on number one (the left outboard engine) and shut it down to avoid possible damage."

At that point, about 300 miles west of Oregon, Captain Hoey declared an emergency and changed course to land at Portland. He dropped from his normal cruising altitude of 21,000 feet down to 9,000 feet, most efficient altitude with only two engines, he said. "No sweat," he said. "This Canadair Swingtail will go around on two engines even with a full load."

Based on an article in The Oregonian newspaper of Portland, Oregon of February 10th, 1966.

First Trip To Da Nang, Vietnam

Captain Thomas E. Constable

It was 1966 and I was a second officer, or flight engineer, on the CL-44 'Swing-Tail'. We were operating out of Tachikawa, in the western part of Tokyo, Japan. Our destination was Da Nang, Vietnam. We were hauling supplies to the airbase. Our captain was Jack Bliss, a terrific guy and a mighty fine pilot. His favourite thing to tell us was, "This crew don't take no horseshit." He told us that on the way to Da Nang. Well, after that I knew I was with the right guy, especially on my first trip to the war zone.

It was dark when we arrived and made our approach to the U.S. Air Force base at Da Nang. We were just touching down but little did we know that the base was under attack. We landed on the air force runway and to the right of us and parallel was the marine base runway. They were not very far apart. When we were landing, six mortars hit the marine runway next to us.

We turned off the runway and entered the parking ramp. We shut down three engines, but, without ground power to restart, left one running. Still we had no idea what was going on. I went to the entry door and opened it. Just then, an air force blue crew van drove up and screeched to a stop below the door. The driver jumped out and yelled over the noise of the engine, "Get out of that thing quick, you make a mighty good target, we are under attack."

I relayed to the crew what the air force driver had told me, grabbed the escape rope from the door sill and dropped it down to his van. Jack shut down the remaining engine and we made a hasty retreat out of the plane down the rope. We jumped into the van and drove off at high speed to the bunkers and trenches, and stayed there until the all-clear was sounded.

After all that excitement, we were escorted to a tent and jumped in our racks for the night. The next morning there was a fire fight at the south end of the base. Jeeps were whizzing by with 50 cal. M19s. Soon that was over, so we could so go to the mess hall and

Landing at Da Nang USAF Air Base   *photos Tom Constable*

Da Nang dining room, note the sign above the door

get some breakfast. The entrance to the mess hall had a sign over the swinging saloon type doors which read: 'Check your guns at the door.'

When we were ready to depart, they briefed us to not make a left turn over the jut of land that goes into the sea; an old fellow had dragged a 50 cal. out there and he would shoot at you if you went that way. We assured them that we would take their advice. We took off and headed back to Japan.

Well, as Captain Jack said: "This crew don't take no horseshit."

Why Captains Become Crabby Old Bastards

Captain Garry Duff (FTL employee #19349)

One of the secrets to the Flying Tiger Line's success was the corporation's frugality when it came to non-essential expenditures. For example, the airline did not equip its fleet with air traffic control transponders until required by law. Similarly, the altimeter settings in the Canadair CL-44 fleet displayed only inches of mercury and not the millibar equivalent used in many foreign countries and provided on fancier altimeters. For this reason, when flying internationally, Tiger co-pilots routinely converted the reported altimeter setting from millibars to inches of mercury and passed the conversion on to the captain so that the captain's altimeter, as well as the co-pilot's, would read correctly when approaching the foreign destination airfield. This adjustment is essential since atmospheric pressure is quite different from place to place and time to time. Without accurate height information, flying approaches to airports in inclement weather would be dangerous – if not impossible.

And so it was that in early January 1969 that I, as a young captain, was assigned to deliver N449T, one of the last Tiger CL-44s, to its new owner, Mr. Mike Keegan of Transmeridian London at Southend airport (EGMC) near London, U.K. On board also was Mr. Keegan's wife and young son. The flight engineer was Art Vance, who later played a major role in the Unlimited class at the Reno Air Races.

Tigers' Bill Gelfand, right, concluded an agreement with Mike Keegan, chairman of the board of Transmeridian Air Cargo, Ltd., for the lease/purchase of the last four of Flying Tiger' CL-44's

photo Flying Tigers Club Archives

The ferry flight of N452T, the last Flying Tigers CL-44, took place on January 28, 1972. From left to right, Captain Kevin Keegan (brother of Mike Keegan), Second Officer Bob Stickler and First Officer Luis Salazar prepared to take off to Stansted, Essex.

photo Flying Tigers Club Archives

I had been assigned a co-pilot who had never flown outside of the United States, so much of the transatlantic flight time was used explaining to copilot (known as Marvellous Marv to spare the feelings of his family) what was to be expected in European airspace and particularly how he was to assist me with the altimeter setting information.

Not surprisingly, due to a typical winter low pressure weather system prevailing over England, there were clouds and light rain covering the airport for our late-night arrival, so the approach and landing would be made with reference to instruments and low frequency radio signals.

When Marvellous Marv converted the reported millibar setting to inches of mercury, he thought the result must be in error since it was much lower than any setting he had experienced stateside, and so, without telling me, he added one inch to the result. The effect of his addition was that, after setting the altimeters, the aircraft was flying approximately 1,000 feet lower than the altimeter indicated.

During the approach, and for no good reason other than I felt the urge, I turned on the landing lights while still in the clouds. Within seconds of doing so, we broke out of the clouds and the lights illuminated a huge electric power transmission line a few hundred yards in front of us and cow pastures a couple of hundred feet below us. The muscular response of the four Rolls Royce Tyne turboprop engines and those huge propellers skimmed us over those wires and back up into the clouds for a review of what had happened, followed by a successful approach and landing.

The subsequent arse-chewing Marv received in the crew car, had it been heard during World War 2, would have made General Patton feel inadequate. I was on my way to becoming a "crabby old bastard", and a believer in guardian angels.

Mr. Keegan never knew how close he came to losing his wife, son, and his new CL-44.

Correction, Not Perfection

Captain John "Dizzy" Dziubala

Captain John "Dizzy" Dziubala   *photo Flying Tigers Club Archives*

I was first officer on a DC-8 freighter service from Los Angeles to Tokyo in the late 1960s at the time we were still carrying navigators on transoceanic flights. Navigators had a sextant that they placed up through the top of the cockpit roof, above the observer seat.

To achieve precision in their work, the navigator had to prepare for the flight and study the weather charts. In flight, over the ocean, using a sextant, they would take measurements, plot on their navigation chart, send position reports. In doing so, the navigator could monitor the progress of the flight and issue course corrections to the pilots.

To issue course corrections, our navigator was hanging up small paper bands with headings on them, handing them over to the second officer who would hand them over to me. I would stick them on the glareshield and we would then proceed with required adjustments using the autopilot controls to capture the new heading.

The routine was established and on our trip to Tokyo, every so often he would hand over a new piece of paper with a few degrees, minutes or even seconds. As we got closer to landfall, all of a sudden he noticed that he was starting to catch the non-directional radio beacon (NDB) reading in its instrument pointing at a station. He then suddenly turned around and shouted "Come left 30 degrees!"

Flying Tigers 707 In A Blockbuster Motion Picture

Guy Van Herbruggen

Flying Tigers Boeing 707-349C N324F (msn/ln 19354/503) starred in the classic and blockbuster disaster motion picture Airport. It was one of seven 707s operated by Flying Tigers from 1965 to 1969 and subleased by Universal Pictures for production of the movie between January 28 and March 8, 1969.

For the movie, N324F sported a previous lease El Al cheatline over its bare metal finish, with fictional Trans Global Airlines (TGA) titles and tail. The film portrayed an airliner limping back home after suffering an explosive decompression caused by a bomb blast in the rear lavatory. It also was the 'other' 707 which became mired in mud and snow adjacent to the runway. Scenes at the Chicago's fictitious 'Lincoln International Airport' were actually shot at Minneapolis/St. Paul International Airport and many of the film's extras were Northwest Airlines employees.

Based on the novel of the same name by Arthur Hailey and released a year layer on March 5, 1970, the action thriller starred Burt Lancaster as airport manager Mel Bakersfeld, George Kennedy as TWA mechanic Joe Patroni, Dean Martin as Trans Global captain Vemon Demerest, Jacqueline Bisset as Trans Global stewardess Gwen Meighen, and Helen Hayes as stowaway Ada Quonsett. Hayes won a Best Supporting Actress Academy Award for her performance.

By the time the aircraft was returned to Los Angeles on March 8, 1969, Flying Tigers was in the process of standardising on the DC-8, and Boeing sold N324F to Aer Lingus as EI-ASO in April. The aircraft

N324F leased to El Al, Paris Orly, August 25, 1968

photo Jacques Guillem

"This plane is built to withstand anything, except a bad pilot," said Joe Patroni, a TWA mechanic played by George Kennedy, to a captain, while he is trying to move the aircraft out of the mud and snow during a first attempt   photo Universal Studios / Flying Tigers Club Archives

had a long and varied career and was leased to several carriers, including Qantas, British Caledonian and Zambia Airways. On October 30, 1986, the aircraft was purchased by Omega Air, an Irish-based leasing company specialized in 707s and it reverted back to N324F. On January 25, 1987, it was leased to TransBrasil for use by its cargo affiliate Aerobrasil and re-registered PT-TCS.

After two years of hauling cargo in South America, the aircraft met its end in a fiery crash on March 21, 1989 in a heavily populated suburb of São Paulo during a high-speed approach west of the city airport, killing 3 crew members and 22 persons on the ground. Over 200 were injured on the ground. An ironic twist of fate that the aircraft used to portray in the dramatic landing of a crippled airliner in the 1970 motion picture should end its career two decades later a mile short of a runway. N324F wasn't the only airliner in the Airport movie franchise to crash in real life – the 'Federation Airlines' Concorde in Airport '79 was lost on July 25, 2000 in Paris.

FORGOTTEN MOVIE FILM REELS
Charles "Chuck" Marshall, LAX Line Maintenance

I was working swing shift maintenance at LAX when our 707, tail number N324F, came back from Minneapolis where it had been the centre of two stories in the blockbuster movie, Airport. As I recall, Tigers had leased the aircraft to El Al, the Israeli airline, before the lease to Universal Studios. That was the basic paint scheme that was on it when it came in. I was the one driving the aircraft tug. After pulling the aircraft into the hangar bay right in front of the interior shop, we started our post flight inspections.

Upon opening the lower belly cargo doors, we found many large movie film reels that had been left there. We assumed the movie people had flown on the plane back to Hollywood and forgotten the movie film reels were in the belly cargo compartment. We notified the maintenance foreman and moved all the reels of film to his office. Thankfully, it all ended up where it was supposed to go because a good aviation movie was put together and released in 1970.

N324F on March 8, 1969 - back in Los Angeles Tigers base
photo Ted Gibson, via John Wegg

DC-8-63 N792FT, the aircraft involved

photo Charlie Straeche and Frank de Koster

21

"Prepare For Emergency Descent!"

Captain Dwight Small

UNABLE TO CONTROL THE CABIN PRESSURE, THE FLYING TIGER DC-8, WITH 229 SOULS ABOARD, PLUNGED TOWARD THE EAST CHINA SEA.

The crews that flew the Vietnam MAC flights share a bond that perhaps only we can fully understand. The war nearly tore our country apart and many of us that flew the airlift had the same worries, doubts and misgivings. Emotions were high with most everyone. To keep the conversations light and friendly, the more controversial aspects of the war were rarely talked about.

We were keenly aware of the lives being lost and it did not escape us that some of those that we took to Vietnam would not come back. I tried not to dwell on this but it was sometimes inescapable. I tried to focus on the joy we shared with the ones we brought home. I smile as I recall the whooping, hollering and foot stomping as the wheels touched the home runways at Travis or Mc Chord or Norton. But: I cannot forget the fear and sadness of many of those young men that we took over there; many were sure they wouldn't return. Because the flight attendants were in the cabin for hours on end with these young Americans, some got caught up in the swirl of emotions: fear, loneliness, despair.

I poignantly remember a flight attendant coming into the cockpit and losing her composure. The cockpit door opened and then closed quickly behind a young flight attendant. I turned and saw her put her hands to her face as she began to cry. She turned away from us as much as she could and wept quietly. In a few minutes she collected herself, wiped the tears from her face with her inflight apron and bravely went back to the cabin to resume her work. As she exited she turned to us and said, "Sorry guys." Later she said that she fell apart, as she put it, because she had been trying to comfort a 19 year-old army guy that was sure he would not come home.

This was the backdrop for the ten crewmembers of flight 4643 as we departed Yokota, AFB Japan at sunrise on September 25, 1970 with 219 soldiers aboard. Our passengers had already been on the plane for 12 hours but this flight leg would be the most difficult for them. Next stop would be Vietnam.

We were scheduled to fly to Cam Ranh Bay, Vietnam and then back to Yokota, AFB. Flying time for each leg would be about five hours with a two hour ground time so it would be a long day. Each of us had made this trip many times before but today would be different, very different.

The crew bus unloaded the flight attendants and the flight engineer at the passenger terminal. They would go directly to the airplane, N792FT, to do their preflight checks. The captain, navigator and I went to the weather briefing on the second floor of operations. "No problems today," the weather man said. "You'll be CAVOK all the way." Another short ride in the crew bus and we were at the airplane. A blush of orange from the coming sunrise reflected off the shiny aluminium fuselage of our two year old DC-8-63. I was very proud to be flying the stretch DC-8. I was a senior first officer and would be a captain in two years.

We did our usual cockpit preflight checks and I contacted ground control for our ATC clearance. "You are cleared," the voice said, "To Cam Ranh Bay via Yaezu, Transition Mullet, Jet Green 81, Flight Planned Route. Cross five miles northeast of Yaezu and maintain flight level two-eight-zero." As we taxied to runway 36 the captain said, "Tell the tower to lower the barrier." The barrier is a cable webbing network at the end of some military runways that can stop an airplane from going off the end in the event of a brake failure.

It would not, however, stop a heavy DC-8 such as ours and would cause a disaster if our landing gear tangled in it as we were lifting off. The tower confirmed

119

that the barrier had been lowered. Runway 36 is over two miles long so we should be airborne before the barrier but weather and performance variables could change that.

The flight to Cam Ranh was smooth and routine. We had a particularly congenial and professional group of flight attendants aboard and military passengers are almost never a problem. In the cabin were flight attendants Brigitte, Jan, Sandy, Barbra, and Maureen. Regrettably I don't remember the name of the sixth FA. All went well and we landed about 1100 Vietnam time.

In the fall of 1970 the war was winding down for some but changing for others. There was now occasional infiltration at our military bases by locals with ill intent. Flight crews were warned to monitor their airplanes carefully when on the ground and not to let anyone unknown to the flight crew board the planes or use the lavatories. There had been, we were told, at least one case of plastic explosives (C-4) being placed in a lavatory and another incident where it was attached to

a landing gear strut. We were also told that the C-4 was, in both cases, found before takeoff. I'm not sure if these incidents were fact or fiction but we were, nevertheless, briefed. An hour into the next flight leg we would wonder if perhaps we had been sabotaged.

The takeoff and climb-out from Cam Ranh was normal in every respect. We soon reached our initial cruising altitude of FL290 and I'd had my first cup of coffee. One of the first tasks of the flight attendants was to brew coffee so I always requested it as soon as it was ready. It doesn't take long for airplane coffee to taste stale so I always chose to get it while it was at its best.

About an hour into the flight, Captain Al, sniffed the air and asked if anyone smelled smoke. None of us did so he decided that it must have been his imagination. But soon after that a flight attendant came to the cockpit and said, "There's a smoke smell mid-cabin." This indeed got our attention. Captain Al ordered her to "All Call" the other flight attendants and tell them to quietly check the entire cabin to find the source.

Flying Tigers DC-8-63 at Cam Ranh Air Base, Vietnam

photo Flying Tigers Club Archives

We thought that it was most likely a bored GI playing with matches but nothing is more concerning than the possibility of an inflight fire so best to be proactive. A few minutes later the flight attendant came back and said she could no longer smell smoke so we shrugged it off and got back to the usual flight monitoring tasks. We had burned off about 15,000 pounds of fuel so the captain told me to request a climb to FL330.

We were nearing FL330 in the climb when suddenly there was a big change in cabin pressure. My ears popped a couple of times and I turned toward the flight engineer as I wondered what was happening. The captain asked: "What the hell's going on with the pressurization?" Our flight engineer, Doug, said, "I don't know but I've selected manual and seem to be able to control it." The cabin pressure had suddenly climbed to 10,000 feet from about 7,500 which would be normal for FL330.

Could there be a breach of fuselage integrity I wondered? And, could the previous concern about smoke in the cabin have something to do with it? We were now on high alert. For a few minutes things seemed to be stable. The flight engineer said that he had been able to manually bring the cabin altitude down to where it should be so we begin to relax.

But then something happened that raised our alert level another notch. We heard a United Airlines flight call ATC and report an engine failure and we immediately realized that it was the United Airlines DC-8 that was on the ramp with us at Cam Ranh Bay and had departed just after us. I wondered, and I expressed my concern, about the possibility of a connection between the United Airlines flight's engine problem, our smoke in the cabin and our pressurization problem. Could these two airplanes have been sabotaged on the ground at Cam Ranh, I wondered? Maybe a little paranoia on my part but...

A few minutes went by and again we began to relax. The flight engineer told us that he had successfully brought the cabin pressure down to 7,200 feet where it should be for this altitude. All was well, but not for long. Suddenly, as before, my ears popped and the

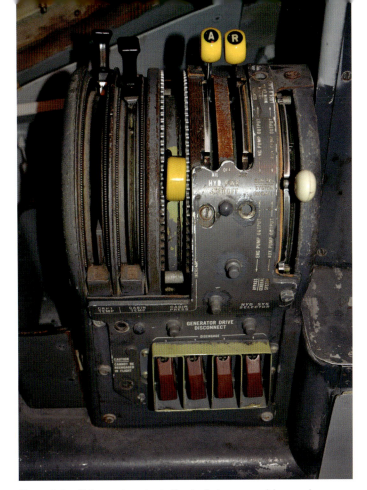

Part of the flight engineer's station includes several levers, known as 'lollipops'. The middle yellow lever is cable connected to the outflow valve, allowing manual control of the cabin pressurisation system
photo Guy Van Herbruggen

cabin pressure rose rapidly. My head felt like it was going to explode.

I heard rattling behind my seat as the flight engineer grabbed the manual controller and attempted to increase the cabin pressure. The captain had now turned sideways in his seat to observe the flight engineer's panel as the engineer worked feverishly to regain control. Doug said, "Look, I can't control it, the outflow valve is completely closed, but the cabin pressure is still climbing."

But then, just as before, the cabin began to repressurize. This time the cabin pressure had climbed to over 10,000 feet so we thought it fortunate that the passenger oxygen masks hadn't automatically deployed. We were anxious now and didn't relax or let our guard down. The captain said, "If that happens again we're going to take the high dive." He meant that if it happened again he would order an emergency descent. We didn't have long to wait.

I felt the abrupt pressure change in my ears, it was happening again. Immediately the captain called: "Prepare for Emergency Descent!" At this point it became very much like a simulator check ride. Each crewmember performed his immediate action memory items section of the emergency checklist. Mine were oxygen mask on, establish communications, squawk 7700 (emergency transponder code), declare an emergency, reset altimeters, call out altitudes in descent.

The captain's Immediate Actions called for putting his oxygen mask on, then throttles to Idle, inboard throttles to full reverse, slow to 265 knots in level flight, call for gear down, descend at Mach .83/BP (Barber Pole - redline) and begin the level off passing 12,000 feet, level off at 10,000 feet, retract the landing gear and bring the inboard engines out of reverse.

Our steep, diving plunge from 33,000 feet to 10,000 feet took less than four minutes. Everything had gone as expected up to that point but then the inboard engines wouldn't come out of reverse and the landing gear would not retract. We now had a whole new set of problems to deal with.

The engineer had announced a hydraulic system failure just as we were levelling off but, rather than proceed directly to the hydraulic failure checklist, we had to deal with something more immediately important. "First things first," the captain said. "We've gotta get these two engines out of reverse." With that, I reached up to the overhead panel and activated the reverse bucket dump switches. There had been moderate buffeting in the descent and mild buffeting when we leveled off, but when the buckets dumped we once again had smooth flight, noisy but smooth.

The buckets were now faired but the reverse translating rings remained extended so we would have a 10% thrust decrement on the inboard engines for the

EMERGENCY DESCENT PROCEDURE

CAPTAIN ANNOUNCE:	
PREPARE FOR EMERGENCY DESCENT	
OXYGEN MASK.	ON
AUTOPILOT	YAW DAMPER POSITION
INBD THROTTLES	REV PWR STOP
DESCENT SP SCHED	M.88/BP
WITH PTC INOP.	M.83/BP

F/O	
OXYGEN MASK	ON
SEAT BELT & NO SMOKING SIGN	ON
TRANSPONDER	7700
RADIO	NOTIFY ATC
CALL OUT ALTITUDES	

S/O	
OXYGEN MASK.	ON
PAX OXY MASK SWITCH	EJECT
MANUAL PRESS CONTROL . . .	UP (locked)
PNEU PRESS CONTROL SWITCHES	HIGH
ALERT COURIERS TO DON OXYGEN MASK.	

NOTE: DO NOT EXCEED 15° BODY ANGLE IN DESCENT.

Recovery should be initiated in sufficient time to regain level flight at the desired altitude. Do not remove reverse thrust at airspeed in excess of 300K, or remain in reverse below 190K, in order to prevent undue trim changes. Do not trim less than 0° on horizontal stabilizer.
NOTE: Oxygen capacity has not been evaluated for any particular route.

Emergency Descent checklist   *author's collection*

duration. We can deal with that, I thought. As long as the two outboard engines continued to operate normally we would have sufficient power to get there and land safely. The cockpit noise level would remain high because the cockpit is located above the nose wheel well. Flying between 250 and 265 knots with the landing gear extended and the gear doors open is loud.

The captain called for the appropriate abnormal check lists to deal with the failed hydraulic system and to deal with the two inboard engines remaining in reverse. We then assessed the overall condition of the airplane and considered the options. Senior flight attendant Bridgette came to the cockpit wanting guidance. We were busy and the captain may have been a bit impatient with her so she started to leave. I carefully interjected, telling her that we were now headed for Kadena AFB Okinawa, and that everything should be alright from here on.

When I had earlier declared an emergency, air traffic control told us to let them know if there was anything they could do for us. I responded with, "For starters, you can clear us direct to Kadena," which they immediately did.

We had a lot of things going on, but under Captain Al's leadership we remained cool and composed.

Methodically we dealt with each problem in order of significance, and because of the excellent Flying Tiger training, we had no doubt as to the outcome. We had faith in our airplane because of system design redundancy which covered primary system failures.

About 50 miles directly ahead of us was Miyakojima, a small island with a 6,000 foot runway. Captain Al had a major decision to make. "Should I put this thing on that island or not?" he wondered aloud. A few minutes ago the answer would have been, hell yes, but now things had stabilised. Air traffic control asked about our status numerous times. They became especially concerned after our emergency descent when we reported hydraulic and reverser problems. I now realize that they had decided that our situation was deteriorating and the outcome was uncertain.

The controller told us that there were two F-4 Phantoms in our area on a training mission and that they had offered to assist if we would like an escort or an assessment. Yes, yes, the captain said. A minute or so later air traffic control said that the F-4s were headed our way. "They are 125 miles at your three o'clock on an intercept heading and closing fast at high mach. They will be there in six minutes."

The lead Phantom formated with us, his wingman a couple of hundred yards to his right. He positioned his cockpit about 30 feet below our right-wing tip. He was in that position for a minute or two and then crossed underneath to take a look at the left side. He was in that position for a minute or so and then the controller asked

if we were ready for a "configuration" report. We were not able to talk directly to the Phantom pilot because military aircraft use a different frequency band so the assessment was relayed through the controller.

"OK, he says you're a mess," and then he went on with the report. "Your landing gear appears to be down and in place but your main gear doors are open and one is hanging at an odd angle. Your inboard engines appear to be partially in reverse with the reverser mechanism about two or three feet aft of the exhaust nozzles but both sides are the same. The right inboard engine is trailing a white vapour that could be fuel or oil but doesn't look like smoke." The controller then asked us if there was anything else we'd like for him to look at and then the Phantoms rejoined and quickly disappeared ahead of us.

10,000 feet is not an efficient jet altitude. Additionally, because the gear was extended with gear doors open and with the reversers not stowed, we had a huge amount of drag. We were aerodynamically dirty and were consuming fuel at a prodigious rate. There were no performance charts in the operating manual for our situation so the captain asked the engineer and navigator to come up with a fuel remaining number for our ETA. After some quick computation the navigator said, "You'll have more than an hour of fuel remaining and that's conservative." Good, I thought, at least we don't have to worry about fuel.

We were now one hour from landing and Captain Al told us to again review the emergency and abnormal checklist, to be certain that nothing was overlooked. He wanted to be absolutely sure what systems capabilities we had and what we might not have for landing.

The abnormal hydraulic checklist reminded us that we had unpowered ailerons. That was concerning because roll control in a DC-8 with failed hydraulics is very, very heavy. We would have a crosswind from the right at touchdown which could require significant aileron input. This would be similar to trying to steer a car without power steering. Captain Al told me to be ready to assist him if more muscle was needed at touchdown. The abnormal checklist also reminded us that we would have normal braking but that the brakes could fail if the antiskid was on and heavy braking was applied.

Captain Al said, "Turn it off, we'll land without antiskid." We should have several normal brake applications available because the brake accumulator pressure gage indicated fully charged. One of the engineer's duties in this situation would be to monitor the brake accumulator pressure and call it out loud and clear if it dropped to near 'air charge' pressure.

Another item on the checklist pertained to nose wheel steering, also normally hydraulically powered but, like the brakes, in our situation would be limited to what energy was available from its accumulator. The accumulator should allow two 90 degree turns which would be enough to allow us to taxi clear of the runway after landing. We were now 15 minutes out. The checklists were complete. The Senior Flight Attendant had briefed the passengers and we were ready for the landing.

It was a beautiful clear day and we could see the runways from 20 miles out as we switched to tower frequency of 126.2 and we began to follow the ILS (Instrument Landing System) glide slope and localizer signals toward the runway. The controller said, "You are cleared to land runway five left. Be advised that there are numerous emergency vehicles on both sides of the runway. Please confirm souls aboard and fuel remaining." I responded, "We have 229 souls aboard and 15,000 pounds of fuel. Cleared to land."

It was almost surreal. At this point everything seemed incredibly normal. Normal but we knew that we had a seriously impaired airplane in our hands. We had discussed what might happen if we incurred additional problems such as an outboard engine failure, remote as it might be, at length. With the flaps fully extended, and a landing gear that could not be retracted, we were now in a vulnerable high-drag situation. An engine-out missed approach would not be possible. The relationship between drag and power available would not be in our favour and the margins would be narrow indeed. Occasionally Al would make light groaning sounds as he muscled the control wheel to the left or right.

We crossed the threshold at the usual 50 feet and Al eased back on the control column bringing the big DC-8 to the flare attitude. Just before the wheels touched the runway, the upwind wing rose. Al put his right shoulder over the control wheel to apply more force and said, "Help." I assisted him slightly but he had it well handled so it would not have been a problem. The landing and roll out were as expected. We were on the ground! I'm sure the passengers and flight attendants were relieved. But...the excitement wasn't over yet.

As we taxied off the runway and were cleared to the ramp, the flight engineer monitored the brake and nose wheel steering accumulator pressures. We had made two 90 degree turns when the engineer said that we no longer had nose wheel steering pressure so Al brought the plane to a stop and set the parking brake and I told the tower that we had gone as far as we could go.

We didn't immediately shut the engines down because, with the engines shut down, there would be no operating generators and so no radio communications. Within a minute or so the tower asked if we were done with the emergency equipment. We said that we were and, at that point, shut the engines down. We were busy securing the cockpit and doing the shutdown checklist. I had noted that emergency vehicles were driving away.

Moments later the fire trucks were hurriedly returning to our airplane. On the right side, firemen, with hose in hand, rushed to the belly area near the right main landing gear. "What the hell's going on?" the captain asked. I opened my side window and extended my head and shoulders and saw smoke coming from the area near the right main landing gear. I reported what I saw to the captain and he immediately called for an evacuation. "Evacuate, evacuate!" he said over the PA system.

Within a very few seconds I heard multiple loud thumps as the emergency exits opened and the evacuation slides deployed. I could also hear loud voices coming from the cabin as our well-trained flight attendants directed the passengers toward the emergency exits. 219 young and able-bodied military personnel probably set an evacuation time record, which may have been less than one minute.

Captain Al and I were the last two out. We used the slide at the most forward door on the left side just aft of the cockpit. Everyone moved well away from the airplane and congregated in small groups, wondering what would come next. I looked back and saw no smoke coming from the airplane.

Soon, dark blue Air Force buses arrived and began transporting our passengers to the terminal. They were later transported to on-base quarters and some to local hotels where they would stay for 2 days while our DC-8 was being repaired and made ready to fly again.

The flight crew, all ten of us, stood together waiting for nobody knew what. A colonel approached us and identified himself as the wing commander. He asked if everybody was OK and expressed his gratification that no one was injured. He then invited the crew to the Officer's Club to have a drink on him.

Two and a half days later the airplane was repaired and ready to fly. A maintenance crew was brought in from Los Angeles and they worked around the clock. Ten new escape slides were installed and the oxygen system was restored. The hydraulic leak was found in the right-inboard reversing mechanism. Apparently, the vibration and buffeting during the high-speed descent with the inboard engines in full reverse caused the breach. The smoke I saw, which led to the evacuation, came from hot brakes on the right main gear. The hydraulic line break had allowed fluid to spray onto the right gear brake assemblies. There was enough air movement around the right main landing gear when the engines were running to keep smoke from being visible. But when the engines were shut down the crash/fire crew took notice of it and came back to the airplane. That is when I saw the smoke and reported it to the captain, hence the evacuation.

It was never determined exactly what caused the pressurization problem. It is certain that the pressure relief valve popped open three times but why? The mechanics changed the cockpit cabin pressure auto controller and gauge. The gauge may have indicated incorrectly, causing the flight engineer to over-pressurize as he attempted to manually set the cabin altitude. But why did it happen the first time when the system was set to auto? No evidence was found that the airplane had been tampered with while on the ground at Cam Ranh Bay.

Two and a half days later we departed for McChord, AFB near Tacoma, Washington. We stopped in Yokota, Japan for fuel so it was another long day but we got our troops home. The airplane flew normally but we were somewhat on guard. Both inboard engine reversers were mechanically locked in place and the pilots' panel was placarded for that. I made the takeoff and at about 300 feet, when the gear was retracting, there was a sudden jerk in the control wheel. Apparently, an air bubble surged through the hydraulic system.

After that little glitch all went well.

Captain Dwight Small

22

My First Job At Flying Tigers

The Story of Glenn Van Winkle, Manager of Ops Control at Flying Tigers

Leigh-lu Prasse (Flight Planner/Aircraft Dispatcher Flying Tigers/FedEx 1987-1994)

Janitor. Yep, just two days after graduating from the University of the Pacific, Stockton Campus, Glenn drove down to the new Tigers HQ at LAX without any appointment, walked in, and inquired if there were any jobs in Tiger's Vietnam ops. He had been told about the opportunity by Tigers pilot Bill Franklin. How did he know Bill Franklin? Well, he just happened to date Bill's daughter in college.

Ned Wallace, the man himself, manager of charters and MAC flying at that time, spoke with Glenn and said there were no current openings in Vietnam but he did have an opening in Cold Bay (CDB), Alaska, as a janitor. Glenn did not hesitate to accept the job on the spot (as it was only temporary) and three days later he found himself on a Tiger DC-8 enroute to Anchorage (ANC). It was January 1971.

After hopping on Reeve Air's DC-3 for the ANC-CDB trip, and many mail stops later, during which Glenn got his first cargo experience by helping toss freight from the plane, Glenn alighted on Cold Bay's ramp into one of the coldest winters on record! (The bay actually froze over and an ice breaker was sent in to carve a path to the dock for the lifeblood of supplies to the town – food and, most importantly, strong alcohol!)

Glenn's first day on the job was in WOXOF conditions with temps at zero degrees and just eight hours of sunlight a day. His job? Clean the 20-room hotel, restaurant, bar, grocery store, and other concessions that Tigers operated at Cold Bay, which served as a fuel stop for Tigers DC-8s from Anchorage to Haneda (HND) or Yokota (OKO). Additionally, Glenn was the plumber, electrician, stock boy, and did any other odd jobs that needed to be done. Having grown up on a farm in California's central valley, Glenn's work ethic of, whatever it takes, get it done, gave him free hours after completing his chores to spend on the ramp learning how to service planes – flight paperwork, weight and balance, fueling, and dumping the lavs (!).

Tigers also serviced other transiting airlines such as Seaboard, Capitol, TIA, World, and ONA, giving Glenn great experience that would foreshadow his Vietnam years to come. The weather and remoteness of Cold Bay never deterred Glenn, and thus began his long storied career at Flying Tigers/FedEx that he refers to as "the most exciting and best adventure of my life."

Five months later and laden with the ways of the aviation world, Glenn was notified of an opening in Vietnam and sent to LAX for training in flight operations and charters. He would spend the next three years in war-riddled Vietnam, including Saigon, Ben Hoa, and Da Nang.

Flying Tigers staff in Saigon, New Year's Eve 1972. From Left to right, George Miller, unknown lady, Bob Lapole, unknown man, Gary Kangieser (station manager), Grant Swartz (aircraft maintenance), Dick Dunn, Lee (George Miller's wife) and Dave McElroy (aircraft maintenance).

photo Glenn Van Winkle

Vietnam staff awaiting inbound freighter, January 1973

photos Glenn Van Winkle

In early 1975, Glenn transited back to LAX to work in Operations Control (OpsCon), over to charters, and had a blast several years as loadmaster (you should hear about Glenn's five hour delay in Nome, Alaska, trying to load a herd of loose reindeer!). He eventually became manager of charters, and onto the iconic Manager of OpsCon. At FedEx he was Manager International Global Operations Control in Memphis, took the GOC Manager position in Oakland, and eventually became Senior Manager of SFO. From his illustrious beginnings with Flying Tigers in Cold Bay and Vietnam, Glenn rallied to meet life's journey head-on, never hesitating to accept the next crazy, oftentimes dangerous, but incredibly exciting adventure. He retired in 2010 after 39 years of 24/7 airline operations at Flying Tigers/FedEx and lives in San Ramon, CA.

His first assignment would be Da Nang, where upon his arrival was greatly welcomed by ops agent George Miller (retired 2018 Tigers/FedEx charter manager), who immediately took off for R&R in Saigon. There Glenn was, all of 22 years old, not a year yet at Tigers, working solely by himself turning around not just Tigers aircraft but any other commercial carrier that came into Da Nang. Glenn had asked George why there were holes on the side of the Tigers Operations truck, to which the reply came, "Oh that was just a rocket that landed too close." Okaaay.

A couple months later, Glenn was personally introduced to incoming rocket fire on his very first night in Ben Hoa. Having just gone to bed, he was awoken by rockets hitting the air base and said, "I hid under my bunk with my pillow over my head!" This event would become more frequent as war wound on; however, it did not daunt Glenn on his mission to turn planes around. On his much deserved days off, Glenn jumped on Tiger planes to meet up with his college roommate in Japan, based at Atsugi AFB. There the two had great outings taking navy nurses on dates to the beach!

Break time for Glenn Van Winkle after offload in Tehran, July 1975

Unusual Animal Charter

H. Paul Rebscher

Flying Tigers carried many farm animals to Asia and Europe to increase the country's milk, meat and fertilizer production. I was the second officer on a DC-8 charter from Chicago to Vietnam carrying six-month-old pigs.

My leg was from Chicago to Anchorage, about six hours, and was instructed by my boss, Chief Second Officer Al Grant, to keep a very detailed log, to include time of loading, temperature, wind direction and any other parameters relevant to the trip.

Two deadheads were to accompany the shipment representatives of the shipping co-op from Illinois. The first problem arose when the loadmaster questioned the size of the pigs whose weight was now double the contract weight.

According to his math 130 pigs would have to be left behind and the shipper balked at this number saying his contract called for 530 pigs and that was what was going onto the aircraft.

So, 530 pigs were loaded and off we went to Anchorage, six hours away. The flight was routine as I noted all parameters and passed this on to the deadheading handlers who agreed all was well with the pigs. On arrival in Anchorage we had a crew change for the next leg to Japan and the second officer had been instructed to note all the data.

On arrival in Japan another crew change for the leg to Vietnam and again all parameters during the flight were noted. After about 20 hours on board the aircraft, the pigs were offloaded and 130 had died. The exact number the loadmaster had suggested be left behind.

Because of the inbreeding domestic pigs are subject to heart attacks, anxiety and in this case, due to crowding, suffocation. The shipper sued Flying Tigers for negligence and the company went to court in Chicago to defend its position.

I was living in Chicago area at the time of trial and the company asked me to become a witness on our behalf. After about a two days trial before a judge (not a jury), the company was found not guilty.

I spent an hour as a witness and was able to back up my testimony with all data I had recorded during my leg to Anchorage. The company put my wife and I in a first-class hotel downtown Chicago, with meals for my testimony. Wow.

Three decks of swine are loaded on board a 747 at Chicago on September 27, 1982. The 747 carried about 1,200 swine while the DC-8-63 would generally accommodate 540 of the animals. Pigs, which lack eustachian tubes in their ears, are the most sensitive of the animals Flying Tigers regularly carried in large numbers. Water supply, ventilation and temperature control are critical factors in the successful transportation of swine.

photo Flying Tigers Club Archives

A Flying Tiger Line Charter

Charles "Chuck" Marshall, LAX Line Maintenance

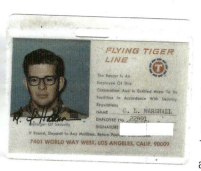

Tigers had a cattle charter out of Helena, Montana. I think it was the late fall of 1973. I was lucky enough to get the maintenance rep position on this field trip. We landed in Helena about 8pm. The aircraft had been prepped at LAX with all the cattle pens and bedding installed so we were ready to load cattle. We were picking up a little over 200 certified pregnant heifers from a ranch in Canada. They were going to some city in Japan.

We learned later in the evening that this DC-8 was the largest aircraft to ever land at Helena. Up to that time they had only 727s and DC-9s. What really amazed me was it looked like the whole town of Helena came out to look at the big aircraft. Since the cattle trucks were running a little late, the mayor wanted to know if the people could look inside the cargo area upstairs. The cargo master (I think his name was Don McComas) checked with the captain and he OK'd it.

We had set up the loading ramp for the cattle to get up to the cargo compartment and people started going up to look inside then they went down by way of the main entry door stairs. It was a great evening.

Later, I was walking around the aircraft just checking it over. I ran into a fellow with about eight high school age kids with him. It turns out he was the instructor for an aviation maintenance class at one of the local technical schools. I walked around with them while the cattle were being loaded. They had many questions about the plane and about working in the airline industry. All the passenger and galley doors had to be opened to allow the heat generated by the cattle to exit the airplane. The difference of the heat in the aircraft and outside made it look like steam was pouring out.

When the aircraft left about 2:30 the next morning, I think we still had the whole town there to watch the departure. It was a good thing it was cold. The aircraft was heavy. It had a good load of fuel and cattle and used up most all of the runway. Since they were headed to Cold Bay out on the Aleutian Chain west of Anchorage, I stayed in Helena. The worse part of the trip was a nine-stop run on Northwest Airlines to get back to LAX.

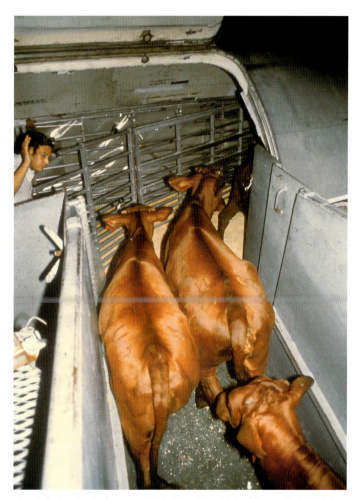

Castle being loaded onto a DC-8-63 photo Flying Tigers Club Archives

Saigon, loading rice for Phnom Penh

photo Flying Tigers Club Archives

25

Tigers Rice Lift To Cambodia

Captain Bob Baird

PART 1: RICE LIFT

11 April, 1975. Tan Son Nhut airport, Saigon, South Vietnam.

We are taxiing to the active runway for the third time today. We, as in Captain Ted Brondum, Second Officer Larry Barrow, and myself, First Officer Bob Baird. I am in the left seat as Ted agreed some days ago to swap seats every other trip out which is great as I had volunteered to the right seat from a domestic captain's position just to fly the Rice Lift missions.

Flak jackets on at top of descent – First Officer Bob Baird en route Phnom Penh April 1975   all photos Bob Baird unless indicated

Ted: "You ready?" I nod my head reply, "Roger, let's go." Ted: "Saigon, Klong 45 ready for departure." "45, roger, climb 160 radial 24 DME then on course, wind calm, cleared for take-off."

Below the line checklist completed, I crank the airplane 90 degrees left and line up on the runway centreline. Larry slides up from the panel and gives me his go to hell grin. Brakes on, I ease the four throttles up and stabilise the power setting. Brakes off and power coming up, we begin our takeoff roll.

I continue pushing throttles forward and call for max power. Larry's hand moves with mine and he sets the final power setting as I am now outside with only a glance at the panel for speeds.

Ted calls V1 and I remove my hand from the throttles and put both hands on the yoke. VR called and I ease the yoke back. We seem to hang for a moment before climbing away. "Positive rate!" is called and I reply with "Gear up!" V2 puts us into our safe three-engined minimum control speed. If an engine blows, the air rushing over the control surfaces is sufficient that when deflected, we will have enough control authority to keep going in a straight line. Flaps are retracted and we climb out on our departure profile. Little do I know, this will be the Tigers' last trip into Pochentong Airport on the Rice Lift.

Who were we and why were we taking a beautiful Douglas DC-8-63 into harm's way? It really started in mid-February of that year – 1975. Although we had pulled all our troops out of South Vietnam by early 1973, we maintained a small number of military advisors in Saigon.

Flying Tigers, along with several other lines, maintained frequent scheduled flights into Saigon, and we had a small operations crew with Vietnamese employees running that station. Gary Kanoisier was the boss there at that time.

Cambodia had been fighting a losing war with the Khmer Rouge, and all supply lines to the national capital Phnom Penh had been cut. Thousands of people were reaching near-starvation levels of malnutrition when the Cambodian government requested US aid. Responding to those pleas for assistance, the United States agreed to several contracts using civilian aircraft only, to fly food and ammunition into Cambodia. Flying Tigers, along with Airlift, Seaboard World and Saturn signed on to fly rice loads from Saigon to Phnom Penh, while Bird Air, using ex-USAF C-130s, would operate out of Thailand flying critical ammunition supplies.

Each of the Rice Lift companies would operate one or two DC-8-63s with crews based short-term in Saigon. Tiger Ops would supervise the operation and would work as much as possible with the USAF advisor assigned to South Vietnam and also use Air America's intel to provide data on the local situation as it evolved.

The February contracts were signed and first flights began on March 2, 1975. The start-up was rather haphazard and crews were assigned from reserve status to operate these missions. From the beginning, the crews realised the actual flying would be very different to what they were used to. Due to the threats in and around Phnom Penh, the DC-8 would have to be flown more aggressively and SOMETHING than the normal FAA-approved guidelines for handling such a large four-engined jet.

By mid-March, a basic mission profile had been worked out and here is how it ran on a normal day's operations. Crews flying missions for the day were alerted in the hotel at 0500 to 0515. Early on during the start-up crews might be assigned to fly morning trips or afternoon trips. When some crews asked to stay full time, these crews found themselves flying all trips scheduled

During the siege of Phnom Penh a DC-8 offloads rice in what came to be the standard manner - quickly. Two engines were kept running for the average of ten to fifteen minutes the aircraft were on the ground.

Pilots' view upon arrival in Phnom Penh. "Tailpipe Bravo" was the command post during the rice lift operations. It appears as though the inhabitants face more danger from an overloading of sandbags than from rocket fire.

During a quick stop over in Saigon's Tan Sun Nhut during the day's activities, the author managed to catch this South Vietnamese A-37 on its way out for a strike mission. Air activity during this period was quite heavy.

Close enough! Rocket strike off the nose while off loading

every day and that meant they were sometimes flying four or even five round trips to Cambodia's embattled capital a day with only an occasional break. By the time I arrived, April 1 – the schedule and crew manning had become more realistic. In our case, we had two DC-8s and four crews. We flew all missions scheduled one day, and the other two crews flew all missions the next day. One on, one off. Worked well.

Crews were picked up with a stop for a quick breakfast, and you could order a lunch that arrive next to the aircraft on the tarmac at midday. On to Tan Son Nhut and meet with the chief pilot for a too-fast brief, get an aircraft assignment, and it's takeoff time. I would, if time allowed, walk over to Air America's briefing and see what their take was. They were still doing a lot of flying all

over South Vietnam and consequently had a great deal of information that we did not get via Tigers. (I admit that out mission at 22,000 feet to Phnom Penh was a bit out of their territory – but still.)

To Tigers and the rest of the Rice Lift crews, the actual threat to us was fairly minimal. The bad guys would launch 122mm and later 107mm rockets at the airfield when we were on the ground in Phnom Penh. Some were close but in fact most were not. They did hit our ramp a few times; the worst incident was a direct hit killed most of a loading crew, shutting down the operation for the rest of the day. Small arms fire was encountered a few times on approach or on departure below 2,000 feet. One DC-8 (not Tigers) was hit in a wing tank.

We were lucky the Khmer Rouge did not have the Russian hand-held missiles that North Vietnam had.

After the briefing, we headed out to the aircraft to prepare the cockpit, finish loading, and run checklists near engine start time. The first aircraft was normally off about 0815 followed every 15 minutes by another Rice Lift DC-8. Total aircraft of all airlines involved each day ran from five to nine aircraft. The first off could fly four missions and later in the flow would fly three missions. The profile was day VFR only – Phnom Penh had no lights after dark.

Phnom Penh, two 122 mm rockets explode near the runway

View from our cockpit, a Cambodian T-28 taxies past. Chance is, the T-28 is almost as old as the pilots

Rice ready for loading onto two World Airways DC-8-63CF tail numbers N801WA and N805WA. Other DC-8 operators were Airlift International and TIA - Trans International. A Flying Tigers DC-8 is in the background.

Once airborne, a standard SID (standard instrument departure) routing was flown, or a radar vector was followed up to 8,000 feet. At this point ATC (air traffic control) would clear us direct Phnom Penh, climb to FL220 (flight level, 22,000 feet). The Phnom Penh DME (distance measuring equipment) was active and at 70 nautical miles from landing we cancelled IFR with Saigon and the fun began!

We had radio communications frequencies for the tower and the Tigers ramp at Phnom Penh. The ramp we unloaded on was almost exactly halfway down the runway and the folks controlling it and us to some degree while we were still inbound were USAF tactical controllers with US Army special forces mixed in. Their callsign was Tailpipe Bravo and they had a small bunker-type building on the edge of the ramp. I seldom saw anyone from Tailpipe and when I did, they did not appear to be in uniform – which meant rather little as none of us were in full uniform either, due to the heat in the cockpit or on the ground.

Descending to land, at 45 nautical miles DME, we would call Tailpipe and get the field condition report red (under fire) or green (clear), runway in use, and possibly conflicting traffic, such as a preceding DC-8 still inbound after a go-around. At this time, we were descending to cross 25 DME at FL 150. From there it was power back to flight idle, slow to 230 knots, then flaps 23 and gear down.

Push over to maintain maximum rate of descent. You were pretty much in this configuration down to the downwind leg. It kept us high to stay out of reach of any lurking ground fire until as late as possible. The DC-8 was rated for the use of reverse thrust in the air, which would have been more effective at creating a very high sink rate than the use of gear and flaps. It was never used as far as I know, most likely to avoid extra wear and tear (ex DC-8 drivers will recall the level of vibration when reverse was deployed in flight), especially as a major technical fault, while unlikely in such a well-built machine, could strand a ship behind enemy lines.

Close in, say 10 nautical miles, a call to Phnom Penh Tower and they would just normally clear you for a visual approach just like the other ten or 12 airplanes and helicopters that were on frequency. Visuals were fine except the early arrival around 0845, 0900, which could expect low scattered to broken cloud, which obscured the airport until reaaaal close. This junk would burn off by 1000 on the norm.

One approach path took us to the outer city built-up areas, then a hard left turn to enter downwind for runway 05. Air traffic control was pretty much non-existent in the so-called traffic pattern. There were airplanes all over the place including opposite direction downwind (one C-130 went 1,000 feet below us on one arrival.) Downwind was flown pretty tight to avoid some areas that reported ground fire. This made turns to base and final sporting to say the least, with 45 degrees of bank common and with a few a little steeper. Pitch and power judged accordingly!

Finals to landing. Base leg more flaps and full flaps as we rolled out on final, two to three miles from the threshold.

Phnom Penh Pochentong Airport as seen from the cockpit of our DC-8. As the author put it, "It's hard to believe there is a war going on down there."

On the way in! Looking out over the nose of the author's DC-8, Pochentong Airport can be seen directly ahead

We are not super heavy, and have a 10,000-foot runway, so plan was to land with a grease job touchdown and reverse thrust. Brake cooling time was a limiting factor for a speedy turnaround so on the rollout we used no brakes until 5,000 feet remaining, then we would use just enough to stop with no hard braking at all if possible, which meant we had to fly the approach accurately; coming in high or fast on approach would ensure much more kinetic energy to disperse and delay our return leg, waiting for the brakes to cool off.

There was no taxiway, so we would turn at the end and taxi back to our midfield exit to the Tigers ramp. Flaps were brought up to 23 degrees and trim set for takeoff as we came into our ramp. As soon as chocks were in, engines number one and two – port side – were shut down and the cargo door opened. The Second Officer usually went back to supervise the offload, or on many occasions we had an extra crew member as a Loadmaster who would do that, with engines three and four (starboard side) running.

We planned on 12 to 15 minutes to offload 90,000 lbs of rice. I think the record was near ten minutes. Must have been rockets coming in on that one. With the last pallet moving off, we were restarting engines one and two, door shut, and calling for clearance which we seemed to always get right away. We would emerge from the taxiway on to the runway at midpoint, checklists diligently complete, power building as we turned to line up. Empty of payload and with only the trip fuel for the short hop back to Saigon in the tanks, at max power the remaining 5,000 feet was sufficient and we would blast off with 1,000 feet of runway to spare, using just four-fifths of a mile.

We would leave the gear down during the climb out to cool the brakes, but flaps up, VSI (vertical speed indicator) and airspeed pegged out away from any possible small arms, and away from other uncontrolled traffic and up to the safety of 22,000 feet. Relax a bit, flak jackets off, have a slurp of water, but still looking for traffic always. Get back on the radio with Saigon ATC – and perhaps another trip or two back to Phnom Penh.

In the end the Khmer Rouge shut us down. They brought their 105mm Howitzers into gun range and shelled the airport. The Rice Lift was cancelled on April 11. I had flown three trips that day and my scheduled fourth was cancelled due to shell fire. On that day, I think on our second trip we flew over a DC-3 that was shot down while entering downwind. A US captain was on it.

Tiger N783FT sporting First Officer Larry Partridge's hand lettering Phnom Penh Ph Nancy, after his wife

photo Larry Partridge / Flying Tigers Club Archives

On the ground in Phnom Penh, Second Officer Jim Winterberg (left) and First Officer Larry Partridge   photo Flying Tiger Line Pilots Association

Back in Saigon we remained on standby until the 14th when all Rice Lift aircraft are sent home. Tiger's last airplane in the region, another Eight with Ralph Mitchell as Captain, was sent into Saigon on the 20th and flew all Tiger personnel and their families our of Saigon. Saigon, and with it South Vietnam, surrendered on April 29 & 30.

PART 2: FROM THE ORIGINAL DIARY OF EVENTS STARTING 3/29/75

3/29/1975 - 1230. Pan Am SFO-HND 747. Good food, bad stews. Tokyo – 2 hours departure lounge, one beer. Press on to Hong Kong.

3/30/75 - Hong Kong. Nice ride down. Hotel excellent. Very tired so off to bed!

3/31/75 - Up at 0500. Tigers called 0800. Breakfast and then off on China Air Lines 727 at 1115. Arrival Saigon 1330. Bill Popp is with me. Saigon. 88F, humid as hell, lots of CBs (cumulo nimbus). Off to Tiger Ops as afternoon crews coming in.

Captain Tom Sullivan (chief pilot now as Oakley Smith is going home) gave us a rundown on what to expect. No real problems with 122mm rockets. A 105mm Howitz fires with accuracy and closes down Airlift. Gun silent last two days. No AAA reported (yet). Approach boundaries outlined and will brief again informally at 1800. Air Force briefs each morning and also Air America is recommended so I will go to AA tomorrow for that. I don't expect to fly tomorrow as Popp won the coin toss. Damn!

Danang evac cancelled as the city has fallen. Complete chaos up there. World 727 had a narrow one as 400 troops mobbed it. Took off with all doors open, people in gear wells etc. Stories of blood bath in Danang (unconfirmed as of tonight).

We are in the Miramar Hotel off Tudo Street. Not bad, cool at least as opposed to living in tents last time I was here (1966-67). 2200. Off to bed. Brief over beer. Main obstacle seems not to be the shelling or AAA but co-op between crews regarding ingress/egress routes, procedures etc. Four or five different airlines on this so need to get it standardised. Oh, steak dinner at

Mynam, excellent $9.00. Popp wants a beer so stop in Annie's. Last I see of him – ha! I mentioned to Sullivan, I would like to ride to Phnom Penh tomorrow. He said not worry plenty of flying coming up. So, no.

4/1/75 - 2100. Was supposed to be an easy day. Went to A for brief at 1030. Fridel was going home so I was put on the 1300 launch for Phnom Penh. Callsign Klong 946. Easy trip over then IFR down to 3,500 feet on a downwind of sorts. Sam Royal flying, did his usual good job. No ground fire. No incoming while on the ground offloading (12 mins!).

I took it back from the right seat. Hell, can't feel airplane, first time in two years back in the right seat and fees like crap – need to ease up! Landed Saigon about 1600. Told to stand by. Tom Sullivan asked me if I had ever been to Nha Trang when I was over here. "Yes, I took a helicopter in there once or twice." Sullivan says OK. Hush-hush emergency evac of 150-200 US citizens from Nha Trang has just been decided on! Sullivan will fly as Captain, I will go as First Officer and Fred Peterson as Second Officer. Also, a couple of young guys who I take as marines walk up and are both armed to the teeth. I am given a miserly .38 revolver. Five rounds in the cylinder. Great! And yes they are going with us.

Later. Too tired to hash it out now so will note comments down for later on the so-called Nha Trang rescue attempt. Couple of rapid ideas while fresh: Victor 07 is Air America in Nha Trang. 197 Zulu is an Air America helicopter outbound from Nha Trang. Unknown garbled Air America used 121.900 for whatever reason. Abort the mission. Orbit offshore. Max confusion and warnings on ARVN troops all over the airfield. Runway partial blocked with vehicles and troops. I will detail it tomorrow. I am off the 0910 lift due to this mess. I will fly the afternoon runs though. Air America said all US were flown out to an LST offshore. Excellent ending but still, our part was a mess! Total flying time for today was VVVS-Phnom Penh-VVVS 1.5h, VVVS-orbit Nha Trang-VVVS 1.4. Grand total 2.9 but it feels like was about 10 hours. Need sleep!

4/2/75 - 0600. Up as usual too early. Can't sleep the right hours. Damn it! Need a couple more days to sort this out I think. Think I am going flying around noon due to the "late show" yesterday. Cambodian government seem to be leaving but airport still open. In Vietnam, Danang is gone. Complete disaster there. Qui Nohn falling, Nha Trang falling. Many refugees trapped. VNAF aircraft all over the place at Saigon. Few flying. Why? Saigon tense the dollar still rules.

Nha Trang evacuation. I need to get this down. After landing from first afternoon trip yesterday, 'asked' to volunteer to fly to Nha Trang for emergency evac of about 150 US people plus 300 Vietnamese. USAF had commandeered our DC-8. Brief was NVN still about ten miles north of Nha Trang with tanks and possible SAMs. Plan runway 33, turnaround at the end, cargo door open, load people. All engines running. Load and go. Not sure if any stairs are available so cargo nets rigged to climb into an aircraft. YGBSM! Airfield will be closed only for us, good security. OK, shit hot, let's go!

OK from the company stalled. 7th AF and USAID people say, go before too late but nothing moving! Second Officer and I went to the bird and set up for departure. Company called us and said move aircraft to another position so cranked up and did so. Cargo tie down nets were installed in the cabin. 30 minutes later

Offloading the DC-8 in Phnom Penh

photo Larry Partridge / Flying Tigers Club Archives

Second Officer John Franzone supervising activity at Tailpipe Bravo

all photos this page Flying Tigers Club Archives

Sullivan, Gary Krugisier, USAID official, mech, and two embassy guards board and away we go!

Route is VVS-Phan Thiet-NHA. FL220. Cancelled with ATC at PT (my old hang out in 66-67!) and came up on 129.1. An Air America frequency. Here's a rundown on radio chatter from that point. "Klong 946 on 129.1, anyone up?" "Klong 946, 197Z, do you read?" "Roger, Klong 946, Flying Tigers 779 USAID inbound, what's the story?" "Klong 946, '97Z advise you do not land at V7 as you will be mobbed. We just departed and we were mobbed." "97Z roger that. What's the situation on the ground?" "Well many people, many, ramp areas, runway, have bikes, motor scooters blocked the runway, ARVN in jeeps alongside with .30s. I think the friendlies may be your worst problem." "Roger 97Z thanks. Anyone else I can talk to there…?" "Roger, call Victor 07." "VO7 it is, thanks."

I now tried Air America on 120.7 and 130.7. No joy. Back to 129.1. "97Z no joy with VO7, another channel…?" "Klong 946 call VO7 here, what, OK, OK. VO7, do you read Klong 946?" The conversation became three-way. "Klong 946, VO7, roger, understood. Inbound, what's your position now?" "VO7, 946 is abeam Nha Trang feet wet (off shore) at 18,000. What's going on? Over." "946 roger, come on in, many people have come here, drop your ramp to load and be ready to go right out."

"VO7, Klong 946, we have no ramp, repeat, no ramp. Can you get stairs for boarding?" "946 what aircraft type are you?" "We are a delta charlie eight, over." "Say again!" "DC-8!" "OK, roger, DC-8, uh, come on in and 180 on the runway, I'll see if I can get some stairs for you." "Klong 946…" garbled radio. "Aircraft 946, my people say there is no way they can get stairs, no way. Do not land, over." (Who the Christ is this now?) "Roger, no stairs, standby."

We orbit right. Could throw out nets for people to climb up on. "Aircraft 946, we have nets." "Roger, Oscar Mike (?), the DC-8 says he has nets." "Tell 46 to use his discretion but safety of the aircraft comes first." "Roger that, thanks." Then, "946, Victor 07, do not land…!" "Do not land?" "Roger, they're not under control down there and you will be mobbed." "OK standby." "VO7, 946, what's going on?" "946, it's not bad, not too bad…" "OK, how many US citizens to be evacuated?" "946… VO7… all US airlifted to LST off shore." "What the hell… VO7 confirm, no US to be taken out?" "Roger, 946, we are running the last chopper out now." "VO7, 946. OK. Can you get out OK?" "Roger, am going out." "OK VO7, think we will be returning to O1 (Saigon)."

2130. God damn it! Absolutely beat again. Three trips. Lots of 'incoming' today. Two pull-ups on last trip! Airlift hit by about 20 rounds of .30 cal auto weapon. Too tired to write now, will do it tomorrow as supposed to be off (ha!). The flying is something else for a heavy jet. Shit hot! PS curfew at 2200 so can't go anywhere anyhow.

2200. Dinner. The 'P' (money) has gone from 700 to 800 per US dollar, 1000-1200 black market I am told. Need to maybe buy gold bracelet and some elephants tomorrow?

4/3/75 - Well really can't complain. Have the day off so slept in until 0900! Then off shopping. The 'P' is now 1000 to 1800. Prices going to hell! Walked around the so-called black market. All sorts of stuff for sale. I bought a US 8 day aircraft clock for $9.00 and a flak jacket carrier (bag to you!). Now for some log notes. Here's yesterday's flying.

First mission. 0900 take off. Ted Brondum and Mike White are crew. Uneventful until 50 out as usual. Phnom Penh appeared to be IFR. We were at FL210 on top, started let down through layers to just on top again at 13,000. Thin layer. Hit the NDB beacon and came on around to the left. Ted did not want to go lower due another aircraft coming out but I couldn't see how he could

Captain Robert "Bob" Bax

Captain Ted Brondum, this was the uniform of the day during the Rice Lift to Phnom Penh

Second Officer "Lord Jim" Winterberg

Captain Paul Crowley en route to Phnom Penh

all photos this page Larry Partridge / Flying Tigers Club Archives

be a factor unless he climbed straight up! Kept my mouth shut of course as he is the captain for a reason. Anyhow we orbited for a while, finally drifting down between layers to 9,000. The deck was covered with broken low stratus, some holes in it. We could see the airfield once we were ref that area. Ted finally decided to come in on (landing on 05) so picked our way through the stratus. Tops were at 1,500 feet, base 500 feet in places.

The airport was on my side so I called the downwind and the turn to base leg. Lost sight turning base so I asked Ted to steepen the turn up and as we rolled out the runway was straight ahead. Good! Landing and taxi in was uneventful. 13 minutes on the ramp and promised Tail Pipe a case of beer on the next trip. Usual helter skelter take off from mid field. By the way, on the ramp we shut down one and two, cargo door open, three and four running. Two minutes prior to unload finished, crank one and two, close cargo door as start taxi. Pretty slick!

Climb out and return to Saigon normal, not much traffic in our area after landing USAF wanted the weather picture at Phnom Penh. I told em marginal VFR but looked better to the north so should improve. Spent above an hour and a half on the ground in Saigon.

Second mission. 1230 take off. Ted flying this one too. Oh well! Guess he is uncomfortable after I told him I can't fly worth a shit from the right seat. Approaching VVPD looks VFR this time. Bravo says green field. We get down into the traffic OK. We are number two behind a C-46 so extend downwind then on in. Notice a burnt-out DC-3 that was not there earlier. The Khmer Rouge must have got lucky. Taxi into our private ramp area. Whump! Bravo starts yelling on the radio, "Incoming, incoming!" We were pretty much up to speed on that. The impact was about 200 yards off, out near the abandoned DC-4 near the runway. No problem. Whump! Another impact. This one looks like it hit in the Cambodian Air Force ramp area down from us. May have hit some helicopters in there. I decide to put my APH-J (my army-issue flight helmet which I by the way had rigged to use civil VHF radios prior to heading over here). The rest of the crew have steel pots on now. Great looking bunch we are!

A few more rounds come in. Nothing close. Kick up a bit of dust, nothing else. Load crew back up and finish the job. Crank and taxi. Bravo is talking to a C-130. "You guys qualify for combat pay today." "Roger that, thanks." Remember those days? Take off and climb out OK, hard right turn direct Saigon. Lunch break on arrival. Watch a VNAF A-37 belly in, shot up somewhere. Lot of folks near our ramp. World Airways are flying 500 babies somewhere. The best-looking girl in this part of the world is in that group of people. Representing some orphanage one of the ops guys says.

Third mission. Take off 1500. Ted says you fly this one. Great. We change seats. Crank and go. Feels much better over here. Climb on course direct NK beacon direct VVPD. 50 out, drift to 15,000 feet. Bravo come up and advises to standby. Burning aircraft on the runway. Klong 930 is ahead of us holding VFR at 8,000 feet. I continue drift down to 13,000 feet at the beacon. Right hand tight turn. Bravo says come on in. Tower advised. 930 rogers and starts down, lots of traffic out here now, C-130s, helicopters, T-28s, some air strikes about ten miles west of the airport. I pick up 930 crosswind in a steep descent so dirty up the bird and honk it over right turn, sink on VSI is legged (about 6,000 feet per minute).

Whoops! C-130 going the wrong way downwind under us. No sweat, continue, roll out 230 degrees out of 4,000 feet. Can't see the field too well, OK there it is again. Note 930 on base leg well ahead. Continue and ask Ted to call abeam threshold. Down to 2,000 feet now. Ted says go on out a bit. Tower calls for a five mile final (Indian Country that far out). What the fuck! Five mile final? Three DME I ask Ted how it looks. "Come on around." Good, turning base. "Tighten it up." Still can't see the runway rolling around now to final. "930's on the runway." Crap! I see 930 taxiing back on the runway. Not going to clear in time. I call for max power, flaps 23, gear up. Tower advised (maybe they could have said something about 930 on the runway but hey, they don't seem to care about that sort of thing too much!). Looking for traffic and press out a bit turning back to 230 degrees, level at 1,500 feet. Downwind.

Tower now says we are number one. Good. Ask Ted to call the turn for base. Down to 1,000 feet now. Ted calls, "Turn now!" Done. Gear and flaps again. Right on around as we are close in, tight turn, speed good, sink a little, correcting, runway coming up, right on down. 500, 400, 300, speed good, 200... "DC-8 go-around, DC-8 go around!"

Rocket burst ahead but not near the runway. Shit! Go around. Max power, flaps 23, climbing, gear up! Right break and slide in behind and outside a C-130 downwind. Line up again. C-130 lands. Right on around for a third attempt, runway looks good. Speed, flaps, gear, all good. Sink good, over the approach end, ease power off, plop. Nice. Too nice in fact. No spoilers. Four in reverse, shake rumble, no braking yet, reversing good, 3,000 feet of runway to go, on the brakes, just enough, no tire change desired here! (A couple of the other companies did have problems and no fun sitting on our ramp for two or three hours.)

Runway end, 180 degree turnaround, just enough room for the 8 to do this, taxi back setting flaps to 23 degrees and take off trim so we're ready for a fast exit when ready. Taxi in to our ramp. 930 is still there so park close to Bravo's bunker. Note a lot of Cambodians filling more sandbags. Bravo will be a real fort when they added to it. Offload, ten minutes, wow! 45 tonnes of rice and one case of beer! Crank, taxi, line up midfield, power coming up, call for max power. Airplane lurches right, can't hold it, shit, brakes, still skidding, number four isn't spooling up. Left rudder. Now number four decides to spool up and as it does, so we swing left. Throttles back and I get it back on the centreline again, bring throttles back up even, all good, max power and away we go, rotate, leave the gear down to cool it, crank her around and the rest is normal. What a trip!

Back in Saigon we all walk around checking tires. Not even a scuff mark. Lucky! I look at Ted. "Hey that was fun!" He sort of grins and mumbles something. I wonder if we will swap seats again.

4/4/75 - No fly. Mess around with Larry Barrow who tries to get me in trouble with a money exchange guy. Nope. Larry gets screwed and we have a laugh on him. Not so good, am on roof of hotel and note ominous black smoke coming up in the direction of Tan Son Nhut. Hope that is not someone gone in. Word in lobby later in afternoon a USAF C-5A crashed. Many casualties. Later still, they were taking many orphaned children out, and had a large number of military wives from Clark AB onboard to help with the kids.

2000. Panic! We are told to grab our gear and do so. Moved from hotel to abandoned barracks on the ex-USAF base at Tan Son Nhut. What a rat hole! No blankets, towels, soap, toilet paper. What the hell! Also no food and only water we had with us. What gives! I walked out of area aways looking for coffee. Saw a group of USAF guys all sitting around an outdoors table. Walked up and introduced myself. I was politely asked to keep moving as they were an accident investigation board flown in from Clark and were interviewing the flight crew from the C-5A. Grim.

4/5/75 - 2145. Well four lift trips today. Too tied to sort all details. Had two hours sleep in the rat hole (yup rats!). Nobody telling us why the panic and BS location put in. Here's today's fun. 0600 wake up. 0630 breakfast. 0730 ops and sit reps (situation reports). 0800 first mission. Normal. Three rounds on airport while on ground. 1000 second mission. Six to eight rounds. One about 50 metres right in front of us on ramp. No damage. Got a photo of it! One 100 metres left of us right on the bunker or next to it. Four Cambodians wounded. Some aircraft hit down the field and burning. 1245 Lunch on the ramp at Saigon. A-37 crash on 25L. Down to one runway now. Chaos as about 100 airplanes seem to need to go somewhere else all of a sudden. 1315 third mission. Normal. Quiet. No rounds. Maybe too hot to shoot at people today? Lots of t-storms to dodge just to keep it interesting. 1700 fourth mission. One round. Getting dark (whooooo!). Seaboard blew two tires and spend two or three hours on the ground. 1930 moved back to hotel. Dirty, tired, hungry. 2200 that's it for today. Yes sir!

4/6/75 - Saigon. Off today. Boring! 1700 call from field, one DC-8 needs some maintenance. Oakley is there. He says, come on Bob, I'll give you a checkride to Hong Kong! What? We launch at 2015. Oakley flies. What a great guy he is. Always my favourite and will never never forget him as my IP on the Connie in Newark in 65.

4/7/75 - Hong Kong to Saigon. Oakley swaps seats. Check ride? I ask him how did I do when we are walking in after shut down. He gives me his famous laugh and says, Gosh, Bob, I plain forgot to do that!" None like him anywhere. I am scheduled for late lift trip. It is cancelled. Word is an AC-47 shot down northwest of the airport last night. Missile?

4/8/75 - Went up on deck at hotel for a cup of coffee just as a VNAF F-5 flew over and bombed the palace! Place in an uproar but calming down now. Near panic again and we are told to stand by to move again. Lots of news people (ABC CBS BBC etc.) running all over the place. Calm down people! 24h curfew imposed. Now how do we get to the airport? The "white mice" (VN police) will shoot you. Who is running the ops show here? No word, no worries? BS! Streets deserted. Hey I think maybe the F-5 pilot just pissed off with no leadership and sent a message. (Added much later after surrender: F-5 pilot was embedded NVA guy and his mission was to kill as many high ranks in palace as possible. He then flew to North Vietnam.)

4/9/75 - Up at 0530 for 0600 pick up. Breakfast on the way out at Steve's. Super food. He brings our pre-ordered lunches out to the ramp also. No white mice around so we did not get shot. Good! First trip. 0820 off blocks. No problems. No incoming! Second trip. Same. Normal. CBS News guy onboard. Lunch. Talked to some RNZAF chaps flying a twin piston south to some island, they said all going well on their op, no ground fire yet etc. Third trip. 1320 off blocks. OK going over, two rounds on the approach. Seaboard on the ramp so we taxi in behind them. A 107mm went off about 500 feet in front of us, blew up next to a bunch of fuel trucks. Some Cambodians were right there too and no one hurt! Pure luck. Lot of Cambodian T-28s taxiing out. Waved at one guy. He ignored me. I think he wishes he was flying that big DC-8 today! Airstrikes going

in about two and half miles southwest of the runway. Khmer Rouge getting close.

Fourth trip. More incoming as we taxi in, a lot of them. Most not too close. The load crew really hustling, want us out of here! Example, this a.m. no incoming, 15-18 minutes to unload. Now under fire, ten minutes.

Rice Lift to Phnom Penh "uniform"   photo Flying Tigers Club Archives

Yes sir! Got out OK, Saigon was a mess though. ATC not the best on a normal day and today no radio contact, got them for a minute and cancelled with them and came in VFR. No radio contact while doing that either. Finished up about 1850. Beat. Four trips and the lack of sleep plus heat get to you.

4/10/75 - Off today. Shopping. Picked up elephants and got them to airport. Much later, they made it home. Xuan Loc (38 miles southeast of Saigon) heavy contact. VN airborne holding on, NVA have tanks, much artillery. Understand Phnom Penh embassy evacuating now. Lift off. Heavy fire just prior to first lift arriving so they returned. Lift on again at 1300 so crews today will get only one or two trips. Bet we get three or four tomorrow!

Lift shut down. 107mm hit load crew on ramp in Phnom Penh. Three dead, 15 wounded. Lift resumed late, maybe two or three trips. News crews and others are overflowing in the lobby. Whoa! Some gal just came in and stopped traffic. Almost forgot what a round eye looked like.

4/11/75 - Up at 0630. Two or three hours sleep, no aircon, sweating. Off for food and to fly airplanes. Three trips. Not much incoming at least on our trips. Only saw one and not very close. A Cambodian Airlines DC-3 spun in. No one got out. US captain on it. Phnom Penh hanging on but grim. I had talk with Udo, a new's guy who flew with us one mission. He said film he shot with us was used by Cronkite CBS News yesterday. He was still unhappy no one fired at us while he was filming. Bully! Had a few drinks with the troops. Talked with RNZAF guys about flying with them tomorrow if I am off (I'm still a reserve officer so they are good with that!). They are flying a Bristol freighter!

4/12/75 - Lift closed down! Direct artillery fire now on the airfield. USMC/USAF helicopters evacuating all embassy folks (and Tailpipe I hope!) out of Phnom Penh. My last flight in yesterday is the last lift flight to operate. Not good news. I wonder how Cambodians will survive. We are milling around the lobby. No word from Ops. I would guess we will be moving airplanes out of here. Late afternoon. Be ready to leave any time. Bill Popp says he wants to stay. I don't think so Bill!

4/13/75 - Officially we are done. Crews to take our airplanes and some people out.

4/14/75 - Toughing it. Offered first class on Pan Am's last scheduled flight through Saigon. Franzone and I with great regret accept and mid-afternoon are headed home. Two day trip took us six days and that's another war story!

1979: BACK TO PHNOM PENH

On November 24, 1979, Flying Tigers was the first commercial U.S. carrier back into Phnom Penh, with mercy again the mission. A DC-8 jet carried 77,000 pounds of food, medicine and supplies sponsored by two private American relief organizations, Operation California and the American Friends Service Committee, for the first direct United States to Cambodia mercy flight since the oppressive Pol Pot regime was overthrown in January 1979. The trip to Phnom Penh took 31 hours including stops in Anchorage, Japan and Hong Kong.

Members of Los Angeles' Cambodian community expressed their thanks. Next to DC-8-63 tail number N787FT, actress Tippi Hedren, Captains Harold Ewing and Arch Hall are standing behind at right.   photo Flying Tigers Club Archives

Tiger Evac Flight From Saigon

Captain Ralph F. Mitchell

APRIL 18, 1975: SEOUL, KOREA

Our regular schedule calls for my crew, First Officer Ted Freedell, Second Officer Rick Middel, and myself to fly from Seoul to Bangkok via Manila and Saigon as flight 43 tomorrow. We have been following the news developments in the Saigon area with close interest as we will be going there tomorrow night. As the situation is disintegrating very rapidly, I feel that the company may want to evacuate the Tiger personnel soon, although I haven't been contacted. As it seems that our arrival there

First Officer Ted Freedel

tomorrow night may coincide with such a request, I talked it over with my crew to be certain that they would be willing to go along. They were eager to do this, if called upon.

I calculated the maximum number of people who could sit on the floor of a DC-8-63F, in case such a situation arose. I was much more worried about the problem of panicky people trying to get on the airplane than about any military attack on the airport. Having had some experience in evacuating refugees from war areas in China in 1947 and 1948, I was aware of the difficulties which can occur in a time of panic.

I also did a lot of thinking about the probability of having to use emergency pilot's authority in modifying a lot of FARs concerning the carriage of passengers, and also the possibility of carrying passengers without complete immigration papers. I had been reading about the difficulties people were having in getting exit visas and passports in Saigon. A figure of 400-500 persons seemed to be a realistic figure, if these conditions prevailed.

APRIL 19, 1975: LEAVING SEOUL FOR MANILA

The Seoul manager tells us that last night's flight had been ordered to overfly Saigon. Also, ours is to overfly Saigon tonight. The situation is getting much worse in Saigon and the Congress is getting impatient with the slowness of getting Americans and "endangered" Vietnamese out of Saigon, so I still expected a possible stop in Saigon to get out Tiger people or perhaps a lot of others.

After leaving Manila for Bangkok, we decided that we were not going to be used for the evac operation. Passing abeam Saigon, Ted called the Tiger Operations on the radio. They reported all is normal. We went on to Bangkok and got there about one a.m.

Second Officer Rick Middel

Captain Ralph Mitchell   *photos Flying Tigers Club Archives*

APRIL 20, 1975: BANGKOK

At eight a.m. at the hotel, I received a call from Oakley Smith in LAX. He explained that Joe Healy and others in a meeting had just decided that the time had come to evacuate the Tigers from Saigon. I think that I surprised him by saying that my crew and I had been planning for this for several days and that we were ready to go at any time. He explained that the company had intelligence reports from the USAF in Saigon that SA-2 Russian anti-aircraft rockets with a range of 19 miles were expected to be within range of Tan Son Nhut airport within 48 hours. They expected an airplane to be shot down at that time, and that would effectively close the airport.

The plan was to take the airplane to Saigon at three p.m. Saigon time, pick up about 100 passengers, and proceed to Hong Kong. First, the plane had to offload the Manila-bound freight and get fueled up for the flight.

I alerted my crew members to the change in departure time since we had not planned to leave until later that evening. I was lucky to get them before they went out shopping or on a city tour or whatever crew members do in Bangkok! I called the Tiger station at Bangkok, but got no answer. Then I called R. C. "Andy" Anderson, our super-reliable maintenance and operations expert in Bangkok, at his home, and informed him of the operation. He called fellow Tiger employees and got the unloading and fueling taking care of.

While checking out of the hotel, we received another call from LAX. Larry King at Crew Control said they had not been able to get the Bangkok station on the teletype about the change in schedule. (Normally there would be no one in the station in the early morning, since the only flight was not leaving until that night.). I reassured him that all was taken care of and that we would be in Saigon at three p.m.

We were concerned about being swamped by too many demanding passengers, as a World Airways 727 had been leaving Da Nang. We took the precaution of having the baggage door handles covered over with speed tape (wind resistant metallic tape used for running repairs on non-structural elements of the plane's exterior),

in order to make access to those doors inaccessible. Rick was assigned Senior Flight Attendant duties and the duty of keeping the passenger load within limits in case of a panic. Ted was in charge of communications and navigation. He had only recently come back from the Phnom Penh Operation.

APRIL 20, 1975: ARRIVAL SAIGON

We rushed off to Saigon after being held up on the Bangkok tarmac for a few minutes by a Royal Australian Air Force plane unloading people from Saigon right in front of the terminal. Shortly after three p.m. we were talking to Tiger Saigon, asking where to park and whether to shut down all our engines. They said shut down all engines, and they didn't seem to be in any hurry to leave!

We parked in an area adjacent to the end of runway 25L. Dick Dunn, Tiger Ops man, said that all was well, but they did not want the plane to leave until evening, as a lot of the passengers could not get to the airport until after dark. Apparently they were to come onto the airbase in some "hush-hush" manner that we were not aware of. An engine cowl was opened to feign maintenance on an engine, so that the tower would not become suspicious.

I was not very pleased to leave my accustomed mode of transportation, and a little put out that we had rushed over here to save these people and now no one was ready to leave. We were driven off the airbase to Steve's Cafe run by an American. All seemed quiet around the airbase, although we had noticed some smoke in the Bien Hoa area to the northeast as we came into land.

We spent the afternoon sitting around Steve's drinking ice tea. I was facing President Thieu's portrait on the wall. Next to him was Presidents Kennedy and Johnson, and Martin Luther King. I couldn't escape Thieu's stare and felt uncomfortable, so I moved to the other side of the table. There he was still looking at me, now via the bar mirror. Waitresses kept asking us what is happening, when are the Americans leaving and where are the VC? We were evasive. Steve, the owner, told Ted he didn't have any plans to leave town.

Finally, at nightfall, we were taken to the Tiger operations building at the airbase. It was full of Vietnamese relatives of Tiger employees, all looking rather nervous. The destination of our flight had been changed to Guam, but we were still filed Hong Kong on our flight plan. We got a briefing from two USAF Majors who confirmed the rocket situation. They told us the safest ways to depart and had full knowledge of our flight, its destination and purpose.

At 8:40 p.m., the crew went out to the airplane with some of the Tiger family personnel and station manager Gary Kangieser who had had a very hectic day trying to arrange all the details of our departure. Grant Schwartz, maintenance rep in Saigon, had been taking care of the airplane all this time and supervising loading of Comat (company material), spares, et cetera. Many of our passengers had been already loaded on through the cargo door in so-called igloos, as though it was a freight operation.

As we approached the airplane, the last load was being lifted on a flatbed loader. The occupants were all squatting so they could not be seen. It was dark and it looked much like a normal cargo operation. Since some of the expected passengers did not arrive, we waited until the very last minute before closing the doors. Apparently, many people were having a difficult time deciding whether to go or not to go.

At nine p.m. we taxied, received our clearance to take off, and took off one minute after the hour. With the South Vietnam government dragging its feet about letting people out, there were fears that the tower would make us come back or perhaps have us intercepted if the real nature of our flight was known, nothing of this nature happened. With a very easy rotation of the airplane on takeoff, none of the unseated passengers had any trouble hanging on to the ropes and nets provided.

After climbing out over the ocean, we changed our flight plan destination to Manila. Ted suggested this instead of directly changing to Guam, since we operated more frequently into Manila. Later, after entering the Manila Flight Information Region (FIR), we changed destination to Guam. Manila, at first, was inquisitive about our diplomatic clearance but when we explained the nature of the flight gave us no further trouble.

Enroute, we talked to Captain Al Silver and First Officer Bill McCune, who had just taken off from Manila, bound for Bangkok. They seemed happy to hear that we had gotten out of Saigon alright. McCune made some remark about not knowing that 791 was in a passenger configuration. They promised to get us legal help, if needed. They also gave us a briefing from their charts of the weather east of Manila. I had only been able to get terminal forecasts and was worried about the possibility of thunderstorms enroute, with our unstrapped and unseated passengers.

Meanwhile, Gary Kangieser and Grant Schwartz and others were making sure that everyone was getting along alright. In Bangkok, Andy had put on ten large fruit baskets, so that was served. We also had brought along a lot of extra water jugs. The toilet facilities were very limited, with 104 persons using the crew facility. (We did bring some wastebaskets and other recepticles from Saigon for emergencies!)

All passengers were employees and families of Flying Tigers, World Airways, Trans International (TIA), American Express, and others who had in some way or other contributed to the safe departure of our Tiger Saigon staff. We had only one sickness on board, a child with a slight fever. We also had a pregnant woman (eight months), but just in case, also a doctor.

APRIL 21, 1975: GUAM

After a smooth flight, all the way in the clear, we landed at Agana, Guam after a flight of five hours and ten minutes. Having arrived with little notice, we created quite a bit of confusion. The commander of the Naval Air Station had several questions to ask of us before we landed, regarding personnel on board, papers, et cetera. The Governor's assistant in charge of a "possible" refugee program shaping up was unhappy since we arrived with one hour of notice at four a.m. Guam time. The passengers were temporarily cleared and taken to an apartment complex that the government of Guam had arranged. There were very few bureaucrats arriving

Saigon Tigers and families exit aircraft at Agana, Guam, after 5 ½ hour flight   *photo Flying Tigers Club Archives*

on the scene – only second-in-command or lower. No one seemed to know what to do with us. After talking with the home office on the phone and clearing customs, us crew went to a hotel to rest, in preparation for departure at eight p.m.

Many telephone calls came in as we tried to sleep. The FAA, the press, a ladies group interested in getting orphans out of Saigon. To the Immigration Department I kept insisting I wanted to sleep. The FAA man wanted to talk to me about the radio aids in Vietnam in the captured areas and whether they were still operational or not. He didn't seem too worried about the unusual nature of our flight. He said that there

wasn't too much to worry about, since the governor had a police car parked in front of our nose wheel and the aircraft was impounded. It seemed to be some dispute between Governor Bardello and Henry Kissinger, as near as I could ever find out!

The press wanted interviews, but on orders from Joe Healy, we refused. Grant Schwartz and Gary Kangieser were with the passengers (fellow refugees) at the apartments, but were let out the next day to go to the airport. Gary did the arrangements for the passengers to continue on to LAX on Pan Am.

I concentrated on getting our airplane opened up and liberated. It finally came to the point where the Governor would let the airplane go only if and when the whole group of passengers had departed the island on Pan Am. So the departure of our ship was delayed until the following day.

The police had been instructed not to let anybody onboard the DC-8. I wanted to get papers out to plan our next flight, but he wouldn't let me on. Finally, after much pounding of fists on the airport administrator's (assistant, that is) desk, they let me send Grant Schwartz on to look around and get my papers. He said the airplane had not been cleaned, so I went over and pounded my fist on the Health Department's assistant desk warning of an impending health hazard to my crew. Finally, they let Pan Am people clean the airplane, reluctantly.

According the Guam papers, on April 21, Governor Bardello's task force on Vietnam refugees lacked a basic ingredient – refugees. We brought him a bunch, and what did he do? Impound us. I wonder how he feels about it now that 100,000 have passed into Guam?

APRIL 22, 1975: HONG KONG

Ae we finally arrived at Hong Kong after ferrying out of Guam early on the 22nd, a final note was added to our clandestine operation, as Rick Middel wrote in the aircraft logbook: Please reconfigure aircraft from "refugee" to "cargo".

Watch This!

Captain Thomas E. Constable

The captain was Bob Zalusky also known as "Skee", and I was the first officer on a freight flight to Asia. Our aircraft was a DC-8-63F. We were taxiing out at Los Angeles to take off on runway 24 left. It was so foggy on that day that we had to get vectors from ground control to reach the runway threshold.

Captain Bob Zalusky
photo Flying Tiger Line
Pilots Association

We lined up on the runway but we could not see far enough to be legal to take-off. We asked what the runway visual range (RVR – forward visibility at surface level) was and the tower's reply was below minimums for take-off.

As Bob was putting his right hand on the reverse levers, he said, "Watch this." He reversed the inboard engines, applied power for about 10-15 seconds and blew away the fog in front of our DC-8. He then turned to me to ask the tower what the RVR was now. The tower replied that it had suddenly cleared up and that we were cleared for take-off. Bob said to me, that's how you do it. I was very impressed. Over the years I learned many other things from "Skee". We had many fun layovers and he will always hold a very special place in my heart as my favourite captain I flew with.

Years later I was a captain on the DC-8 and the situation was the same. I remembered what "Skee" had taught me, so I did the same thing at runway 24L and it worked like a charm. My first officer was also impressed so my crew asked me where I got that idea from and I told them, Captain Bob "Skee" Zalusky taught me that trick.

At every Flying Tiger Line Pilots Association reunion, I would thank "Skee" for teaching me to be a good captain.

First Officer Tom Constable in 1974   *photo Tom Constable*

All In The Tiger Family

Captain John F. Dickson, President, Flying Tiger Line Pilots Association

The former employees of the Flying Tiger Line enjoyed an esprit de corps unmatched by any other major airline in history. Personnel from all departments are more inclined to refer to themselves as part of a family than as fellow workers. This revered Tiger Spirit has not diminished since T-Day on August 7, 1989 when the airline flew into the history books after the acquisition by Federal Express. Even after 30 years have passed, this close sense of connection between former employees is evident in the form of associations, clubs, books, and social media sites dedicated to their good fortune and heritage as members of this larger family.

Nepotism, the practice of showing favoritism during the hiring process towards relatives or spouses of current employees, has been used as a hiring practice for as long as business organisations have been in existence. However, this practice became controversial during the 70s and 80s when equal opportunity laws were enacted in America. To avoid the appearance of such favoritism, some airlines used anti-nepotism guidelines during the initial application process. Prescott, on the other hand, knew the value of family relationships in the workplace and did his best to promote the hiring of relatives.

Meeting with Bob in Fall 1971. Left, Captain Gene Taylor and his son, new Second Officer Bob Taylor. Second Officer Mike White, Wayne Hoffman and Mike's dad, Captain John White; Bob Prescott, Second Officer John Drake (rear), John Dewey and his son Second Officer John Dewey, Jr., and rear, Captain Howard Bayne. Captain Bayne is Second Officer Drake's father-in-law.

Memorable last flight #178 on January 7, 1979 for Captain J. Parker Goldsmith, left, with his sons John, center, second officer; and Skip right, first officer

Captain Gene Taylor teamed up with his son First Officer Bob Taylor on his final final flight for the airline in late 1980

Tymczyszyn's family reunion on Father's Day Sunday June 16, 1996 in a FedEx 747-200. From left to right, Joe "Pop" (FAA), John "Tym" (FTL), Jym (AAL), Bill (CAL, UAL), John G. (FDX) and Bob (FTL).

photo Bob Tymczyszyn, all other photos Flying Tigers Club Archives

Boeing 727 Captains Jon, Sandy and David Szigeti during a stopover at the Columbus hub. All three Szigetis were promoted and qualified 727 captains on the same day, October 5, 1987. Sandy met her husband, Captain Oscar Szigeti, while he was serving as an instructor for the company.

All former employees of The Flying Tiger Line often refer to one another as part of the Tiger Family, especially those crewmembers in the front and the back of the aircraft who had to work together for days at a time. The following is an alphabetical list of related family members who flew for FTL as either cockpit or cabin crewmembers, often times never together, sometimes not even in the same lifetime, but with a true bond that the rest of us can only imagine. NOTE: Marriages are not included in this list.

COCKPIT CREWS AND SONS			
FATHER	*HIRE DATE*	*SON*	*HIRE DATE*
Arthur L. Flanagin	6/14/1950	Dennis M. Flanagin	12/1/1976
John P. *'Goldy'* Goldsmith	3/11/1946	Skip E. Maison *(changed named from Goldsmith in 1996)*	8/28/1972
		John P. Goldsmith, Jr.	2/14/1977
William R. Greentree (Flight Engineer)	9/28/1956	William J. Greentree	6/8/1987
Arthur W. John	5/3/1965 *	Philip C. John	4/13/1987
Richard M. *'Dick'* Keefer	9/6/1955	Richard B. *'Rich'* Keefer	2/10/1987
Alfonso R. Lopez	11/10/1956	Guy S. Lopez	3/27/1978
Larry F. *'Dad'* Luccio	8/11/1950	Gary R. Luccio	1/17/1977
Dwight J. Metcalf	7/11/1961	Chet R. Metcalf	2/14/1977
Frederick C. Peterson	6/27/1966	Nathan C. Peterson	3/1/1987
Robert H. Poindexter	11/17/1961	Mark T. Poindexter	4/13/1987
Donald E. Riggs	7/25/1962	Donald E. Riggs, Jr	7/6/1987
Lamont W. *'Shad'* Shadowens	4/29/1953	Lamont W. *'Shad Jr.'* Shadowens, Jr.	2/14/1977
Gene K. Taylor	8/7/1950	Robert G. Taylor	8/9/1971
Arthur A. Stolting	6/26/1966	Kenneth A. Stolting	1/3/1978
Bobbie V. Tharp	7/12/1950	Ernest A. Tharp	8/28/1972
John T. White	12/20/1950	J. Michael White	8/9/1971
COCKPIT CREW SIBLINGS AND OTHERS			
Thomas E. Constable	9/27/1965	William H. Constable [nephew]	10/23/1978
Daniel W. Dill	3/14/1977	John C. Dill [brother]	3/27/1978
Eric A. Ermert	7/29/1968	Terry L. Ermert [brother]	8/9/1971
Tom T. Grider	4/11/1957	Timothy R. Grider [nephew]	12/18/1978
Joseph L. King	2/4/1980 *	Donald R. King [brother]	8/26/1968 *
Skip E. Maison *(formerly Goldsmith)*	8/28/1972	John P. Goldsmith, Jr. [brother]	2/14/1977
Oscar Szigeti	4/2/1973	Jon F. Szigeti [brothers]	1/23/1978
		David J. Szigeti [brother]	2/13/1978
John S. *'Tym'* Tymczyszyn	6/3/1974	Robert S. Tymczyszyn [brother]	5/8/1978
Arnold M. *'Arnie'* Visnick	5/3/1965 *	Harold I. Visnick [brother]	1/11/1989

OTHER RELATIVES HIRED AS FLIGHT ATTENDANTS			
Michael E. Arcamuzzi	11/20/1978	Georganne 'Gigi' Arcamuzzi [sister]	8/8/1987
John H. 'Jack' Bliss	7/19/1950	Kristianne Bliss Peake [daughter of Jack and Patti Bliss, FA]	10/1/1978
Joseph L. DeLazerda	9/17/1956	Annette DeLazerda Lusk [daughter]	10/1/1978
Gaylord H. 'Burgie' Burgwald	3/01/1962	Christie Burgwald [niece]	6/1/1979
M. Ray Foster	9/1/1950	Brian Foster [son]	7/1/1975
John P. 'Goldy' Goldsmith	3/11/1946	Sondra Goldsmith Morrow [daughter]	10/1/1978
John C. Grago	9/6/1956	David Grago [son]	6/30/1981
Harry G. Huckins (Navigator)	10/29/1956	Vivien Huckins [daughter]	8/24/1968
John T. Keenan	3/1/1965	Louise Kennan Busler [daughter]	5/1/1980
Ray A. Lamb	8/15/1956	Jeannie Lamb [daughter]	10/1/1978
Robert R. Lindberg	8/28/1967	Cindy Lindberg [daughter]	5/1/1980
Howell G. 'Rick' Rickman	12/6/1956	Debra Rickman Martinez [daughter]	5/28/1981
Wayne W. Peake	5/25/1951	Roger Peake [son]	10/22/1974
Arthur F. Seymour	11/1/1946	Dawn Seymour Adams [daughter]	6/30/1981
Spencer E. Sidney	7/4/1961	Dayna Sidney-DeHertogh [daughter]	6/30/1981
Starr K. Thompson	7/24/1950	Starr Thompson [daughter]	Late 1960s
Robert F. 'Skee' Zalusky	11/15/1950	Michelle Zalusky Hill [daughter]	5/1/1980
OTHER FLIGHT ATTENDANT RELATIVES			
Jacqueline Lange	10/9/1967	Jeraldine Lange [sister]	4/15/1980
Juanita Danewitz	June 1962	Lousie Danewitz [sister]	2/6/1964
Ellen Dillon	5/28/1981	Robert Dillon [brother]	6/30/1981
Lorraine McCaig	6/1/1979	Marilyn McCaig Jankowski [sister]	4/15/1980
Martha Maxham	5/28/1962	Mary Maxham Healy [sister]	Unknown
Martha Monahan	5/6/1964	Molly Monahan [sister]	6/1/1979
Reita Forbes Gunderson	10/22/1969	Diane Forbes [sister]	6/1/1975
Guia Academia	10/12/1974	Catherine Fune [cousin]	5/1/1980
Ellen Weidman	5/6/1964	Inge Weidman [sister]	Unknown

FDX CHILDREN HIRED BY FEDEX AFTER MERGER			
Ronald L. Burson	9/27/1965	Timothy L. Burson	9/6/1995
Paul E. Cassel	3/20/1978	Victoria Port	2/19/2007
Lane D. Chenoweth	3/14/1988	Cody L. Chenoweth	5/16/2005
Louis R. Furlong *	5/6/1968	Colin B. Furlong	4/12/2004
R. George Miller	3/27/1978	Bradley C. Miller	7/11/2011
Frederick C. Peterson	6/27/1966	Aron F. Peterson	5/16/2005
Thomas W. Rustemeyer	1/3/1978	Chris T. Rustemeyer	12/9/2011
R. Scott 'Scotty' Simpson	8/22/1966	Timothy S. Simpson	4/18/2005
D. James 'Jim' Stenger	1/22/1979	Matt Stenger	2/20/2017
John 'Tym' Tymczyszyn	6/3/1974	John G. Tymczyszyn	11/1/1995
James S. Wilson	4/30/1973	John A. Wilson	6/12/2000
Paul W. Mlinar Sr. **	3/1/1947 *	Paul Mlinar Jr.	8/26/1968*

*   Date of Hire at Seaboard World Airlines which merged pilot lists with the Flying Tiger Line on 3/17/1981

** First pilot hired at SWA and the first to retire at age 60. Although Paul Sr. never flew for FTL, his son did so after the two companies merged and is therefore included on this list for its historical significance.

SONS OF THE AVG - FLYING TIGERS

Although never an employee of the Flying Tiger Line, Robert F. Layher was a Flight Leader in the 1st American Volunteer Group, 2nd Squadron, "Panda Bears. More can be found at https://flyingtigersavg.com/layher-robert-f . His son, Robert F. Layher Jr., was hired by FTL on 3/6/1978 and is the only known descendant of the famed group which our airline and association is so closely related to.

Dennis And Art Flanagin On A Last Flight

Captain Dennis Flanagin

My dad Art Flanagin was with Tigers before I was born. He was hired by The Flying Tiger Line in 1950. He worked until January 11, 1981, a 30 year career. I was hired by Tigers on December 1, 1976 and retired on December 1, 2013, a 37-year career, 26 as captain. I wouldn't have traded my flying career for any other.

I did not go into flying because of my dad. When I graduated high school, I went into college to be a lawyer. For a graduation gift my dad gave me flying lessons or nothing, something I was not thrilled about. I got my private license in the summer of 1971. At Easter break in 1973, I flew three college friends to the Grand Canyon and then to southern Arizona.

When I got back from that trip I decided that I would try to get into aviation because I enjoyed the flying. I could always go to law school. While in college I got my commercial and instrument licenses. I tried to go into the Navy and Air Force after my senior year of college but was turned down because the Vietnam War was winding down and they were letting pilots go. The only pilots that they were taking were academy grads or Reserve Officers' Training Corps (ROTC) cadets.

After graduating I got my instructor's license and started teaching at Burbank airport. During that time I got my flight engineer writtens out of the way. A friend of my dad heard about that and got me a chance to get my sim time for my flight engineer ticket from Tigers. That cost me $3000. I would get a call while I was working at Burbank to tell me there was open time in the simulator and be at LAX within two hours. It took five months to get my required time in. I was hired in the first class in two years, December 1st, 1976. The 16 of us (at 24, I was the youngest) became famous because it was the first hiring class at Tigers to hire a female pilot and became known as Norah's class, for Norah O'Neil, the first female pilot at Tigers.

I flew my dad's last trip with Tigers which began January 4, 1981 and ended January 11, 1981. I had just checked out as a first officer on the 747 a few months before this trip and I was based in JFK. My dad was a 747 captain based in LAX. To be able to fly his last trip I had to get the approval of both the company and the union since this was a LAX trip. It took about a month to get the approval from both groups to make sure a LAX first officer would be paid for this trip. We began the trip on January 4, 1981 with my dad, myself, and Second Officer R. Mollman on aircraft N749FT. We flew from Los Angeles to Anchorage via Travis AFB. My dad was a perfectionist when it came to flying. I remembered that after I got my first leg from Travis to Anchorage I told him he should take the rest of the legs. That means take all of the landings. He said if I did not take every other leg, he would remove me off the trip.

On January 6, we flew a passenger trip from Anchorage to Osan AFB in Korea via Yokota AFB in Japan, again on N749FT. After take-off we got a call from Anchorage tower that we had left debris on the runway. They sent out Tiger personal to check the debris. After examining the debris, they concluded that we had blown two tires on the right side. We continued the trip to Yokota.

During the flight we had asked the senior flight attendant up to brief the passengers on a possible emergency landing. With the right tires blown we planned on landing on the left wheels first, then slowly letting the right side down.

The landing was uneventful. Once we got out of the aircraft, we noticed that the right tires had not blown, but two tires on the left side had blown. After determining that there was no damage to the 747 we continued on to OSN. On January 8, we flew from Seoul (Kimpo airport) to Anchorage via Osaka (Itami) and Tokyo

Captain Arthur L. Flanagin with his son Dennis Flanagin in cockpit of N816FT   photo Flying Tigers Club Archives

(Narita) on N811FT, an ex-Seaboard World machine. On January 11 we flew my dad's last leg from Anchorage to Los Angeles on N816FT.

Flying his last trip was a big event because at the end of it he said to me, "Son, you can fly." Once my dad retired, he enjoyed hearing my stories of where I was flying and the places I went. He was very proud of my career.

A Trip Of A Lifetime

Captain Guy López (FTL, FDX, Ret.)

Ring… Ring… Ring… Arghhh! I didn't want to go anywhere. I wanted to be lazy and have the day off. But the dreaded phone foretold otherwise.

The dreaded phone was the dedicated line for crew control. They were the only party which had that specific number. This was back in the days before cell phones, ring tones, or caller ID. If that phone rang, it could only mean one thing.

"Bill Long here, crew control. We have a problem here." I had the problem. I was on reserve. Bill continued, "We have a captain no one will fly with." There was a pause, and since Bill had cast the hook, I took the bait. "Who is it?", not that I had any choice. Bill replied, "Captain Al Lopez." The day suddenly brightened. Bill started laughing. The joke was on me. Captain Al Lopez is my father.

I was one of the pilots who benefited from Tigers' policy of nepotism. With Flying Tigers, once a prospective pilot, who was a Tigers' pilot's son, met a minimum number of flight hours, he was given preferential treatment in the hiring process. Like the 30+ other pilots' sons, I dreamed of flying with my dad professionally. The dream was finally about to come true.

Captain Al López and his son First Officer Guy López on a flight between Miami and San Juan PR

The trip was a sweet one. It was five days long and consisted of a mix of day and night flying, easy domestic legs, and one international trip to San Juan, P.R. It was all for which I had hoped. The trip proceeded as hoped. Nice layovers, decent weather, and, most of all, the joy and pride of flying with my dad.

As the trip was approaching the last couple of legs, we ran into a problem. In Miami, waiting for us in the ramp office were six Chicago mechanics. All of them were commuting to Chicago for work, with their shifts starting later the same day. For the MIA-ORD leg, we were flying a DC-8-63F; a beautiful plane, one of the prettiest airliners ever built. Regardless of its visual appeal, it had only four jumpseats. Two were in the cockpit, and two were in the back, near the lavatory and the cargo net.

There was no clear, legal solution, except to strand two would-be distraught mechanics. In this situation, sometimes seniority was used for deciding who gets priority. Other times, the order in which jumpseats were requested would take care of seating conflicts. Flipping coins, or playing rock, scissors, paper, all failed to net a satisfactory solution. All of the preceding would result in at least two mechanics failing to show for work and getting in trouble. Undoubtedly, two would be disciplined with time off and zero pay, or termination. In addition, the shift missing any absent mechanics would likely be overburdened and result in flight delays or cancellations. Nothing good would come of any of the possible scenarios.

The beauty of Flying Tigers was that it was the "Can Do" airline. There was always a solution. There was always a way to make things work. And there was the Tiger ethic of taking care of each other. My dad, the captain, had the easier choice of assuming no risk to himself. He could have followed the FARs and left the mechanics behind, at great risk to their careers. Or he could do otherwise.

In our legal system, there are the concepts of malum in se and malum prohibitum. Malum in se is Latin meaning morally wrong or evil in its own right. Malum prohibitum, on the other hand, is a wrong prohibited only because it violates a technical rule not based on morality. Driving 40 mph in a 35mph zone is an example of malum prohibitum. Murder, by contrast, is so universally evil as to be malum in se.

Now my Dad did not raise me to be a rulebreaker or to ignore laws. And he did not practice hypocrisy in what he said and what he did. But he was faced with the choice of following a hard and fast regulation or breaking it to save some fellow employees from trouble and

the company from unnecessary loss. With Solomonic judgment, he announced to the mechanics that he was going into the cockpit and they would have to decide for themselves who would go. He did not tell them to decide who would stay. Furthermore, he would not require them to brief him on their decision. It was very clear he was not going to return for a headcount.

Sealed in the cockpit and ready for pushback, my dad asked the second officer, Dale Hargrave, to close the door quickly and return. There was no need to inspect the lavatory or beyond the cargo net. The mechanics sitting in the back were smiling, relaxed, and happy. Evidently, their priorities had been resolved.

Upon blocking in at the Tiger ramp in Chicago, Dale opened the passenger door for the jumpseaters, while my dad and I casually extended our parking and shutdown checklists. The two jumpseaters followed Dale out of the cockpit, while smiling widely and thanking the captain profusely. The jumpseaters in the back happily shouted their many thanks. And surprisingly, even the agents and working mechanics entering the cockpit were joyous and grateful for our arrival. They knew secrets we could only surmise.

The remaining leg of the trip was wonderful and uneventful. Although, upon leaving Chicago for Los Angeles, everyone around the Chicago ramp treated my dad with extreme graciousness, friendliness and respect. If there were secrets upon arriving in Chicago the day before, they did not last. I'll never know what really happened between Miami and Chicago, but no Tiger employee ever got into trouble as a result of the previous day.

And, so ended a dream come true and the trip of a lifetime. I loved flying with my dad and I will be forever grateful he got me the job. But I will never be able to express how special it was to work for such an incredible airline. Fun and adventure were a working way of life at Flying Tigers. And it all was the result of the spirit of the "Can Do" airline; the spirit generated by people like my dad and so many others. But in my own personal story, that moment watching my Dad make all the people and parts work together, for everyone's benefit, was my proudest moment.

29

Flying Tigers Passenger Operation 1945 To 1989

Diana Smith Nagatani and Sharon Schlies - Flight Attendants

In June of 1945, the National Skyway Freight Corporation – subtitled The Line of the Flying Tigers – was born on a handshake and a hope. This was to be Bob Prescott's dream come true: the nation's first all-cargo airline. What was to become the world's largest air cargo carrier did so by flying not just freight alone. A contributing factor to the success of Flying Tigers was the operation of tens of thousands of passenger flights.

In the early days, after the first three shipments of air freight, there was a lull; the bills piled up and airplanes sat idle. It was in October that the Navy unintentionally threw the company a life raft. A group of 115 sailors wanted to charter some planes to get home to New York. Thus began Tigers first venture into passenger transportation. This was the crude prototype of thousands of passenger charter flights that, in the days ahead, were to furnish Tigers with some of their finest moments as well as a substantial source of revenue. Tigers were advertising themselves as an airline that would and could fly "anything, anywhere, anytime." Passenger loads included everything from hockey and football teams to orchestra and motion-picture casts.

In December of 1946, the largest military contract ever awarded to a commercial air carrier went to the Flying Tigers. For the next eleven months, Tigers flew the Pacific transporting troops and resupplying the occupation forces in Japan. A total of 42 C-54s ran eight flights a day linking the United States with Hawaii and Tokyo. In addition to over half a million dollars in profit, Tigers had gathered a wealth of experience in operating a long-haul international route. They had met the challenge and had become a seasoned airline operator.

Bob Prescott's attitude of uniqueness and initiative propelled Tigers into the era of economy air travel. Chartered DC-4s flew freight from west to east and passengers for $99 a seat from east to west. The concept of high-density seating was introduced and the DC-4's passenger capacity jumped from 40 to 60 to 82 and finally to over 100 for special flights.

In June of 1950, the Korean conflict erupted. Tigers was the first to operate a civilian plane for the Military Air Transport Service – with just 24 hours notice. For the following two and a half years, military personnel were transported from the west coast of the United States to Tokyo for the Korean War. During this period Tigers carried 64.5% of all passengers flown to the Far East.

The DC-4 and the C-46 were both launched into air coach travel for student groups, religious groups on pilgrimage, and displaced persons from Europe to the United States and to Australia. These planes were pre-radar, unpressurized aircraft that flew below 14,000 feet.

October 1945, the first passenger transportation, 115 homesick sailors chartered a Tiger Budd Conestoga from Long Beach to New York
photo Flying Tigers Club Archives

Mexican "wetbacks" boarding a C-46

photo Flying Tigers Club Archives

A group of Yemenite Jews flying to new futures in Israel

photo Flying Tigers Club Archives

A C-54 Hungarian refugee flight arriving in New York in 1956

photo David Pratt / Flying Tigers Club Archives

Stewardess Fran Drew seems to attract soldiers, Burbank 1951 during the Korean airlift   photo Peter Gowland / Flying Tigers Club Archives

A DC-4 charter flight from New York to Dusseldorf for the United Singers of St. Louis on July 25, 1956 (and returning on Sep 25, 1956)

Aviation News picture / Flying Tigers Club Archives

A contingent of Flying Tiger stewardesses at Travis Air Force Base in 1959 prior to departure on a military passenger flight to the Orient. Left to right are Arlette DeBuck, Betty Frazer, Julie Prikosovich, Lilah Casey, Anita Niederer, Anne Clausager, Anne Klaesener, Treso Koken and Patricia Wassum. Super H N6922C is in background

photo Flying Tigers Club Archives

A Super H Connie in 106 seat military passenger version. Tom Haywood (center), supervisor of technical training, makes a last minute check of the planeload of Connie passengers just before an evacuation test starts at Flying Tiger's Lockheed Air Terminal base in Summer 1965

photo Flying Tigers Club Archives

Flying Tiger Stewardess Treso Koken and Korean war orphans on the Seoul-Portland flight in April 1959.

photo Flying Tigers Club Archives

By the early 1950s, Tigers had 44 aircraft flying both domestic and Pacific routes. The DC-4, the C-46, and soon, the DC-6 were all utilized to support the passenger charter business that had by now become very successful. Tigers' mass movements of civilians included Yemenite Jews from the Arabian Desert to Israel, the return of striking Indian sailors to Bombay, and the airlift of thousands of illegal alien farm laborers back to Mexico. Another airlift occurred during this time as 11,000 Puerto Ricans were flown north to work on farms in the eastern United States.

The movement of displaced persons and immigrants became a Tiger specialty during the 1950s. In 1956, there were the homeless Hungarians with little more than a rucksack to begin life in the new world. There were foreign born military wives and families coming to the States. English and French immigrants to Canada, Chinese war brides brought to Honolulu and San Francisco, Greek mail-order brides flown to Australia. Perhaps the most poignant of all were the Korean war orphans who were transported in special cradles designed to lay across folded seats. Between 1956 and 1963, 3,500 unwanted children were brought to the United States for adoption.

By the end of 1956, Tigers was flying 20,000 passengers annually to London, Paris, Frankfurt, Rome, and Tel Aviv. In this year the airline become the largest independent air carrier across the North Atlantic. In 1957, Flying Tigers inaugurated their first modern fleet of 15 Lockheed Super-H Constellations; the Connie. This successful transatlantic passenger aircraft carried over 70,000 travellers.

Tigers passenger operation is not without its tragedy: On March 15, 1962, somewhere between Guam and Manila, a Super Connie carrying 96 military passengers and a crew of 11 disappeared without a trace. Sabotage was not ruled out as a possibility. This was the first passenger accident in the company's 17 year history. Six months later, on September 23rd, another Super Connie with 68 passengers and eight crew members ditched in high seas in the North Atlantic after losing three of its four engines; 45 passengers and three crew members were rescued after seven hours in a single raft.

The 1960s brought new changes in aviation. The impact of the jet age was beginning to be felt and Tigers enjoyed strong growth and expansion. The first Rolls-Royce turbine-powered CL-44 prop jets were added to the fleet. The planes boasted the newly designed circle-T logo on the tail, easily identifiable even at a distance. These aircraft were outfitted with a passenger interior and pressed into MATS transpacific service in July 1961.

The CL-44 carried 150 passengers plus crew from Travis Air Force Base to Tokyo in under twenty hours. Both the CL-44s and Connies were used to support the burgeoning passenger business in the early 1960s. There were exchange students returning to the Philippines, Vienna-bound school chorus members from Newark, a group of dentists and their families traveling to Holland.

Tigers had initiated a $99 fare from Europe to the United States to encourage westbound passenger travel. The See America program brought in groups of military and civilian officials including the Lions Club of northern Italy and the German Poodle Club. On the domestic scene, there were students from Brigham Young University flying to New York over Christmas vacation, a group of Michigan residents transported to Florida to view a new housing development and a group of scouts traveling to the Boy Scout Jamboree.

Crew on a CL-44 in 1961, left to right, Dena Millard, Captain Oakley Smith, Jean Manning, Captain Ernest "Bus" Loane, Pat Siemens, Flight Engineer Gene Olsen, Myrnalee Scott. Kneeling in foreground are (left) Doc Powell and Joe Healy, operating the swingtail mechanism and announcing system. photo Flying Tigers Club Archives

Joyce Oslund (left), flight attendant, and Betty Bernard, flight attendant instructor, serve some welcome coffee to crew and deadheads on board a CL-44 in 1961

The 6 Watson Bros. Photography / Flying Tigers Club Archives

February 1964, deadheading from Tokyo to San Francisco, flight attendants Juanita Hennesey, Lee (?), Marlesa Berger and Marjorie Evans are having fun riding a Honda across the Pacific Ocean

photo Juanita Hennessey

Record passenger load of 165 dentists board a Flying Tiger CL-44 at Los Angeles to Amsterdam and Cologne on July 2, 1962

photo Phil Glickman / Flying Tigers Club Archives

Graduating class of July 7th, 1970 in Tacoma. Front Row Sitting (from L to R): Bonnie Colton (Instructor), Laura Thompson, (?), Jenny (?), Cathy Smoke, (?), Margi Walker, Ginny Slotvia, (?), (?), Brenda Brown (Check Flight Attendant). Middle Row (from L to R): Marci Massey, (?), (?), Laurie Lockhart, Barbara Crawford, (?), (?), (?), (?), Peggy no last name known, Margaret Hink, Marge Hough (Chief Flight Attendant), Nancy Gilbert. Back Row Standing (from L to R): Marilyn Breen, (?), Mickey Manion, Marie Bird, Karen no last name known, (?), (?), Joanne Koncan, (?), (?), (?), Jean Sedgeley, Charlene Towner

photo Richards Studio / Flying Tigers Club Archives

Flight attendants with LAX ramp and maintenance personnel in front of the first 747 passenger aircraft (N747TA) before departure for the first MAC trip in January 1980   photo Flying Tigers Club Archives

Flying Tigers DC-8-63 inaugural flight to Saigon Tan Son Nhut in September 1968   photo Flying Tigers Club Archives

Cam Ranh Bay, South Vietnam March 1970, Flying Tigers flying military troops and cargo into Vietnam during the war years. In the background is a TIA – Trans International DC-8 MAC flight ready to depart

photo Flying Tigers Club Archives

Boeing 707-358B N317F in New York JFK in July 1966 and leased with Flying Tigers crew due to El Al crew strike

photo Jacques Guillem

There were plane loads of missionaries from New Zealand and religious guilds flying to Rome. There was even a wedding conducted on board a special charter flight from Denver to Europe. There were weekend charters to the Bahamas and flights to Korea with anxious parents eager to bring home their newly adopted children. This was a growing revolution in group air travel – Tigers was a forerunner and a leader in the field.

Flying Tigers graduated its first class of flight attendants in San Fransisco on February 6, 1964. Formalised instruction had replaced on the job training. During these first handful of classes from 1964 to 1970, the flight attendants were based out of McChord AFB, South of Tacoma, WA. Later their base was moved to San Fransisco where they operated out of Travis AFB. Later their base and training was moved to LAX.

In 1965, Tigers acquired Boeing 707 jets. This aircraft was put into service on the transpacific routes supplying the United States military forces in Viet Nam. Layovers in Saigon were common for flight attendants in these days. The wet lease of a 707 to El Al Israel Airlines saw a temporary flight attendant base established in Tel Aviv from May until the end of September of 1966. Shortly thereafter, Tigers ceased all passenger operations and all flight attendants were furloughed for a year.

In 1968, flight attendants were recalled and trained on the newly-acquired DC-8-63. The war in Vietnam was escalating and Tigers was back in the passenger charter business flying GIs in and out of Asia.

The passenger business continued to grow strongly into the 1970s. There were special charter flights carrying the Ice Capades to Honolulu, the Spanish Circus to Tokyo and plane loads of Bell Helicopter personnel to Tehran. By 1975, Tigers was transporting more than 60,000 passengers around the world annually on military and commercial charters.

In December of 1979, Flying Tigers brought home from Singapore the first 747 passenger aircraft. The 747 was immediately put into MAC charter service flying across the Pacific to Japan and the Philippines. There were also special military missions which filled the 747 with nearly 500 battle-ready, equipment laden troops.

From 1979 through 1981, Tigers was once again involved in the airlift of homeless people. Southeast Asian refugees were evacuated from Bangkok and Manila, through Hong Kong to the States. These were a people, as so many before them, heading for a new life in America.

In 1980, another of Tigers' mass movements of people was occurring on the other side of the world – the annual Hajj, muslims making the annual religious pilgrimage to Mecca. The first year of Tiger participation was with flights out of Libya; the following year, Tigers returned to Africa for the Hajj, this time flying out of Kano, Nigeria.

In March of 1981, Tigers passenger business was entering a new phase, Scheduled service between the east coast of the United States and Europe was established and the operation was given the name Metro International. Sales offices opened in New York and slick advertisements were placed in magazines, newspapers, and on billboards.

Tigers 747s were painted with the Metro logo and flew scheduled service from New York to Brussels

Kristi Bliss Peake serving coffee to Cambodian refugees onboard N747TA in July 1980

Flight attendants Michael Colombo and Lynn Bucknell are relaxing during a Cambodian refugee flight in July 1980

photos Flying Tigers Club Archives

Enhancing the 1983 MAC program is Boeing 747 passenger aircraft LV-MLO on lease from Aerolineas Argentinas. From left to right, D. Falvey, manager inventory planning; M. Edwards, facilities & equipment (F&E) mechanic; D. Nielsen, flightline shift manager; R. Hatcher, F&E mechanic; J. Toro and T. Moore, maintenance supervisors; mechanics K. Kelly and E. Comacho, sheet metal (SM), J. Caceres, F&E N. Daniels, H. Bergman and E. Larson, SM; M. Harris, F&E lead mechanic; R. Hawn, SM lead mechanic; mechanics R. Clayton and V. Le, SM, D. Warner, F&E, E. Paliungas, SM, and B. Bonnell, F&E: J. Butts, material planner; M. Kealy, F&E lead mechanic; R. Fleming and R. Young, F&E mechanics; and R. Wier, maintenance supervisor
photo Flying Tigers Club Archives

and Tel Aviv. Special charters carried passengers to Amsterdam, Paris, and Rome, as well as to Athens, Lisbon, and Madrid. The Metro operation was new and exciting. It was staffed by hard working and enthusiastic people determined to make it work and it did. By the end of 1983, after two and a half successful years, changes in corporate strategies directed attention away from the passenger service business and Metro ceased operations.

The famine in North Africa in 1985 caught the attention and aroused the humanitarian spirit of many Americans. Lifelift was an Ethiopian-bound relief mission conceived and accomplished by Flying Tigers employees. Tigers participated in five other relief missions during the first few months of 1985 including the USA for Africa flight in June. Most of the relief flights were staffed with volunteer crew members including Flight Attendants.

The devastating earthquake in Armenia in December 1988 once again saw Tigers responding to a people in need. One of the passenger 747's was utilized to fly medical personnel and disaster specialists along with medical supplies and equipment on a special relief mission to Armenia.

By mid-1989, Flying Tigers was operating two passenger 747's, each FAA approved to carry 520

Freshly repainted with the Circle Tail which was re-introduced in January 1987, next to Boeing 747-133 EI-BPH are flight attendants, from left to right, Jone Amaral, Kristi Bliss Peake, Carolyn Inglis, Mary Schulte, Carol Everhart, Betty Carver, Debbie Quintero Sweeley, Marge Hough, Molly Monahan, Jeri Lange, Patti Keown DeLuna, Lee Baliukas Pollitt, Andarin Arvola
photo Flying Tigers Club Archives

people. Both 747's were flying regularly scheduled MAC flights in and out of Asia as well as special missions to destinations across the world.

After the merger with Federal Express, the passenger element of the airline continued with Boeing 747 passenger charters, primarily on behalf of the United States military. At its peak, Federal Express employed 250 cabin crew for its three passenger jumbos. The operation was gradually wound down as the aircraft left the fleet and the last passenger flight operated on September 30, 1992, from Los Angeles to Saint Louis, with a positioning leg back to LAX the next day. The passenger-carrying history of the Flying Tiger Line was at an end.

This chapter was edited by Charles Kennedy and Guy Van Herbruggen. It was first published in March 1989 in the "Tiger Track", a publication of the Flying Tiger Pilot's Master Executive Council, affiliated with ALPA and AFL-CIO.

photo Flying Tigers Club Archives

The last Federal Express crew with flight attendants took place in September 1992 with aircraft N621FE, a 747-133 from Osan to Yokota, Anchorage, Los Angeles and St. Louis. At the Hilton Hotel in downtown Anchorage, left to right, Captain Gayle Lane, First Officer Tim Alfred, Susie Clikeman, Arnie Blomquist, Terri Lane, Jan Manning, Jenny Schueneman, Marge Hough, Gael Okicich, Betty Carver, Carol Horton (hidden), Gigi Arcamuzi (laughing), Peggy Yost. Second Officer John Hall is standing in the back on the left side. Kneeling in front are Chris Puccio and Kristi Bliss Peake.

FTLPA Flight Attendant Recognition Reunion in Palm Springs 2018   *photo Eliot Shulman / Flying Tiger Line Pilots Association*

30

The Clipped Wings Club

Captain John F. Dickson

President, Flying Tiger Line Pilots Association

The earliest Flying Tiger flight attendants, known as stewardesses then, enjoyed a very special relationship with Bob Prescott. Most were hired on the spot and trained on the job until more formalised procedures were mandated in 1964. They possessed a charming eloquence, a desire for adventure, and a willingness to fly anywhere at any time.

Their salaries were low and it was a requirement that they remain unmarried, a standard at most airlines during the time. They often worked under very tiring conditions in converted military aircraft without the modern day amenities taken for granted today.

This group, often referred to as Bob's Girls, formed a close bond and were extremely loyal to Prescott. In turn, he personally rewarded their dedication by involving them in as many social functions and public relations opportunities as possible. A lot of these women met their future husbands in the line of work, including businessmen, attorneys and, of course, pilots.

As they began retiring, there was a strong desire to remain socially connected, to sustain the friendships that were formed during those early years. The Clipped Wings Club was created around 1958 as a way to stay in touch. Although organised primarily as a social club, the women also engaged in charitable efforts such as volunteering at local Veteran's Administration hospitals, and creating fundraising events for well-known organisations such as the Crippled Children's Society.

Annual reunion dinners were held at larger venues and each member hosted less formal luncheons in their own home. At first, their meetings were arranged in Los Angeles, but later were generally held in the Palm Springs area, where many had relocated for retirement.

Bob Prescott was the guest of honour at most of their functions, and he paid tribute to the group

The Flying Tiger Clipped Wings Club held its first annual fashion show luncheon at the Sportsman's Lodge in North Hollywood on November 20, 1958 for the benefit of the Crippled Children's Society. From left to right are ex-stewardesses, Billie Welsh Garrick, Peggy Jones Herness and Marsha Eubanks Biggs.　　　photo Flying Tigers Club Archives

whenever he could. At the 1967 Christmas party, he honoured the group by saying, "The Clipped Wings deserve a vote of thanks from all of us because through their organization they continue to spread goodwill in the name of the Flying Tigers."

It's believed that the last luncheon was held at Ann Ludwig's home in Indian Wells in 1992.

Another annual luncheon to honor Bob Prescott, a bash which took place late 1969 in Sherman Oaks. Former Flying Tigers stewardesses present were, left to right standing, Donalda Towne, Ann Ludwig, Bobbie Fowles Van Norstrand, Pamela Trott Hunter, Joan Lambrose, Maggie Morgan, Michelle McKenzie, Nurse Duke, Jan Marshall, Maggee Thompson, Marsha Eubanks Biggs, Patti Bliss, Peggy Jones Herness. Seated, Skip Lawson, Mary Lee Rodenbaugh, Del Florzak Noland, Bob Prescott, June Pagano, Trudy Trudell Bogart and Joy Belli.

photos Flying Tiger Line Pilots Association

A Clipped Wings event with Patti Bliss (standing, right), Del Noland (sitting, second left) and Dixie Richards (seated, right)

Surrounded by a bevy of beautiful smiles that once charmed passengers on Flying Tiger Line charter flights, Bob Prescott poses with former Flying Tigers stewardesses. Back row (standing): Fran Drew Whitesides, Billie Welch Garrick, Donalda Towne, Patti Bliss, Skip Lawson (stooping), Marsha Eubanks Biggs, Bob Prescott, unidentified, Lenore Brenan, Peggy Jones Herness. Front row (sitting or on their knees): Trudi Trudell Bogart, B.J. Lee, Ann Ludwig, Dixie Richards, Anne-Marie Prescott, Michelle McKenzie, Bobbie Fowles Van Norstrand, Maggee Thompson

photo Flying Tiger Line Pilots Association

Ammunition Flight To Guatemala

Captain Thomas E. Constable

March 1976. Captain Jim Nezgoda, Second Officer Barney Szymaniak and I as first officer flew a 90,000-lb load of 5.56mm rifle ammunition to Guatemala City, from Lisbon via Santa Maria in the Azores and San Juan PR, on a DC-8-63.

The weather forecast was not good at Guatemala City, reported to be completely fogged in. Our alternate airport was in Honduras. On the way to Guatemala City, I was reading a magazine that reported geopolitical conditions around the world. In one of the articles, I learned that Guatemala was at war with Honduras. I showed the article to the captain. Since they were at war with each other, it seemed inadvisable to use to the Honduras alternate. Obviously OpsCon did not know that they were at war.

When we arrived at Guatemala City we entered a holding pattern over the airport. A nearby volcano was erupting and throwing giant boulders and lava into the air, which was an entertaining sight as we circled over the cloud layer. We were getting low on fuel, so we decided to go to San Salvador, the capital of neighbouring El Salvador, as an alternate, a wise decision.

We landed at San Salvador where the weather was good. We waited for the weather to clear at Guatemala City. When it was reported to be clear we fueled our Diesel Eight and took off for our original destination.

We took off after a Pan Am flight, which was also going to Guatemala City. Jim said, "Watch this!" and we levelled off below and behind the Pan Am 707 plane. We caught him and went shooting by underneath. We beat Pan Am to the airport and landed first.

The fork lift at Guatemala City was not strong enough to unload the ammo, it was too heavy. So we had to help the Guatemalan Army unload the cargo by hand. By this time we were running out of duty time and had to cancel the return empty leg, and go to the hotel and get some rest, which we all needed. If I had not seen and read that article about the war between those two countries, and if we had landed in Honduras with a full load of ammo for their enemy, I shudder to think of what would have happened to us! Just lucky I guess!

First Officer Tom Constable

Quarantined In Torino, Italy

Captain Thomas E. Constable

March 18th, 1977. Captain John Keenan, first officer Tom Constable and flight engineer Paul Phillips were flying a DC-8 charter to Kano, Nigeria.

We took off from Amsterdam Schiphol and arrived over Nigeria. Our destination was Kano in the north of the country. Our alternate airport was in the next country to the west, Ouagadougou in Upper Volta (now Burkina Faso) or we could use Bobo Dioulasso, also in Upper Volta. The weather was supposed to be good in Kano but at this time of year the winds come from the north off the Sahara Desert with a red dust that reduces visibility to zero.

By the time we reached Kano, visibility was very bad and we had burned too much fuel over the original flight plan because of head winds, to hold or go to the alternate. Captain Keenan did a marvellous job of finding the runway and landing safely. We later found out it was a good thing we didn't go to our alternate due to a terrorist attack the day before that was not reported to us.

When we taxied into the ramp and parked, I looked out the window and noticed the locals running around with red hair. I thought this to be strange indeed. Maybe it was a mysterious northern tribe that had this characteristic. When we deplaned, the mystery was solved. The Sahara red dust was all over everything, even the people.

Tired, the next step was to go to a hotel. We drove and drove for a long time. There was a traffic accident that stopped us at an intersection. A Nigerian policeman dressed in the classic uniform of the French Foreign Legion was hauling the person out of a car who caused the accident. With his crop he was beating the daylights out of this poor soul.

Finally we arrived at what barely passed for a hotel. We were informed that they were full except for the wedding suite, which was expensive. We all five of us

A Flying Tigers DC-8-63 during a stop in a Nigerian airport
photo Flying Tigers Club Archives

said we didn't want to do that. We voted to pass on the wedding and go back to the airport and fly away. Our next scheduled destination was all the way to Torino, Italy.

We flew to Italy and landed at Torino. We got a hotel, had dinner and crashed in our rooms. We were very tired by this time. I had just dozed off when the telephone rang. It was a call from our representative at the airport. We had to get up and go to the immigration office at the airport. When we arrived, we were informed that we had entered the country at a port that was not allowed from a country which suffered outbreaks of cholera – the only two authorized ports were Rome and Milan. Tigers hadn't done their homework

We were told by the Immigration officer that we would have to be quarantined. John Keenan was so tired and mad that he would not speak, so I was the spokesman for the group. I tried to reason with them but to no avail. And to make matters worse, all five of our cholera shot records had expired. We were taken to a hospital that looked like a castle; it literally had a moat around it. At the entrance was a sign in Italian that said Hospital for the Terminally Ill.

*Captain John Keenan
photo Flying Tiger
Line Pilots Association*

The procedure to admit us was very long. I saw a room that had a table so I flopped on to it and went to sleep. When I woke up, I realized that it was an operating room. It's not a good idea to do that in a hospital. I wasn't missing anything, so off we went to get our rooms. While we were waiting for that to happen, Paul and I noticed some children had awakened and were staring at us, strangers in the middle of the night. So, Paul and I grabbed some toys and began to entertain these terminally ill children. They laughed at our antics and seem to enjoy the show. At least we brought a little joy to their lives.

My bed was the last to be to ready. The nurses carried out an old man in a sheet, and wouldn't you know it, that was my bed – ugh. We were stuck there, and our beautiful DC-8-63 was equally stranded, sitting at the airport.

The next morning, we were fed a bowl of consumé and a zwieback cracker; we made plans to escape. We had Plan A and Plan B. John Keenan our resourceful captain had smuggled a bottle of scotch into our prison. Plan A was to pass the bottle around to everyone in the room and get so drunk and disorderly that they would throw us out. Plan B was to go to the lavatory, climb out the window, down three stories of sheer stone walls, cross the moat, over the outside wall, somehow get to the airport, jump in our airplane, and fly away. We were not exactly thinking straight.

The nurse issued each of us a little plastic vial with a tiny shovel as part of the cap. They wanted us to give them a sample of our stools. That didn't happen.

Paul and I knew some Spanish so we attempted to have a conversation in broken Italian with the lady doctor who was in charge. It went pretty well and she said she would contact our embassy. She did but they said they wouldn't do anything to help us. Then she said that the British Air Ministry might be of help. She called them and was given permission to release us. Thanks to her and the Air Ministry. We were free at last. We went to the airport, jumped in our good old DC-8 and flew to Amsterdam. What a trip!

Tom's plastic vial kept as a souvenir of his ordeal

First Officer Tom Constable

33

Tiger Nicaragua flights

Captain Dwight Small

I made two Red Cross flights to Nicaragua in the Summer of 1979. My first flight there was on July 29, 1979, my second and last was on July 31st. My first officer, Chuck Cozad, had been there a few days earlier on one of these flights so he was able to prep me for what I might encounter. He told me that we would find near chaos on the airport and that I would be approached by people desperate to leave the country. Some of the people were desperate to leave had been on the wrong side of the Sandinistas (Communists) victory so they might do anything, including hijacking, to get on our plane when it was leaving. I briefed the crew, the ops representative and the maintenance rep that, if we were hijacked, we would "…treat them like gentlemen and take them anywhere they wanted to go." I included in that briefing, "No heroes, unless there was a clear and certain opportunity to get the upper hand."

As we approached Managua I could see fires burning in the city so obviously the civil war was still going on. I elected to make a dog-leg, diagonal, approach to the runway so as to not overfly the city where I thought there could be small-arms fire directed toward our DC-8. Martial law had been declared in Nicaragua so there were no civil planes were in the air except for relief flights such as ours. At the first officer's encouragement, I elected to make a high-speed pass down the runway. Not many opportunities to "play" in the restrained world of airline flying so I didn't let this opportunity pass. I flew down the runway at 350 knots and at less than 500 feet. It was a thrill I won't forget and later, when I told my United Airlines pilot friend about this, his eyes glazed over with envy.

Once safely on the ground, I was immediately approached by several males desperate to leave. They all had compelling stories and I made the decision to take two of them with us. We had only two seats available but, after hearing their stories, would have taken many more

Captain Dwight Small in Managua, Nicaragua; the first of two aid missions, July 29th, 1979   *all pictures Dwight Small*

if that had been possible. We unloaded our 100,000 pounds of mercy and were on our way back to Houston. The next flight would be even more interesting.

We landed in the early afternoon. It was a showery day so the ramp was wet but I liked it because it was cooler. I was immediately approached by a Red Cross doctor requesting passage out of the country. I agreed to his request especially because these were Red Cross flights. The decision was easy. Then I was approached by an official from the US Embassy with papers requesting passage, another easy decision. A few hours later, these guys would play an important part in getting us out of the country before sundown when the unfinished war would flare up as it always did during the night.

While on the ground we saw an East German Il-62 arrive with a very small amount of relief supplies. It was a token amount of what appeared to be blankets but they made a big showing with cameras rolling, etc.

The offload took longer this day but we were taxiing out for take-off about 3pm when a brake locked on the left main landing gear. I applied as much power as I dared but the DC-8 had stopped and would not move. The tail pipes were pointed directly toward the East German Il-62 and I was afraid that too much power might damage that airplane and create an international incident so I shut all four engines down. We got off the airplane and our maintenance rep assessed the situation. He told me that the brake had totally jammed the aft inboard wheel on the left main landing gear truck and that it would have to be changed. We were carrying a spare wheel in the forward belly but the problem would be to get jacks and tools to do the job.

Our passenger from the embassy quickly became the translator. The maintenance rep told him what was needed and he passed it on to the airport staff and things began appearing. It was probably less than 45 minutes until we had it jacked up and were wrenching the wheel off. But, try as we might, the wheel would not come off. Our translator communicated the need for a pry bar and soon one appeared but it was too small. So, another request for a larger one, and that

East German, Russian built Il-62 arrived and, with great fanfare and cameras rolling, unloaded a single pallet of relief supplies. Managua, Nicaragua, July 29, 1979

Taxiing out for departure a brake assembly jammed. It took three hours of blood, sweat and pry bars to remove that wheel. One of our outbound passengers (white shirt and tie) was from the American Embassy and was a very valuable translator enabling us to get the needed tools, jacks and pry bars. The war was still going on at night so we had to be airborne by sundown. At one point we had decided to takeoff without that wheel on the plane if necessary, Minimum risk, we thought, and probably not as risky as being on that airport overnight. Managua, Nicaragua, July 31, 1979.

First Officer Chuck Cozad and Captain Dwight Small. Samoza had just been overthrown and the Sandanistas were now in control but some fighting was still going on. Managua, Nicaragua, July 31, 1974.

Second Officer Rod McConnell and Captain Dwight Small with tough looking Sandanista Hombres, July 29, 1979, Managua, Nicaragua. Fighting in and around the airport was still going on at night so we had to depart before sunset.

too appeared. The pry bar was huge, maybe eight feet long, and several of us were leaning on it but could not get that wheel to budge. Finally, finally, it gave way with a loud thud. Unfortunately for our ops rep, his hand was in the way and the flesh between his thumb and first finger was squished.

Our second passenger, the Red Cross doctor, became useful. For a time worked stopped on the wheel while the doctor cleaned and bandaged our ops rep's hand using the first aid kit from the cockpit.

The sun was getting low in the sky. We knew we had to be in the air in about an hour, and the maintenance guy couldn't promise that he'd have the wheel on by then. We held an informal meeting of the crew including the maintenance rep and the ops rep, and it was decided that we would fly without this

wheel installed if necessary. We were told that when the sun sets, the Samosa loyalists would dig up buried weapons and resume the carnage. In fact, the airport ramp had many, many bullet slugs lying around. I picked up several of these so I knew what would be happening soon. When the sun set, there would be more of these coming in, so my crew and I made the decision: be out of town before dark!

The wheel was finally in place, and we taxied out just as the sun hit the horizon. We were running checklists and starting engines before the belly doors were closed but we managed to get out of Dodge before sunset.

We took the airplane to Charleston, AFB in South Carolina. It had been an amazing adventure for all of us.

34

A Tokyo Tale

Pat Bliss

Time really does fly when you are having fun. May I tell you about an awesome sight that I have never forgotten.

Tokyo Narita Airport on a warm rainy night, in the 1970s, not long after the world had seen the advent of the jumbo jets. The giant 747s, DC-10s, Tristars and A300s, equipped with the latest powerful new jet engines, designed to fly enormous loads of passengers and freight on long routes around the world. Much earlier, I had worked on flights across the Pacific, in smaller and less dependable DC-4s – not as a female pilot, as they had not yet been recognised, but as a solitary stewardess working aboard unpressurised aircraft, early 1950s style.

I was accompanying my wonderful airline captain husband and his crew at the end of a three days layover in Tokyo. Our crew bus was on a mission to deliver the crew to the awaiting Flying Tiger Line Boeing 747 that would soon depart for Los Angeles by way of Anchorage. The whole trip would cover 7,800 air miles on the great circle route.

The rain had slacked off to become a late evening drizzle as the bus progressed along the wet tarmac. All of the bright lights of the busy terminal and parked aircraft were reflecting a very active and colorful scene along our path, like a playful celebration of what was to come.

The giant jumbo jets were lined up with precision and nosed in toward the busy Japanese terminal. We passed beneath the tall tail section of one behemoth after another. Looking up 63 feet (which seemed more like 300 feet) each tail towered above us, proudly displaying their logos. One unique and colorful display after another, as each plane awaited departure. Flight plans were being prepared for their long -distance flights around the globe, before the midnight curfew that would close down the airport for the night.

The towering aircraft tails seemed to represent the whole world above us. There was Air Canada with a big red maple leaf displayed on the tail, Air France with streamlined red and blue stripes, Air-India with great red exotic lettering, and Qantas, whose 747s sported a large kangaroo dancing on the tail. Qantas was world famous for navigating the early years of the jet age accident-free. We wheeled by British Airways, China Airlines, and Egyptair, all standing wingtip to wingtip.

photo Teka77 / iStock Images

Next, KLM, loaded with wonderful cheeses and chocolate treats, then Lufthansa with great beer onboard to quench the thirst of its passengers, SAS preparing for the long frozen polar flight to the land of the midnight sun, Singapore Airlines, well known for the most luxurious flights the Pacific, Iberia Airlines in from Spain, and on the end was Saudi Arabian Airlines.

All of the impressive towering tails on these beautiful airplanes conjured up amazing thoughts to me. It seemed all of the nations of the world had gathered to depart the land of Mt. Fuji. People with one common intent, drawn together to spread their wings in every direction, that one memorable, rainy night.

Passengers would be numerous tourists and diplomats, the well heeled and the well recognized, some servicemen, students, and perhaps a handful of religious travellers – monks, priests, nuns, and many more. An fascinating assortment of people, ready to begin an air journey to all corners of our world.

Was all of this busy scene a breathtaking sight, or just another well planned night's work in aviation. An evening of intercontinental air travel preparing to cross distant oceans like a flock of oversized birds heading homeward. "Sayonara and Happy Landings!"

I close my eyes and there the beautiful airplanes with the colorful tails awaiting start up and push back. For airline crews everywhere, a very common sight, but for me, that rainy night at a far away foreign airport, it was an awesome sight to remember forever.

Pat Bliss was an airline stewardess for the Flying Tiger Line, flying worldwide. She met her future husband on her first trip, flying from New York to Frankfurt, Germany. Her husband, Captain Jack Bliss, a 32 year Tiger pilot, passed away on July 22, 2010. They have a daughter, Kristianne, who also flew 13 years as flight attendant for Flying Tigers, daughter Merrilee, who worked 17 years for Continental Airlines and son, Mike flew for Alaska Airlines.

Captain Jack Bliss and his daughter Kristianne 'Kristi' Bliss Peake

Captain John "Jack" Bliss and Patti in the cockpit of a DC-4 in 1952

Kristianne married Roger Peake, a former Flying Tigers flight attendant who later became a ramp agent, Roger Peake was the son of a well known Tiger Captain Wayne Peake, the Friendly Fighter Pilot, a non Jewish, American pilot who flew combat missions for Israel during its fight for independence in 1948, was buried in the Christian section of Haifa Military Cemetery in Northern Israel with full military honors of the kind reserved for Israel's war heroes.

The Tigers' Vladivostok Incident

Captain Joe Crecca (FTL, FDX)

Joe Crecca in 1973 right after his release from the Hanoi Hilton

It was around 1979. We were flying a DC-8 cargo flight to Tokyo, Japan. George A. Gewehr was the captain, Thomas J. O'Connor was the first officer and I was the second officer. I am busy with the fuel sheet and something is coming on 121.5, VHF guard frequency.

It was not very clear but what it sounded like was like, "Ahdeen, dva, tree, cheteri, pyat, cheteri, tree, dva, ahdeen" – one two three four five four three two one in Russian.

George hands me the microphone and says, "Joe, you speak a little Russian, talk to this guy." I responded, "For chrissakes George, I do not want to create an international incident." We were only 40 miles from the Russian border. George turned back to me and says "Well, say something to him!". So, in Russian I said, "Kto govorit ahdeen, dva, tree ee tak dalya…?" Who is saying one two three four five…etc.?

Short pause.

Then a crystal clear voice on the radio says "Hey you Russkies, stay the hell out of this frequency, this is an emergency frequency". I handed the microphone back and said "See, I told you so" and he responded "Keep him going, wind him up!"

I thought this would cost my job, as I was just on the edge of a period known as twelve months' probation.

I said "U nas serdityy amerikanskiy pilot" – sounds like we have an angry American pilot. After a short pause the same American voice said: "You've goddam right, I am an angry American pilot, you Russki son of a bitch, now get the hell off of this frequency."

Now I am positive someone, somewhere – CIA, NSA etc – have heard all this shit and we will go to jail as soon as we land at Yokota Air Base. I just said "I want to bail out", and I was looking for an ejection seat like I had on the F-4.

So, I said very, very politely on the mic, "Dobroye utro," which means good morning, and he said "Up yours too!" I finally got rid of the microphone and handed it over to George.

Captain Bobbie Tharp

We landed at Yokota an hour later or so and we got to the New Pony Hotel in Tokyo where the rooms were never ready on time. 45 minutes later, the Tiger crew that was behind us arrived in the lobby. The crew was headed by Captain Bobbie V. Tharp and his son co-pilot, Ernest "Ernie" A. Tharp. Bobbie, who is five foot seven, walks up to George, who is six foot five, and says, "Hey, did you hear that Russki pilot out there, George?". George started to drop the news, and I was thinking, "Oh shit!". George, then looking down from his towering height to Bobbie and says, "Yeah, I heard that," and Bobbie replied, "I sure told that son of a bitch off."

Captain George Gewehr in the early 1990s

I am then practically on my knees, thinking "For chrissakes George, don't tell him it was me." George saved my bacon and did not say a word. Thank you, George. I might have had to fly with that crazy loon someday.

Sheep Charter To Tozeur, Tunisia

Captain Thomas E. Constable

Around 1979 I was called to help a stranded flight in Casablanca, Morocco. A radio was needed to resume a sheep charter to Tozeur in south west Tunisia. Tigers scheduling asked me to take a communication radio in a large box from our base in Los Angeles LAX to New York JFK on TWA, meet my crew and continue on with Iberia to Madrid, and then Royal Air Maroc, the Moroccan national airline, to Casablanca. The previous crew had cancelled.

When I arrived in JFK, my two crew members were not at the terminal to meet me. I called them and they were still at Tigers cargo terminal. The time for them to make the connection was running out. So, I told them to get there anyway they could.

I had to run to make the connection myself and barely did make it. They were just closing the door when I made a mad dash for it and jumped in. I had a long wait in Madrid for the Royal Air Maroc flight to Casablanca. I finally got to Casablanca airport by way of Algiers and almost dipping a wing in the water off the coast and barely missing a sand dune.

I was very tired coming all the way from LAX with no rest. I was going through customs and they wanted to know what was in the big container. They made me open it and when they saw the radio, they didn't know what it was and confiscated it. I was so tired that I didn't want to argue with them, so I told them to take it.

I finally made it to the hotel, if you could call it that. By that time, I didn't care. I went to sleep and it seemed as though I had just passed out when the telephone rang and woke me up. Our charter agent was on the phone and told me the radio was rescued, installed and the flight was ready to go. My crew had made it by way of London and they were at a different hotel. The first officer was Larry Springer and the second officer was Jim Richards.

I got dressed and took a cab to their hotel. I knocked on the first officer's door and he answered in his underwear and asked, "Who in the f*** are you?". I told him, "I am your Captain, get your cloud suit on and meet me in the lobby." Then I knocked on the flight engineer's

Captain Tom Constable

Sheep in double decker configuration ready for loading

photo Glenn Van Winkle

door, got the same response, and gave him the same instructions.

They were a little under the weather because they had some beers after they arrived in Casablanca and got into a fight with the manager of the hotel bar. They came to an amicable understanding and went to bed. In short, they were in worse shape than me!

The sheep were loaded and ready to go. We took off and had to fly a long route around Algeria because they were at war with Morocco. This made the flight a lot longer than if we had been able to overfly. Tozeur is 400 miles south of Tunis, the capital of Tunisia. The weather was good and we landed with no problem. Unloaded the sheep, turned around and flew back to Casablanca.

Now we were really tired. On arrival we were informed that the second load of sheep was ready to go. We said, "No way, José." We are too tired to do a second rotation. Then the owner of the sheep and the man who chartered it came to the cockpit and begged us to take it. Well, the Tiger motto of Can-Do made us rethink the situation. He begged and begged and blessed the DC-8. With all that and the threat of cancelling the charter, we said yes, we will go.

This is a DC-8-63 and it could carry 1,200 sheep on a double decker configuration. The max take-off weight is 355,000 lbs. We blasted off again and flew around the Mediterranean Sea, the long way, to get to Tozeur, Tunisia. When we arrived the weather had deteriorated with thunderstorms everywhere. I was dodging them on the approach. It was so rough that I was turning the yoke right and left lock to lock to maintain a level attitude. I remember the rain was very heavy. Just as I got close to the runway I centered the yoke and we touched down very smoothly. Boy was I lucky!

When they were unloading the sheep down a stairway with a carpet over the stairs, you could tell which ones were on the bottom deck because they had raisins on their heads.

We went to a hotel and slept for 14 hours. We had been on duty for 23 hours. That's what I call the CAN DO SPIRIT.

International Override

Captain Rex Cotter

I was hired on July 7, 1979. My seniority number at the time was 714 and I was at the bottom of the seniority list. It took me two years to get off probation and I was still at the bottom of the seniority list. It was until October 1980 when Flying Tigers acquired Seaboard World Airlines that I started to gain seniority.

Prior to that, when the bid package came out, the first choice was always for 747 captain, second choice was DC-8 captain, then first officer, then flight engineer. Crew members had international bids, domestic bids, and we also had five to ten lines called charter lines outside of the scheduled flights, but charter was also either domestic or international.

One day when bids came out, and crew scheduling needed another flight engineer on the DC-8 aircraft on a charter line so I bid for it. Nobody else spotted it and consequently, I was awarded three months as DC-8 flight engineer, international charter.

After taking a couple of charter trips around the world, Doug Happ – at the time DC-8 chief pilot in Los Angeles – called me and said, "Rex, I got bad news for you and you got me into a lot of trouble." I enquired what he meant. "Because of you being at the bottom of the seniority list flying international, per our Air Line Pilots Association (ALPA) contract, we have to pay everybody senior to you international override for three months!". Because I was the junior guy and anybody senior to me could have held the international route, someone complained, "Why is the bottom guy on the list doing international?" Bottom line, the company had to pay everybody (including those flying domestic) three months' international override.

I became known as "714" and had people buying me drinks all over the world everywhere I went. The company was then forced to put an all new system-wide bid just get me off the bottom of the list in order to stop paying everybody international override.

Rex Cotter next to 747 N806FT "Robert W. Prescott"

Norah O'Neill: The Flying Tigress

Dr. Cameron Byerley

When I was 10 years old, my mom, Norah O'Neill and I stood in front of her mannequin at the opening of an exhibit about women pilots at the San Diego Aerospace Museum. Inside the glass case were a number of photos of mom and Lynn Rippelmeyer. The museum had dressed Norah's mannequin in her uniform and had clearly struggled to find a wig that remotely resembled her waist-length red hair. Lynn had been the first woman to fly a revenue trip in the 747 and mom had been the first to fly a planeload of passengers on the 747.

I was puzzled by the spectacle of the exhibit. To me, mom was an everyday mother. She was mostly nice and occasionally annoying but all in all a normal person with normal flaws. I asked her, "Mom, this is all really neat. I'm glad your being honored on TV with all your friends, but I don't really get it. You and Lynn were the first women in the world to fly the 747. That's cool. But who taught you to fly it?" "747 check airmen." "They were all men?" "Yes." "Who taught them to fly it?" "Check airmen from the Boeing company." "Were they all men?" "Yes." "Well, if a whole bunch of boys had already done it, how hard could it have been?"

Today I much better understand her response to my question in the museum that day. She explained that learning to fly the 747 was not more difficult than learning to fly other planes and that she was not being honored for learning to fly it. She was being honored because she had continued flying despite the difficulties of being the first woman pilot at Flying Tigers and the only woman pilot during her time at Alaska Central Air.

At the end of her life, my mom was nothing but grateful for her time at Flying Tigers. She had many Tiger friends who helped her through her four-year cancer battle. However, to fully understand Norah's strength, it's important to have a few examples of what she was up against. In her first flying job in Alaska, passengers and copilots routinely refused to fly with Norah. Her check pilot at Alaska Central Air said that he would not give her an FAA check ride because, "He would not be a party to my eventually killing people. He said my becoming a murderer was not a matter of if, but when." Other pilots told her she would "crash, burn, and disappear."

Think how much confidence it takes to keep doing something difficult when you are told you are bad at it. When I was kindly told I was tone deaf in high school, I quickly learned to stop auditioning for musicals. I did not know I was bad at singing until I got external feedback. As a young woman in Alaska, how was my mom to know if she actually had talent as a pilot when people with more flight hours told her she did not? What if their criticism wasn't due to her gender, but she was actually just bad at flying?

photo Flying Tigers Club Archives

Contact sheet of Norah O'Neill when hired in December 1976 as second officer together with fifteen other pilots; James W. Bailey, David V. Caruso, Ray A. Churlonis, Greg T. Cotton, James W. Courant, Robert W. Douroux, William A. Eck, Dennis M. Flanagin, William N. Hebert, Philip A. Jones, William M. McCaverty, Richard A. Rothstein, Lewis C. Shrader, Michael Todd and Angel L. Vasquez

Flying Tigers Club Archives

Norah O'Neill in 1977

photo Flying Tigers Club Archives

Reflecting on how my mom pushed through many years of criticism, I see three huge factors that made it possible for her to get to the point in her career where she could fly a 747. The first were the dear pilots like Paul Haggland, who gave Norah her first flying job because he wanted to give someone who loved flying a chance. He put up with a lot of complaints to employ her and stayed friends with her right up to his visits during the last week of her life. Paul was one of many supporters.

Another was Captain Dick Stratford, one of the men who interviewed Norah for Flying Tigers. He told her, "Someone with thousands of hours in the Alaskan bush has to be either very, very good or very, very lucky. I hope you are both," and was part of the team who decided to hire her.

I think mom was still wondering if her survival in Alaska was mainly due to luck when she entered Tigers' ground school and realised that she was woefully unprepared to understand the lessons on electrical systems in jets. Tiger instructor John Adcock was one of her favorite teachers who saw her potential to learn instead of her lack of knowledge about electricity. She wrote, "You would think that being an A student in high school and college would have given me the confidence that, with effort, I could learn anything. But my confidence was undermined by years of men telling me I didn't belong and wouldn't fit in and it took 'balls' to be a a good pilot. John helped to restore my confidence." Thank you to Paul, Dick, and John, who were some of the first of many good guys who welcomed my mother into the sky.

The second reason for my mother's perseverence was her love affair with flying and seeing the remote wonders of the world. Her ability to experience joy, time and again, in the wonders of the world buoyed her up in hard times. Her first experience in a small plane was landing on a glacier with bush pilot Don Sheldon. She wrote, "I found that waking up to the sky-roofed cathedral formed by Mount McKinley, Mount Foraker, and Mount Hunter towering over the vast whiteness below them was to breathe in splendor — daunting, savage, and incredibly beautiful. Living those days was akin to constant conversations with God."

She returned from her time on McKinley and lived in a basement to save all her money for flying lessons so she could see more of Alaska. She quickly realised she needed a job as a pilot to fund her flying and that most flight schools were not interested in hiring a woman. She persisted until Paul gave her a job. She wrote, "I couldn't stop flying. It was already a part of me, as essential as air and water." She braved long nights, frigid winters, and her least favorite insect, the mosquito, as she amounted more and more hours. She wrote, "Sometimes we slept under the wings of the plane

Captain Dick Stratford in 1974
photo Flying Tigers Club Archives

nestled in the dirt by its tie down ropes. The spring rains should have made this miserable, but they did not. We huddled with other flight-crazed young pilots under dripping wings, in sodden sleeping bags, and talked about flying. Flight filled our days and minds and hearts."

Norah's love for flying was coupled with her love of being a part of the Tiger family. She loved telling stories of Tiger adventures from flying Shamu the Orca to snakes on a plane to stealing mini-drink carts. She wrote, "And thanks always to my Flying Tiger family, the men and women who launched planes to adventure and held hands during the tough times. Office personnel, crew control, dispatchers, loaders, mechanics, charter representatives, flight attendants and pilots — you are ever in my heart."

Finally, the strength of my mother's character and her willingness to keep fighting helped her not only fly 747s but to overcome alcoholism, depression, and PTSD. As a child I did not understand how special it was that she fought to heal herself and how rare it is for

Norah O'Neill in 1983
photo Flying Tigers Club Archives

people who cope with their feelings through alcohol to get sober. I better understood her strength as her caretaker in her cancer journey. She had a remarkable and inspiring ability to keep going in the face of emotional and physical suffering. Her skin was cracking, her bones aching, and her body filled with toxins that could extend her life but not save her. Still she wrote gratitude lists and thanked God for being able to fly 747s around the world in her cancer journal. We wore brightly colored dresses she painted to chemotherapy to cheer everyone up. She corresponded with new women pilots in Africa and the Middle East and felt joy that even on her sickest days she was able to reach out and inspire women around the world. She corresponded with teenage girls in Africa. One wrote back that Norah's messages, "Made me think differently about life. Thank you for inspiring me to do everything I can to the best of my ability." In the end, Norah was grateful for things as simple as feeding the crows on her balcony, and as extravagant as our trip to touch baby whales in Mexico. It was a testament to her great strength that she was able to focus on the good even without hope of a cure.

It took years for me to recognize how lucky I was to have Norah as my mother. I consider my childhood ignorance of the magnitude of her accomplishments a privilege because when I was deciding on my own career, it seemed entirely plausible to me that I could pursue anything I was best suited for, regardless of my gender. I thought it was truly normal for women to fly around the world as most of the pilots I met were women. I never experienced the crisis of confidence my mom faced or worried about entering the male-dominated field of mathematics. Like my mom told so many others, she always told me I could have my dream job if I kept working towards it. Norah's life has been an example for me and so many others of what is possible with passion and spirit and grit.

Norah's excerpts are all taken from her book Flying Tigress.

DIVAS

Flight Attendant Gael Okicich

Norah had many interests outside of flying. She loved arts and crafts and was herself a painter. We would attend craft shows together. The Northwest Flower and Garden Show was also an annual event for us.

But our true passion as friends was a love for the pop-opera group Il Divo. We called ourselves 'divas' and attended as many of their concerts as we could, which numbered at least 15 over the years. We always bought VIP tickets which included front row seats, meet and greet, and photos with the group. Our travels took us from Victoria and Vancouver in Canada to New York, with all the venues in between. I will miss those times with my friend.

Norah O'Neill and Gael Okicich in New York

A Tale Of A Tiger

A First in US Cargo Commercial Aviation

Captain Reyné O'Shaughnessy-Goetze

It was March 14, 1988 when I found myself sitting in a room full of Tigers – Tiger pilots that is! It was the best of times and the worst of times. The best of times because I was elated to be part of something bigger, something that I had ever experienced in aviation - my first heavy jet job. Wow! My classmates were from all walks of life with a variety of aviation experience, and like me, thrilled to be part of the Tiger legacy.

There were ten total in our class. Nine men; I was the only female. It was the worst of times because women were seriously ostracized from the skies, yet, then and now, I consider myself one of the lucky ones hired, along with pilots who were the best of the best. Much like my husband (a Tiger pilot as well), my classmates were gentlemen as well as aviators. Looking back at my Flying Tigers and FedEx career, without hesitation, I am able to say it was a brilliant career path.

As my story begins, I trained on Boeing's first commercial heavy jet aircraft, the 747. After probation, I joined the line as a second officer, also known as flight engineer. It was said that very few women pilots held engineer ratings on the Boeing 747 jumbo jet liner. However, due to the merger in August 1989 between Federal Express and Flying Tigers my time as a second officer in the Boeing 747 was short lived. Soon after T-day, I became a second officer on the Boeing 727, and subsequently a first officer on type. I chose not to upgrade to captain in the Boeing 727; the Airbus was the newest aircraft on property, it was automated and it went to cities that I desired.

On May 2, 1989, I was second officer in an all-female crew on Flying Tigers flight 110: Captain Sandy Szigeti, First Officer Sheri Graybil and myself as second officer. There wasn't any particular briefing or celebration before or after the flight. It was only while in the hotel in

Boeing 727s at Colombus Rickenbacker Airport (LCK)

photo Flying Tigers Club Archives

The first all-woman flight crew, May 2, 1989. From left to right, Second Officer Reyné O'Shaughnessy, First Officer Sheri Graybil and Captain Sandy Szigeti. *photo Reyné O'Shaughnessy*

The first all-woman flight crew, May 2, 1989. Captain Sandy Szigeti, Second Officer Reyné O'Shaughnessy and First Officer Sheri Graybil.

photo Reyné O'Shaughnessy

767 Captain Reyné O'Shaughnessy, in January 2019

Sandy Szigetti became the first (and only) female captain at Flying Tigers on October 5, 1988   *photo Flying Tigers Club Archives*

Columbus next to the Rickenbacker Airport (LCK) that we received a call from the ramp. Evidently someone had noticed it was an all-female crew. Lights! Camera! Action!

It was a mild spring-like morning when we departed Rickenbacker for Charlotte, and history was made: the first Tiger all-female flight crew. At the time Flying Tigers had approximately 500 pilots and only 22 were female (4.4%). We were the first all-female crew in US cargo commercial aviation history. I was quoted, "Other than a routine flight, our pride in being part of Tiger's 44-year history was 'fantastical.'" We were Tiger proud!

My priority in life was always to bid for trips that would create some quality of life. The Airbus schedules allowed balance for years, but eventually I decided to transition to the Boeing 767 that FedEx introduced in

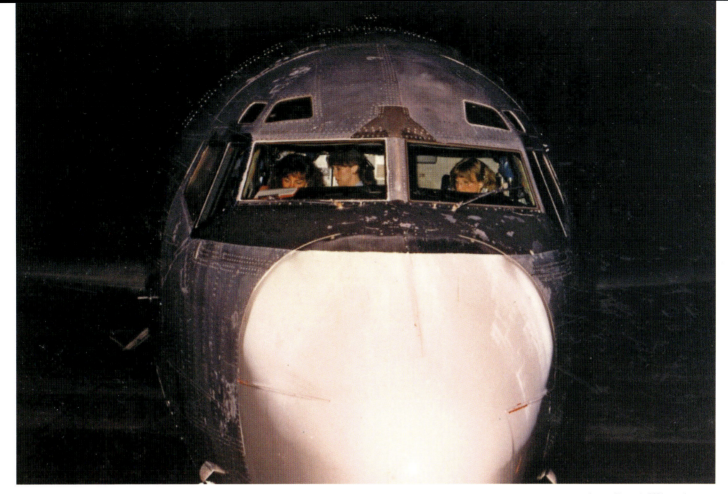

2013, my third type rating in a heavy jet. It struck me as funny when one day a person in my hometown shouted "Hi there, Heavy Metal Mama!" Me? That was funny; I never thought of myself other than "mom."

Flying heavy metal jets is certainly an accomplishment for anyone, male or female, and I never took myself too seriously. Being a mother and raising three awesome sons has been my greatest joy and life accomplishment. The credit is theirs; it's been my privilege to be their mother. Every working mother out there knows being a parent is not for wimps, and quality of life can be hard to achieve. However, most may agree that there is no higher calling than being a mother. I believe both Sandi and Sheri (both mothers) would agree!

As tailwinds go, from the original first US all-female flight crew, I am the only remaining Tigerette.

Sandy Szigeti retired from FedEx on the last day of 2006, and Sheri Graybil also separated from FedEx at one time. Talented. Smart. Genuine. Warm. That's how I remember them. I miss them both.

Sandy, Sheri, and I were only three who paved a path for future female pilots. Today's female pilots have it easier than the three of us did, but the path remains not an easy road to travel for women. Maintaining a "won't stop" perseverance is the key that keeps most women pilots moving forward. When I'm asked by younger women about my trailblazing days, I simply smile and say, "Always reach for the moon and settle for the stars!"

Happy Trails (blazing) to all,
With love, Reyné

Secret Escapade In Saudi Arabia Revealed

Flight Attendant Deborah Paul (McCoy)

The summer of 1981. I had absolutely nothing exciting going on in my usual hectic life. No classes, hobbies, sports, or boyfriends, only flying junior trip after trip for Flying Tiger Lines as a flight attendant. The Nigerian Hajj was coming up, so my girlfriend Lucinda Johnson and I decided to take a few months out of our lives and work the Jeddah, Saudi Arabia to Kano, Nigeria trips. After two months of a continuous cycle of flying, sleeping, sunbathing, never-ending shopping, and a few forbidden parties at royal family members' homes and chalets, we found ourselves very bored one day.

The Sands Hotel is situated in the fashionable al-Hamra consulate area of Jeddah and hotel management did everything they could to keep us happy and comfortable, but women had so few privileges in Saudi Arabia, we decided to play, what we thought, was a very hilarious trick on all the male crew members. There were four of us: Lucinda Johnson, Michelle Harrison, Cynthia Harvey and myself.

We collected all the stationary from our rooms and began writing "admiration letters" to every male crew member among our team of flight attendants, pilots, mechanics, and ramp agents. Imagine us laughing so hard, tears rolling down our cheeks as we complimented each other on our cleverness and creativity. We made our notes look like they could have come from Taiwan or someplace equally exotic by giving curlicue finishes to our letters and dotting our speech with "accents" by way of incorrect verb tenses and dangling participles.

A typical letter was scribed like this: My name is Miko. I stay at hotel, too. I see you in lobby and think you wery hansome. Please, you meet me for drink in lounge near 5 o'clock, so we talk and have laugh. I wearing pretty flower dress and have rose in hand. Escuse English, I from Yokohama. Miko.

Deborah Paul recalled to flight attendant duty on a DC-3, operating passenger charters at the 2018 FTLPA reunion, Palm Springs

photo Eliot Shulman, Flying Tiger Line Pilots Association

We managed about 20 or 30 variations of this, then sealed the letters and slid them under the doors of all the male crew members.

Then we went on our trip to Kano. When we got back a day later, the hotel was all abuzz. Someone said, "The hotel management is really upset. Police are checking everywhere – they think there is a prostitution ring in the hotel!"

I can't remember exactly, but the four of us got together and vouched we would NEVER tell anyone. We could have gone to jail in Saudi Arabia for life (or worse) had we been caught, not to mention getting fired. Fortunately, since we immediately went on a trip and were out of town when the oil hit the fan, no one suspected anyone from our crew.

There were tales of guys going down to the lobby to look for their secret admirers. Sweet, trusting Dave Lusk, for one, comes to mind, but the whole mess scared us so bad, we never revealed our part in the "prostitution ring" until 35 years later.

Flight Attendant Shopping, Saudi-Style

Flight Attendant Deborah Paul (McCoy)

Starting in September 1981, some 44 flight attendants, seven mechanics and nine operations personnel were based in Kano, Nigeria and Jeddah, Saudi Arabia for ten weeks to facilitate the airline 's Hajj charter operation carrying Muslim pilgrims to Mecca.

A Souk is a covered market found in every Arab town and city, where you can find most of everything you need – with a bargain. All the preparation - in the form of company briefings, friends' advice or literature – hadn't prepared us for our first trip to the souk in the heart of Jeddah's old town. Our hotel manager guided us to bus stop #6 in front of the hotel. We waited… first on the wrong side of the street where we missed the bus, then on the right side where we pounced on the next double-decker.

BATTLE OF THE SEXES

Jeddah buses are immaculate, spacious, and quiet. Men enter from the front and pay the driver; women enter from the back and pay a box attached to the wall. A swinging door that doesn't stop banging, almost purposely, unless it's secured shut, separates the sexes. Fellow flight attendants Gary Sopher, Dave Lusk and Bob Dillion sat smugly in front enjoying a clear view of the road. Lucinda Johnson, Ann Bier and myself sat aft, peeking through holes, ducking to see the sights from large glass windows whose paneling blocked our view. A woman entered our section, undid her long black veils and gave us a beaming, toothy smile. This was our cue that we were allowed to converse with her, and immediately our hands and facial expressions set to the challenge of communicating outside the auspices of a common language. She showed us a beautiful tablecloth she had just bought; we tried to explain who we were and why we were in her beautiful, modern city.

A young Egyptian lady in dark Arab attire entered and became our translator, since she spoke a little English. She graciously welcomed us to Jeddah and explained that business brought her and her husband here to live for a few years. She then explained to Menira – our first lady friend – what our gestures were about, and Menira bobbed her head in understanding, welcoming us to take pictures of her with Ann. The follows, said they could hear us all gibbering in back while their Arab and other multinational bus mates peered askance at them. Leaving the bus, we once again felt our lowly, humble positions in this society as we watched the men file off first. Other than having separate swimming pools at the hotel, this was our first real encounter with taking a back seat to the men folk. (It's not really so awful – we sort of developed a casual attitude toward their prejudices – mainly because we didn't want anyone jeering or spitting at us!) The souk itself harbors every kind of specialty shop you can think of. If you can't find it here, the next best place is Hong Kong. Fabric, electrical appliances, watches, stereo equipment and gold are the most predominant products.

GOLD FEVER!

Shop after shop, row after row of gold, gold, gold. Chains, bracelets, rings, grams, earrings, coins – gold everywhere. 14-carat is almost unheard of – the walls of the small shops were covered in only 18 kt. and upwards, much visited by spangled and bangled sheiks' wives. We staggered from store to store, our faces clearly flushed with gold fever. The ability to bargain is a must in the souk, and Bob Dillion, having lived in Greece for two years where the practice also abounds, was good at it. We kept him two paces in front and mercilessly plumbed his talents until we "blew the whole wad," as the saying goes. Our families would have a nice Christmas with all their new trinkets and baubles!

Depending on how one fares with the jeweller, a gram of 18 kt. gold costs about $16 U.S. In the

Debbie buying gold at the Souk in Jeddah, Saudi Arabia

Debbie McCoy, above right, with passenger on board Flying Tigers Hajj flight enroute to Saudi Arabia   photo by Captain Starr Thompson

States, the same Swiss gram would weigh out at the gold mart for $40 and up. To give you an idea of the bargains that dazzled us – I bought an 18 kt. five-gram Swiss gold ingot, intricately engraved, and a frame and hang hook amounting to a gram of 21 kt. gold. Bob talked, I watched for a change, and all went well, with the price war coming to a rest at 216 Rials, about $63 U.S. Then we haggled again, this time for an 18 kt. 28-inch gold chain, weighing seven grams, which finally sold for 464 Rials – about $187. At home the package would probably run close to $600! Fortunately for us, for religious and legal reasons the souk closes midday for about 30 minutes. We thought this was supposed to be a time for kneeling down toward Mecca, like they do in Nigeria, but it was actually more like a coffee break to divide up their day. We sat and sipped the water we brought until the shops reopened.

HARSH REALITY

We witnessed a commotion outside one of the gold shops. Everyone including shopkeepers hurried outside. An angry mob of 25 or 30 men were coming towards us, brutally shoving a fellow Saudi who had his hands tied. He had a thick black rope around his neck and two men were tugging, clearly tightening their hold on the man who had a slightly demented glaze in his eyes. People were spitting on him as he passed and according to the shopkeeper, the mob was taking him off to the square to be flogged or stoned for stealing.

We watched in awe until they turned a corner. This was a real-life exhibition of violence and we cringed before it.

CAMERA BUGS BEWARE

Picture taking is permissible although one has to be extremely careful not to take pictures of gold shops, religious or political concerns, military, or anyone who doesn't want their picture taken, which means don't take pictures unless you aren't afraid of what the conspicuous policeman will do.

We asked one currency exchange official what we could take pictures of in the souk. He answered, "Me!" So, we took a picture of him counting money, which would seem controversial to some. Sitting in the back of the bus allows for picture taking in private, but it's not always worth the risk of snapping that captivating shot of a sheik zooming by in a Cadillac or the mysterious veiled women sparsely dotting the streets. The buildings and pavilions are relatively non-descript, anyway, although we've met people who have visited Saudi homes and say they are opulent and ornate on the inside. The buildings look spacious, airy and stark against the flat sandy backdrop of Jeddah, which itself is a city built on a stationary coral reef.

Finally, after three or four hours of stifling heat and having spent all our per diems, we once again boarded bus #6, our men friends gloating in front, us in back revelling in the privacy of talking with the forbidden ladies in black and sneaking pictures to our hearts' content.

42

The Super Seventy

Al Hader

I was hired on November 6, 1978. My employee number was 35916. One of the key highlights of my career at Tigers was my involvement in the re-engine and conversion program of the DC-8 at Flying Tigers between 1981 and 1985.

Facing stricter federal noise standards, Flying Tigers launched a $200 million program to re-engine 14 of its stretched DC-8 jet freighters with the CFM56, a new, quieter and more fuel-efficient engine made by CFM International, a joint venture by General Electric and French engine maker Safran (previously known as SNECMA – Société Nationale d'Étude et de Construction de Moteurs d'Aviation).

Flying Tigers' first DC-8-73 N787FT test bed aircraft for the CFM56 engine

photo McDonnell Douglas / Flying Tigers Club Archives

The DC-8-71, DC-8-72 and DC-8-73 were straightforward conversions of the -61, -62 and -63, primarily involving replacement of the four Pratt & Whitney JT3D engines with the new 22,000 lb CFM54-2 high-bypass turbofan engines. The new nacelles and pylons were built by Grumman Aerospace. Maximum take-off weights remained the same, but there was a slight reduction in payload because of the heavier engines. Fuel burn and noise was greatly reduced.

All three models were certified in 1982 and a total of 110 Super Sixty Series DC-8s were converted to Super 70 standard by the time the program ended in 1988. DC-8-70 conversions were overseen by Cammacorp with CFMI, McDonnell Douglas, and Grumman Aerospace as partners. Cammacorp was disbanded after the last aircraft was converted.

Flying Tigers DC-8 N787FT was selected as the DC-8-73 prototype aircraft. It was first ferried to United Airlines' San Francisco base for a heavy D check.

During the overhaul, fatigue cracks were found on the pylon of engine number one (left outboard). Since the aircraft engine pylons were to be replaced during the conversion, it was decided to leave the defective pylon. Consequently, the ferry flight to McDonnell Douglas's facility at Tulsa Oklahoma was operated on only three engines.

A special flight permit to conduct the three-engine ferry flight was issued in August 1981 on the condition that only the required flight crew would be aboard: VP Flight Operations Captain Dick Wilson, Captain Gary Stearns in the right seat, and me at the flight engineer's panel.

In September 1981, the first 15 furlough notices were sent to Flying Tigers pilots due to reduction in flying from a decline in business, coupled with effects of the air traffic control strike. I was requested to stay in Tulsa where I was working for both Flying Tigers and Cammacorp through the Super 70 series development, and certification of the -73. I became responsible for maintaining the Production Flight Log manual, to contribute to the development of procedures

DC-8-63 N787FT flair landing at Tulsa, OK after a three engines ferry flight from San Francisco   *photo McDonnell Douglas*

In Tulsa, OK with N787FT in the background, from left to right, Charlie Edge, Cammacorp, Second Officer Al Hader, Captain Dick Wilson, Captain Garry Stearns, Gerry Elikan, Jack McGowen, President Cammacorp
photo McDonnell Douglas

The McDonnell Douglas Tulsa facility was so big that the three DC-8-70's on this picture were not noticeable at the far end. A golf cart would take us to see our aircraft. Here are DC-8-73F N787FT, DC-8-61 Saudia N917R (leased from ONA) and DC-8-61 United N8092U under conversion.

photo McDonnell Douglas / Flying Tigers Club Archives

DC-8-70 CHECKLIST	DATE: 16 JUNE 1982

FOR DOUGLAS FLIGHT OPERATION USE ONLY

DC-8-70 TRAINING CHECKLIST
For Use in Traffic and/or ILS Patterns
Initial Entry and Final Departure from the
Training Area Should Be Accomplished
Using the Normal Checklist

COCKPIT PREPARATION

Cabin Air Shutoff Valve	NORMAL	F/E
Ram Air Valve	CLOSED	F/E
Circuit Breakers/Fuses	CHECKED	F/E
APU		
Batt Sw	ON	
Fire Circuit	TEST	
Indicator Lts	TEST	
Bleed Air	CLOSED	
Generator	OFF	
APU	START	
Generator	ON	
Electrical Panel/Ext Pwr	CHECKED/ON	F/E
* Flight Recorder	SET	F/E
Mast Heater	SET	F/E
Radio Rack/Cargo Compartment Blower Switch	ON/NORMAL	F/E
Passenger Oxygen Eject Switch	GUARDED	F/E
Generator Disconnects	GUARDED/SAFETIED	F/E
Cabin Pressure Control Lever	AUTOMATIC	F/E
* Aileron/Rudder Power Controls	OFF	F/E
Hydraulic System Selector	GENERAL SYSTEM	F/E
Standby Rudder Power	OFF	F/E
Alternate Ground Spoiler Switch	GUARDED/SAFETIED	F/E
Anti-Skid Monitor	CHECKED	F/E
Ignition Pwr/Sw	CHECKED/OFF	F/E
Scavenge Pump	CHECKED	F/E
* Fuel Pumps/Lights	PRIMED, CHECKED/OFF	F/E
Fuel Selectors/Crossfeeds/ Fill Valves	SET	F/E
Pneumatic Switches/ Crossfeed	AUTO/NORMAL	F/E
* Pneumatic Manifold Fail	CHECKED	F/E
* Pack Cooling Doors	OPEN	F/E
* Air Cond., Temp Controls/ Recirc Fan	SET	F/E
Airfoil De-Ice	OFF	F/E
* Oil Quantity	CHECKED	F/E
Cabin Pressure Control	SET	F/E
* Smoke Detector	CHECKED	F/E
Engine Hydraulic Pump Sws	ON	F/E
* Crew Oxygen/Interphone	CHECKED	ALL
* All Warning/Caution Lights	CHECKED	ALL
INS/Ramp Coordinates	INSERTED/CHECKED	C-F/O
* Fire Warning/Short Circuit	CHECKED	C-F/E

BEFORE TAKEOFF

Takeoff Data	CHECKED	ALL
Aileron/Rudder Power	ON/REVERSION LIGHTS OUT	F/E
Yaw Damper	ON	F/O
Spoilers	LEVER FWD/LIGHT OUT	F/O
Flaps/Slots	*/LIGHT OUT	F/O
Stabilizer/Trim	*/SET	F/O
Exterior Lights	SET	F/O
Anti-Skid	ARMED/LIGHT CHECKED	F/O
Hydraulic System	CHECKED	F/E
Ignition Override	ALL ENGINES	F/O
Packs	SET	F/E
Before Takeoff Checklist	COMPLETE	F/E

AFTER TAKEOFF

Flaps	SET	F/O
Hydraulic Shutoff	CLOSED	F/O
Ignition Override	SET	F/O
After Takeoff Checklist	COMPLETE	F/E

BEFORE LANDING

Landing Data	COMPUTED/SET	ALL
Fuel System	CHECKED	F/E
Hydraulic System	CHECKED	F/E
Radio Altimeters	SET	C-F/O
Gear/Lights	DOWN/3 GREEN	F/O
Anti-Skid/Brakes/ Brake Pressure	ARMED/CHECKED	C-F/E
Spoilers/Pressure	ARMED/CHECKED	F/O-F/E
Main Gear Spoiler Inop Lights	CHECKED	F/E
Exterior Lights	SET	F/O
Flaps	*/SET	F/O
Ignition Override	ALL ENGINES	F/O
Packs	MIN FLOW	F/E
Before Landing Checklist	COMPLETE	F/E

NOTES

1   6

DC-8-70 checklist used in flight test

and checklists, and to conduct most of the flight tests along with two other Flying Tiger pilots, Ty Turley and Ron Cuiccio, both on furlough. I stayed at Cammacorp through 1985. In September 1981, I attended CFM56 School at GE in Cincinnati and in October 1981, I attended DC-8 Series 70 Environmental Control System School at Garrett Airesearch in Los Angeles.

It was a very interesting and busy period and I kept our Los Angeles headquarters up-to-date on the development. The McDonnell Douglas facility at Tulsa was one of the largest unobstructed hangars ever built. The facility was 4,004 feet long and 200 feet wide, with more than 800,000 square feet of floor space.

Flying Tigers first DC-8-73 N787FT during a flight test over the desert after conversion photo McDonnell Douglas

I remember the overwhelming appearance of the hangar the first time I entered it.

Flying Tigers first DC-8-73 N787FT made its first test flight out of Tulsa on March 4, 1982. The aircraft was then flown to Yuma, Arizona the next day to undergo certification flying through late April 1982.

On April 3, 1983, Ty Turley accompanied Don Mullin, former Douglas test pilot, on a record-breaking flight with Cammacorp's DC-8-72 demonstration aircraft from Cairo to Los Angeles in 15 hours and 46 minutes. On arrival the aircraft had enough fuel to fly for another 1,000 miles!

Even though scheduled for August 1982, our first DC-8-73 was never delivered to Flying Tigers. Instead, in an effort to resize the Tigers fleet, it was decided that four DC-8-73 stretched aircraft were sold to United Parcel Service (UPS) for $80 million. Together with N787FT delivered in December 1982, 784, 786 and 788 were all delivered to United Parcel Service (UPS) by June 1983.

It was not over yet ... more Flying Tigers original DC-8-63 aircraft were sold. Late in 1983, five DC-8s were sold to Emery Air Freight starting with N792FT that was delivered in December. The other four – 791, 794, 795 and 796 – were delivered by June 1984. Before delivery to Emery, the aircraft were re-engined

with CFM56 engines utilizing Flying Tigers' re-engining positions at Tulsa.

Even though the entire DC-8 re-engine and conversion program was mainly driven by growing fuel and noise considerations, other aircraft meeting the 1985 noise standards started to gain attention to Flying Tigers executives, aircraft like the L-1011, DC-10 and the European-built Airbus A300 twin-engine widebody aircraft. It was noted that an A300C4-200 of Hapag Lloyd was flown to Los Angeles from Germany with a single fuel stop in Bangor, Maine, carrying an 85,000 pound charter load of automobiles including eight Mercedes, three Porsches and one Rolls Royce. Flying Tigers LAX terminal employees offloaded the aircraft. The aircraft was then towed to the headquarters hangar for informal employee viewing before it departed for a return flight to Europe. This visit illustrates Flying Tigers'

Hapag Lloyd A300C4-200 D-AHLB in front of Flying Tigers headquarters hangar in Los Angeles in November 1983 photo Reinhard Zinabold

continuing evaluation at that time of various aircraft as possible replacements for the DC-8.

Starting in June 1984, four additional aircraft were delivered to German Cargo starting with N781FT and followed by 790, 793 and finally 783. N783FT was the last Flying Tigers DC-8-63 freighter to take-off from LAX to Atlanta, Georgia on September 23, 1984 for re-engining.

Flying Tigers' DC-8-61 (N860FT, 861, 862, 863, 864 and 868) and -63 (N772FT, 773, 776, 797, 797, 798) were phased out of the fleet in order to meet the Federal noise regulations scheduled to take effect on January 1, 1985. They were all re-engined and converted in 1984 and 1985 and sold to UPS.

When DC-8-61CF N867FT – one of the 61 series added to the fleet in 1978 – touched down in Atlanta as flight 543 on December 31, 1984, it marked the end of an era spanning 16 years for Flying Tigers and a fond farewell to an old friend: the last DC-8 in service for the Flying Tigers. The crew on flight 543, which had routed San Juan-New York JFK-Atlanta, was Captain Dick Andrews, First Officer George Beck, and Second Officer John Dill. After offloading in Atlanta, the DC-8 was ferried to Marana, Arizona by Captain Mike Johnsen, First Officer Thomas O'Connor and Second Officer William Gormly. The aircraft was later converted in June 1985 to -71CF for UPS.

Initially, none of the Flying Tigers DC-8s were redelivered as a Super Seventy. However, at the end of 1986, a lease agreement for six DC-8-73CF freighter aircraft was signed with Guinness Peat Aviation. At the same time, Flying Tigers announced a recall of all 85 furloughed pilots since the 1980-82 period and a new pilot hire program. So, I was again involved in the -73F program when the first of the six DC-8 freighter aircraft, formerly operated by Transamerica Airlines, was delivered with the reintroduced "Circle T" logo on the tail to Flying Tigers on January 20, 1987, and began scheduled service from Houston, Texas operating its inaugural flight to Dallas/Fort Worth and Columbus and back on the same day.

The aircraft was then placed into transatlantic service to Europe over the weekend and returning to Houston on Monday. The flight crew on the inaugural and during the following months were outsourced from Interstate Airlines until we had our training program and operation specifications was approved by the FAA.

Prior to FAA approval, we only had control of the aircraft for training purposes. During layovers at San Francisco, we would ferry the aircraft to Sacramento for training flights, and during that time, we were very busy writing the DC-8-73 manuals.

They were initially deployed on routes to Houston, Dallas/Fort Worth, Atlanta, San Juan, San Francisco, Minneapolis, Chicago, Columbus, New York, Orlando and Miami, plus some international trips.

Flying Tigers' officers were on hand at LAX headquarters to meet with the crew members operating the inaugural DC-8-73 flight. Standing in front of the aircraft just prior to its departure is, left to right, Ron Marasco, senior vice president-operations, Captain Bob Taylor, Chairman of Flying Tigers Stephen Wolf, Check Captain Art Vance, Check Second Officer Alvin Hader, and Captain Donald Pritchett, vice president flight operations. photo Flying Tigers Club Archives

Flying Tigers cockpit crews finally commenced operation on the DC-8-73CF freighter aircraft on August 17, 1987. The inaugural flight with our own crew originating in Los Angeles, marked the pilots' completion of an intensive instruction program at the company's Samuel B. Mosher Training Center in Los Angeles. Crew members for the inaugural flight were Captain Bob Taylor, Check Captain Art Vance and myself – now a Check Second Officer. Besides being inaugural flight, it was also our proving flight for the new subtype and we were observed by FAA Air Carrier Inspector Tex Hutsell.

The trip was a scheduled run from Los Angeles to Minneapolis via San Francisco, Columbus and Chicago.

On August 7, 1989, after the merger with Federal Express, the six DC-8-73CF tails N701FT, 702, 703, 705, 706 and 707 were re-registered N401FE, 402, 403, 405, 406 and 407 between December 1989 and February 1990 before being progressively sold to UPS starting in July 1990. None of the fleet ever received Federal Express livery but spent a year performing valuable service for Tigers' new owner.

Federal Express DC-8-73CF N702FT in 1989

photo Guy Van Herbruggen Collection

43

Under House Arrest

Captain Douglas Happ

The Boeing 747 flight originated in Frankfurt, Germany during the Iran/Iraq war in the early 80s. It was a charter flight for the Indonesian government. Our call sign was Delta Delta 2647 which was unusual because it was not the normal Flying Tigers call sign. Our final destination was supposed to be Sharjah, United Arab Emirates, where another crew would then take it on to Jakarta, Indonesia.

Our first stop was Ostende in Belgium. There we took on a load of class C explosives. The first trucks brought the missiles with warheads. The next trucks brought the solid propellant motors which were to be mated to the missiles and loaded onto the airplane.

The airport manager pulled me aside and said that we were not to return to Belgium under any circumstances with that cargo. Not even for an emergency! We realized we were now gun runners for Indonesia, who sold arms to the highest bidder. We received a message from headquarters back in Los Angeles stating we did not have an overfly clearance for Saudi Arabia, but we should depart anyway and they would send us one en route. I knew better as this had happened before, but the can-do spirit of anything, anywhere, anytime prevailed and off we went.

The flight went smoothly across Europe and across the Mediterranean, until flying down the infamous Bakka Valley between Syria and Lebanon. It was known at that time for having the heaviest concentration of SAM missiles in the world. We could see the city of Beirut burning off our right wing as there was a war raging there.

We had been trying to reach our company all night for that elusive overfly clearance, but no luck. At about three in the morning, Amman centre handed us off to Jeddah control and we were immediately asked for our overfly clearance number. Of course we didn't have one, so we made one up trying to stall for time.

photo Flying Tigers Club Archives

We gave them our Master Card numbers, and any other numbers we could think of. They were having none of that nonsense.

They wanted us to turn around and we didn't want to do that. We asked to land in Riyadh so our company could straighten everything out, but with that Delta Delta call sign, we were no longer Flying Tigers and we were not welcome in Saudi Arabia. We were told in no uncertain terms, "Reverse course, climb to FL350, contact Amman or suffer the consequences."

That is when things got tense in the cockpit. My first officer was relatively new at that time and went into a kind of shock and could no longer speak on the radio. Now all the Jeppesen charts came flying out, as we tried to figure out what to do with this airplane full of live rockets.

We reversed course and climbed to FL350, and when we contacted Amman, they immediately asked our intensions. After assessing our fuel status, we requested a clearance to Ankara, Turkey. Amman then asked the nature of our cargo and we told them the truth, "Class C explosives."

Minutes later they came back with, "The Turkish government will not allow you to enter their airspace, what are your intentions?" "We would then like to go to Athens, Greece," I responded.

Did we have enough fuel? The flight engineer was calculating when Amman came back with, "The government of Greece will not allow you to enter their airspace, what are your intentions?" I said, "We want a clearance present position direct to the Larnaca VOR to hold at FL350." Amman center then cleared us as requested with instructions to contact Cyprus Approach. We then woke all of our passengers up (charter reps, flight mechanic and other deadheads) for a pow-wow on our plans.

They gathered in the cockpit and I told them I had no intention of ditching this 747 in the Mediterranean. "So when we get down to 50,000 pounds of fuel, I am going to descend and land at the Larnaca airport with or without a clearance and we will all probably be arrested." They all agreed it was a good plan and that is just what happened.

Somewhere in our descent we were finally given a clearance to land with instructions to roll out to the end of the runway. There we were met by military police with automatic weapons, who secured the airplane and escorted us to a holding room where we were interrogated for over an hour. We were placed under house arrest and driven to a hotel with instructions not to leave the hotel grounds.

The next morning we awoke to find the hotel was right on the beautiful Mediterranean Sea and all the European women were sunbathing topless. We were all hoping that this house arrest would last a few weeks, but alas it only lasted a mere 20 hours. After this brief sweet arrest, we were on our way with our Saudi overfly clearance in hand and very sad to leave this paradise.

Although we were able to accomplish our mission, I was informed that it had caused a big ruckus at the State Department.

Captain Douglas Happ　　　*photo Captain John Tymczyszyn*

Having Fun With Flight Attendants

Captain Curt Dosé

STORY ONE

Most of us freighter guys would fly just cargo 90% of the time and only every now and then got a MAC charter passenger trip. It was especially fun when we had a flight attendant that was brand new.

We would be starting the DC-8 in the chocks and for fun would call back to the new flight attendant to come up and help us in the cockpit. When she entered the cockpit, we would tell her that we were having trouble getting engine #2 started, and would she please help us. We would show her that we were trying to start the engine, by pulling on the microphone, like starting a lawn mower. Every time the captain would pull on the microphone, the first officer would secretly test the stick shaker, which would make a "brr brr brr" sound.

We would hand her the mike and tell her to keep trying. Every time she pulled on the mike, the first officer would hit the stick shaker test which would noisily vibrate the control yoke - "brr brr brr". After a few minutes of this, the second officer would quietly hit the normal start and the engine would start and spool up. She could watch the gauges come alive and hear the engine. We would say, "Oh you got it now, thanks very much," and send her, very proud, back to the cabin.

Spring 1982, from left to right, Captain Roger Cumin, First Officer David C. Gilmore and Second Officer Curt Dosé in a DC-8-63 on a trip from Honolulu to Guam   *all photos Curt Dosé*

Second Officer Curt Dosé on the ramp in Bahrain in the early 1980s

STORY TWO

There was fun to be had going across the Pacific on a Military Air Transport Service (MATS) passenger charter flight with a full load of troops and eight flight attendants. The DC-8 had a hatch in the floor behind the captain's seat with a ladder down into the avionics compartment. You could easily fit three pilots in that radio compartment. With the airplane on autopilot in the middle of the Pacific Ocean, the captain and first officer would open the hatch and climb down into the radio compartment. The second officer would ring the flight attendant call button for a flight attendant to come up to the cockpit, and immediately climb down into the radio compartment and close the hatch.

The flight attendant would open the cockpit door and come in to an apparently empty cockpit with the plane flying itself. No pilots! When the screaming stopped and the distressed flight attendant ran from the cockpit for help, we would quickly climb back out of the radio compartment, close the hatch and got strapped back into our seats. Three panicked flight attendants would come up to the cockpit to see what had happened. We would turn around and innocently say, "What's the problem?"

Get It Down!

Captain Robert Stickler

On October 25, 1968, I reported for a flight 2468 at 0700 local, from New York John F. Kennedy airport to Chambers Field, Naval Air Station (NAS) Norfolk, Virginia. It was a flight crew of three, plus two company employees onboard. I was the first officer. The captain was James Baldwin and our flight engineer was Stephen Gagliano. Upon arrival at NAS Norfolk, our flight was to convert to a military charter flight to transport cargo to Keflavik, Iceland.

I did my pre-flight duties and went to the aircraft. We departed from Kennedy on schedule. The captain was flying the aircraft on this leg.

The trip was routine and on arrival at Norfolk we were told to expect a precision approach radar (PAR) to runway 10 and were given the weather. The weather was reported to be 2 scattered clouds at 2,000 feet with an overcast ceiling at 6,000 feet, with the wind at 13 knots out of 020 degrees. The controller also advised us that Norfolk International was reporting winds of 020/13 gusts to 19 but the naval station was not reporting any gusts. The controller continued to give us vectors for the approach and then turned us over to approach control for the final phase of the approach. At this time the new controller gave us the weather again and also advised us to expect windshear on approach. No runway condition or braking action reports were given by controllers.

The captain briefed me on how he wanted the Intertial Navigation System (INS) set up. He wanted the number two INS to show the ground speed vs. true air speed differential so I could monitor the windspeed. He used the number one INS to monitor the drift angle. In addition to monitoring the windshear possibility, he added ten knots to his target airspeed to compensate for a windshear, and used an approach speed of 157 knots as per procedures.

The approach was normal and the captain asked for 12 degrees of flaps, and the check list down to the line. After intercepting the final approach course, the final controller came on and advised us of the missed approach procedure then gave us heading corrections and distance information. He told us we should have our gear down, and the captain then asked for gear down, the below the line checklist and 23 degrees of flaps. The controller said that no further aircraft acknowledgement was necessary.

At this point the approach was normal and all before landing checklists were complete, with just final flaps to go. We broke out of the clouds at approximately 600 feet. I reported the runway dead ahead and we were on the VASI. The wind and drift angle at this time were 30 knots on the nose with 13 degrees right drift. During this phase of the approach the controller reported the winds were 360 degrees.

On flare, the INS winds showed a groundspeed of 161 knots and a three degree right drift. Just before touchdown, the captain removed the crab angle and straightened the aircraft out. When we touched down the second officer called out spoilers extended and reversers flashing.

Shortly after touchdown I said "Get it down!" and the captain replied, "Let it sink."

Soon after I stated, "Four thousand remaining," with reference to the 4,000-foot marker swept past the right side of the runway. When I saw the marker, I became really concerned about our ability to stop the airplane. A second later, I yelled to the captain, "You got three thousand feet left." The captain said he was trying to stop the airplane as he was applying full brakes yet the airplane was not slowing down. We were hydroplaning. We were in trouble.

The captain said to help and I got on the brakes but to no avail. It was like we had no brakes, that they were totally ineffective, and that we had no control of the forward motion of the airplane.

We passed the 2,000-foot marker and, with no braking action, we both kicked the right rudder pedals to try and run the plane into the grass hoping to slow down. All three landing gears went off the right side of the runway.

This seemed to help to slow us down slightly as the airplane went through the grass. Then we saw we were heading right at the cars at the end of the runway waiting for us to land so they could cross the runway. We kicked the left rudder pedals and went back onto the runway. The number four engine went right over the hood of the first car in line. When back on the runway, we actually seemed to accelerate rather than slow down.

At that point we ran off the end and hit chain a link fence. Luckily the post of the fence went between the nose tires. That pulled us around and the right wing wound up on the end of the runway and we came to a stop in a swamp. No one was hurt amongst the three cockpit crew members or the two company employees on the airplane.

The first thing we did was open the windows and made sure we weren't on fire. No fire, so I turned around to see what was next, but the rest of the crew were gone. So, there I sat by myself! I said, "Damn, they didn't even say goodbye." I went through the crash checklist and shut everything off. Then I grabbed my brain bag and started to head for the exit.

A fireman came in and said he was smelling fuel. I told him we had full fuel tanks. He replied, "Holy shit." I replied that if we aren't on fire by now, not to worry.

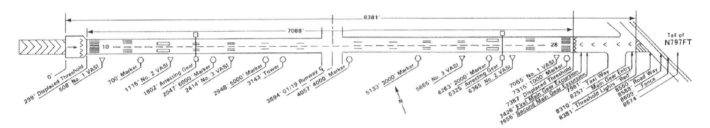

Norfolk NAS runway 10 diagram

NTSB Aircraft Accident Report

The airplane was slowed down as it went through the mud and drifted to the right

photos R.P. Fitzgerald; U.S. Navy / Flying Tigers Club Archives

The airplane came to rest 8,375 feet from the displaced threshold of runway 10. The tail of the airplane was 77 feet beyond the airport boundary road.

Firemen inspect the aircraft. There was no fire.

First Officer Robert Stickler on the right wing soon after exiting the overwing emergency hatch

I climbed out of the overwing emergency hatch. The weather, and thus the wing, was still wet. There was a ladder on the wing so I just climbed down the ladder and walked over to the crew. One of our company agents who was on board went back in the plane and got our suitcases. Luckily Stephen Gagliano, the flight engineer, had his camera and started taking pictures of the plane. We got in the crew bus and the navy guys took us to hotel. But before that, I called the Chief Pilot to tell him what happened. His first question was "Who was flying?" I replied, "The captain. If I was flying I wouldn't be talking to you."

On a side note, at the NTSB hearing they asked Flight Engineer Stephen Gagliano when he first felt when we were in trouble. His remarks were "When I felt the first officer seat was pushing back towards me," which was the moment my seat slid backward as I pushed heavily against the brake pedals to try and stop the airplane. Then he said, "After that, Stickler started yelling at the captain to get this fucking plane on the ground." Every word on the cockpit voice recorder (CVR) that was bleeped out was me yelling at the captain.

After all was said and done, my assessment was that if we had died I would never have known. It happened so fast, all I was thinking was to get the plane stopped. The incident did not have any impact on my career, just another bump in my life.

Captain James Baldwin and First Officer Robert Stickler

photos Stephen Gagliano

Showing Flying Tigers Colours At Oshkosh

John Burke, Vice President Flying Tiger Club

I was hired on March 20, 1978 as a Ramp Operations Supervisor based at New York Kennedy (JFK). My employee number was 34482. Not only was Flying Tigers a great airline to work for but the opportunity to enjoy some unique adventures was always there.

One such adventure was spending the last weekend of July 1983 at the EAA Annual Convention and Fly-In at Oshkosh with a Warbirds of America Board member, Link Dexter, who flew a Tiger DC-8 into Oshkosh.

Meeting up with the crew for this flight, Captains Lincoln Dexter and Nick Tramantano and Second Officer Bob Tymczyszym at Chicago O'Hare, we were off with aircraft N795FT, a DC-8-63, first to Minneapolis–Saint Paul as scheduled flight 443 and then on to Oshkosh as ferry flight 795.

Enroute from Minneapolis to Oshkosh Captain Dexter informed us that he had arranged through the Warbirds to do a low flyby of the airfield with the DC-8 prior to landing. That would have been a highlight of the day but upon reaching Oshkosh the tower advised us that due to excessive traffic in the area they could not grant approval for the flyby.

Once we arrived at Oshkosh, Captain Dexter, who had his Winnebago travel trailer on site, invited me and the other two jumpseaters for a cook-out. A great way to fuel up before starting to walk around the large airfield.

John Burke at JFK (early 1980) when Chief Operations Supervisor just before the Seaboard merger
Flying Tigers Club Archives

Flying Tigers DC-8-63 N795FT on static display at Oshkosh

photo by Bob Lewis / Flying Tigers Club Archives

Romance On The Boeing 747

Paul & Susan E. Rebscher

Every night around midnight, Flying Tigers' scheduled flight 71, JFK-ORD-ANC, departed New York in the form of a Boeing 747. The crew was scheduled to fly the trip to Anchorage via Chicago, rest for 24 hours, then continue to Asia.

I was the first officer and Walter Sahaydak was the captain. As the midnight departure approached we boarded the aircraft and departed on time for Chicago. Walter was flying the first leg and after reaching cruise altitude I went back to the galley for coffee. Our 747 on that trip was a -100 series with only four seats for deadheads and a triple bunk. As I entered the upper deck area I saw two attractive flight attendants who told me they had been recently furloughed and were going to Seoul for Christmas shopping. After I had my coffee

Susan Hart jumpseating on a 747 in November 1985

I invited them to join us in the cockpit for a fantastic view from the front of our aircraft. It was probably the 1,000th time they had been in the cockpit of a 747 but they accepted anyway.

We pointed out various landmarks along our flight path and at one a.m. only the lights were visible. After 45 minutes the ladies retired to the upper deck area to get some sleep for their long trip to Seoul. We landed in Chicago, off/on loaded cargo and after about an hour on the ground, we were airborne again for Anchorage. We never saw the two flight attendants again as they slept the rest of the way. After six hours, we landed in Anchorage around 6:00 AM local time and went straight to the hotel for some much-needed down time.

The best way to get rested for our departure the next day was to sleep about four or five hours, get up around noon, stay up all day, then back to sleep around seven or eight p.m. for a six a.m. wake up call. I managed to sleep until about eleven a.m. and called the terminal to find out the status of our two flight attendants. He told me that several deadheads coming up from LAX with seniority had bumped Miss Hart. Not sure which one was Hart, I asked where she was, answer, your hotel.

I thought a little female company would be nice for lunch so I called the front desk and asked for Miss Hart's room number which the operator refused to disclose, but rang the room for me. Miss Hart answered, I introduced myself as the first officer on the trip up to Anchorage and asked if she would like to join me for lunch at La Mex, an excellent Mexican restaurant one block away. She accepted, we met in the lobby at noon and walked over there. La Mex had a Grande Margarita to die for so we ordered a couple.

Miss Hart was now Susan and we proceeded to tell one another our life stories. I was separated at the time and she was a career flight attendant who had been with several defunct airlines but never married. By now a second round of Grande's was ordered and the biographies continued. At the time I was 50 years old, she was 40 so we had lots of personal history to talk about. A third round kept our conversation going. After many hours and Grande's we ordered some great Mexican food and of course yet another Grande. Not sure what the Grande count was but it was getting to be around six p.m. and time for me to get some sleep for the trip to Asia tomorrow. We walked back to the hotel, I fell into bed for instant sleep and guess Susan did the same and then deadheaded back to JFK and home. I finished my seven-day trip, went home to Chicago and continued to see Susan whenever I was in New York. After two years of courtship we were married on Long Island in 1987 and in September 2017 we celebrated 30 years of marriage.

First Officer Paul Rebscher and Flight Attendant Susan Hart Rebscher holding a birthday cake onboard a passenger flight in 1989

Susan and Paul Rebscher en route to Japan aboard 747-124F N809FT in May 1992   *photos Paul & Susan E. Rebscher*

Susan and Paul Rebscher at the Seattle FTLPA reunion in 2014.

photo Eliot Shulman, Flying Tiger Line Pilots Association

48

You're Going With Us!

Captain Thomas Pierchala

Captain Thomas Pierchala

In early 1984, Tigers decided to try to start a FedEx-type operation using Boeing 727-100s. It was a hub and spoke type operation with the planes starting at the spokes and flying into Chicago (ORD).

One of the spoke cities was Kansas City, MCI, which had a large snow and ice event over the last weekend of December 1984 and the aircraft – tail N930FT – sat outside the whole time without engine inlet covers installed. On the afternoon of Wednesday January 2, the mechanic called TWA to get deiced and they said that he had to bring the aircraft to their ramp. Instead of towing, he opted to start all three engines and taxi over. TWA did the deice but told the mechanic that there was still ice in the engine inlets. The mech said he would take care of it but never did anything about it including not telling the crew, Captain James Levrett, First Officer George Miller and our own FTLPA president, John Dickson as second officer.

Dickson told me later that the crew showed on time that night for Flight 120/03 destined for Chicago O'Hare with a short stop at St Louis Airport. His preflight of the aircraft was conducted on a clear, windless, and very frigid night with an ambient temperature of only four degrees Fahrenheit. Engine inlets were checked but no further than what could be seen from the ground with a flashlight – which was standard procedure.

Engines were started and a routinely short taxi was made to runway 19R which the ATIS was reporting as covered with hard packed snow. The takeoff, made by Levrett, was bumpy due to the packed snow and short in distance due to a light cargo load. As Miller announced V1 from his airspeed indicator, the takeoff go/no-go point, there was a loud bang and bright flash after which all of the number one engine gauges rolled back to zero. The engine had literally destroyed itself, presumably when ice stuck frozen to the lower portion of the inlet finally dislodged and was sucked into the fan section.

First Officer John Dickson next to damaged #3 engine in the maintenance facility of TWA, Kansas City January 10, 1985

photo Captain Arthur Vance

Boeing 727-23F N930FT, the aircraft involved

photo Jacques Guillem Collection

An emergency was declared and the flight was cleared to enter downwind for a visual landing on the departure runway. All three pilots noted at one point that there was significant shaking of the aircraft during the 30-minute air return, all commenting at one point that it must be coming from the shutdown engine. It actually turned out that the number three engine was just as damaged and about to disintegrate also.

The only explanation the crew was ever given on why this engine didn't also fail was that power settings were very low for the return in addition to the fact that the fan blades were damaged in a very symmetrical pattern, all apparently losing the same amount of metal and weight around the rotating hub. The number two engine was X-rayed and showed significant stress fractures. Tigers had to replace all three engines but were lucky not to lose three fine crew members also.

Now enter my side of the story. I was a brand new 727 captain based out of Chicago on reserve. Crew schedule called and told me to deadhead out to Kansas City to test fly a 727! I was rather sceptical that I could legally do this. I thought that a company check pilot or management type should do it. I got a call from the JFK 747 chief pilot and he told me I could do the flight.

So on January 6, 1985, in the Tiger spirit, I headed to the airport to conduct the test flight of N930FT. The aircraft had only been down for a total of three days. Pretty good. We did the preflight and everything was looking good. The mechanic that caused the problem was there. He said that he would see us after the flight. I told him, "NO WAY, you're going with us!" I wanted as many eyes on things as we could get. He didn't like the idea but agreed to come with us.

We lined up for takeoff and I brought all three engines up to full power just to be sure all was good. This is where it could have gone bad again. The aircraft was very light and I was lined up a little crooked on the runway. So when I released the brakes, the aircraft shot forward like a catapult takeoff and we did a little zigzaging down the runway. Quite a surprise!

After all was said and done it was a really fun thing to do. The new engines ran like Swiss watches so we didn't have much to do. We ended up performing a local VFR sortie, flying around for 30 minutes doing some airwork and touch-and-go landings. How often do you get to just go out and have fun with an airliner?

49

747 Flying Lesson

Helena Herceg Burke

In May 1985, I was a 23-year-old gal working at High Tiger in Flight Operations, having the time of my life. My friend and I decided it was time we did a trip to Anchorage, so we planned to jumpseat Los Angeles-San Francisco-Anchorage on the FTO073 up to The Last Frontier state.

We spent four fun-filled days of driving around the countryside and taking in the breathtaking beauty of the surroundings, walking around Anchorage at 11:30 at night with the sun still up, enjoying fantastic food, and, of course, what trip to Anchorage is complete unless you've been to the famous Bird House, one of the most unique bars in Alaska? But that's another story.

We were sad our time in Alaska had come to an end and we were heading home; little did I know that a new adventure was about to begin. We arrived at the airport and boarded our aircraft, an ex-Pan Am 747-100, tail number N818FT. With three cockpit crew members and two other jumpseaters, we were a total of seven onboard for our flight FTO072, routing ANC-SFO-LAX.

After we took off, my friend and the other two jumpseaters fell asleep and I was bored so I went to the cockpit to hang out with the flight crew. I sat in the jumpseat behind the captain and the four of us chatted for a long while and had a lot of laughs. What else are you going to do in the cockpit? The next thing you know, the co-pilot says to the captain, "How much do you want to bet that Helena can fly this plane?" And the captain said without blinking an eye, "Get her up here and let's see."

The co-pilot proceeded to maneuver out of his seat and told me to take his place. So, the captain started talking to me, explaining a bunch of the instruments, gyroscope, engine throttles, steering column, the whole nine yards. I was too excited to pay much attention to anything he said, I was sitting in the co-pilots seat at 33,000 feet! This couldn't be happening!

Helena in the first officer's seat flying the big jet

The captain said there would be a loud noise when he disengaged the autopilot, and then I'll have control. I'm just smiling from ear to ear and can't believe any of this is real and don't believe he's actually gonna let me fly. So, next thing you know, I hear a loud warning sound, the aircraft takes a dip and captain says, "You're flying!"

What? I'm flying? A 747? For real? Yep, for real. I was concentrating so hard, white knuckle'd on the steering column, watching intently out the window to make sure I didn't hit anything, like a cloud, watching the attitude indicator go above the horizon, then below the horizon, then above the horizon, then below the horizon. I realized that I really was flying the plane and I got nervous and asked the captain if we could put it back on autopilot. His response to me was, "You know where the autopilot button is!" So, I put it back on auto and then finally breathed. He asked if I wanted to do it again and the smile on my face just said it all. I ended up flying for about 45 minutes, changing headings and adjusting engine throttles. After a while, my friend woke up in the back, wondering where I was and came in to the cockpit asking "Where is Helena?" Well, Helena was flying the plane! The captain put his hat on me and we took this picture at 33,000 feet somewhere between ANC-SFO.

Flying Tigers And Federal Express In Partnership

Four years before the merger with Federal Express, Flying Tigers joined Federal Express, McDonnell Douglas and Operation California in a unique cooperative effort that resulted in the airlift of more than 100,000 pounds of medical supplies and housing materials from Los Angeles to earthquake-stricken Mexico City. The 1985 Mexico City earthquake struck in the early morning of 19 September with a magnitude of 8.0. The violent event caused serious damage to the Greater Mexico City area and the deaths of at least 5,000 people.

On Sunday October 13, 1985 at Los Angeles International Airport, Flying Tigers built up close to 55 tons of tents, medical supplies including germicides and IV solutions, hospital beds, orthopedic baby cribs, blankets, wheelchairs and a power generator to be flown from Los Angeles.

Federal Express donated the use of a McDonnell Douglas DC-10-30F – aircraft tail N305FE – flown by FedEx crew members, Mc-Donnell Douglas supplied the fuel, and Operation California provided the cargo.

On arrival in Mexico City, Flying Tigers employees volunteered their time to offload the plane, completing the job in just over three of the six hours allotted for the task, and also coordinated delivery of the goods to previously designated recipients.

Flying Tigers manager of terminal operations at LAX, Ian Taylor, coordinated the LAX terminal's role in the effort and was on hand for the Sunday departure along with Cyril Murphy, vice president of international and government affairs, and Joe Hermosillo, director of international and government affairs and coordinator for Flying Tigers' Mexico relief efforts. Also present for the send-off were representatives of the other participating companies and entertainment industry celebrities Apollonia and Rebecca Holden.

In Mexico City, Flying Tigers general manager for Mexico Marco Mendiola supervised the offload and rapid transfer of cargo, destined for leading hospitals in the area, including the Hospital General and American-

LAX send-off. Among Flying Tigers on hand LAX on October 13, 1985 for the loading and departure of the joint effort Mexican relief flight were, L to R, Joe Hermosillo, Bill Mossman (PU & D driver), Ian Taylor, Al Cormier (manager of special projects), Carl Shoemaker (PU & D driver) and Cyril Murphy. *photo Flying Tigers Club Archives*

British Cowdray Hospital, and shelters at Universidad Anahuac and other locations.

In addition to this successful joint effort, Flying Tigers assisted in the aftermath of Mexico's devastating earthquakes by transporting several shipments of relief supplies including pharmaceuticals from Atlanta, Georgia and Southern California, and work gloves from Memphis via Flying Tigers scheduled service to Mexico.

This story was first published in the September/October 1985 edition of Tigereview and has been edited by Guy Van Herbruggen.

16 Years Of Furlough

Captain Ted Loubris (SWA, FTL, FDX)

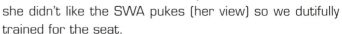

I graduated from Gettysburg College 1962 with a BA in Business Administration, and entered the USAF on August 23, 1962 as a navigator trainee. My military career ended with an honorable discharge as a B-52 navigator and captain on November 25, 1967.

Seaboard World Airlines hired me at age 29 as a navigator on August 23, 1967. The inertial navigation system (INS) furloughed me on November 25, 1970. I then flight instructed and flew air taxi until hired by Air Products and Chemicals in the spring of 1971. I obtained an ATPL on the Beech 18 and two jet type ratings, the Cessna 500 Citation and the North American Rockwell NA-265 Sabreliner. At this point I had 3,500 pilot hours.

I was recalled to Seaboard as a pilot in April 1979 at age 40 and flew the Saudia contract on the DC-8 as a copilot. I was then furloughed again as a result of the SWA/FTL merger. That's getting depressing.

I then flew as a DC-8-55 co-pilot on a subcontract to Zantop in Detroit from the Thanksgiving of 1982 until Easter 1983. Then I was hired by Arista International Airlines for the next two years. They went broke.

Having so much experience with losing jobs, I then went to work for Orion Air to set up an international navigation program for them. Once completed after a year and a half, I become a DC-8 line captain. The old Diesel Eight flew like a truck, and in manual reversion it took a lot of physical strength to wrestle around. When they hung the CFM56 engines on it and added an air cycle machine, it flew like an entirely different, and better, airplane.

I was recalled by Flying Tigers in the spring of 1986, after 16 years of furlough. My peers said I was unlucky. But after all the heartache, I was where I wanted to be, albeit ten years lower in seniority where I might have been.

We were all very happy to be back. It was like a big reunion. Don deLambert and I knew we were going to be first officers on the 747 when the dust settled, and we went up to the secretary in charge of assigning aircraft positions via seniority and she had us down for second officer training on the 747s. We said why not pay us to sit home and save the training costs. No, she said. Obviously she didn't like the SWA pukes (her view) so we dutifully trained for the seat.

After training for the back seat, scheduling sent us home for six weeks. Of course we forgot just about everything. The first leg was JFK to Dover. It was gear up gear down. I was still parking my car at JFK when we landed at Dover. Thank God Kurt C. showed me the way and helped me with the Take Off Landing card.

photo Flying Tigers Club Archives

Captain Ted Loubris

Then we went from Dover to Frankfurt. The captain had been an old engineer and jumped all over me for being really slow and not snapping out the checklist. I repeatedly apologised but nothing I could say or do seemed to satisfy him. Finally I had enough. I said, "You know what I learned as a DC-8 captain at Orion?" He sarcastically replied, "No, what?" I said, "It's a lot easier to be an asshole than to fly for one." There was dead silence – except Kurt, who almost fell off the observers seat laughing.

The captain never bothered me again. But he was right, I wasn't a very good flight engineer. On the other hand, I could fly pretty good, as I had about 7,000 hours at the time. That 747 was a great airplane to fly. It was the highlight of my career. It flew so smoothly and landed like a dream. I was awarded a USAF Desert Storm medal by Department of Defense for civilian flying during the first Gulf War.

After six weeks in the backseat, I was awarded first officer on the 747 along with Don deLambert. What a colossal waste of money to train me as a second officer! Flew in the right seat for two years until Federal Express bought the company on Dec 22, 1988. I loved flying the jumbo, and I really liked the Tiger crews. There were a bunch of really nice people. I had a lot more in common with Flying Tigers than I ever did at Federal Express.

I was on the merger committee for Flying Tigers in the Federal Express merger. That took almost two years. I flew the 747 as a first officer until bumped off by fleet reduction. I was not a happy camper to leave the jumbo, I'll tell you.

I then flew as a 727 first officer for almost four years. The 727 was like a little fighter jet. It was fast and very manœuvrable. If you could see the runway over the nose you could land there. Terrible visibility though.

I then went to the right seat on the DC-10 aircraft. For one month. At that time, I was awarded a captain's bid in New York. Flew as a 727 captain in Europe until reaching age 60. The DC-10 was a great plane to fly. The avionics were initially hard to understand but once the lights came on it did a lot for the pilot. Beautiful visibility.

But it was not over yet! I went to the back seat (flight engineer) for five more years, until the mandatory retirement age of 65, when I finally stood down from flying. Total time was around 24,000 hours in all seats. Fatigue was always the enemy in this job. But I miss it all, to this day.

Captain Ted Loubris on the DC-10 back seat

52

The Little Device That Saved Us

Captain Thomas E. Constable

Flying Tigers was operating a charter to transport military personnel and their families out of Korea with two Boeing 747s in passenger configuration. Of the two aircraft, only one was equipped with a unit called a TCAS – Traffic alert and Collision Avoidance System.

This device would give a warning in both cockpits if two aircraft were on a collision course. First would come an aural warning, "Traffic, traffic," and the small screen on the unit showed a green dot indicating the traffic. When the traffic got nearer, the dot colour changed to yellow; if it continued to be a threat of an imminent collision, it would change to red.

At any time during the warnings it is the responsibility of the pilot in command to manually initiate a maneuverer to avoid a collision. (In today's TCAS systems, the hardware in the two endangered aircraft will communicate in real time with each other to agree a vertical escape path for both aircraft, to avoid both cockpits taking evasive action in the same direction – one cockpit will receive an instruction to climb, in the other, to descend.)

Around 1987 my crew and I, including 15 flight attendants, took off from Yokota Air Base in Japan and flew to Korea, landing at Osan Air Base. Our mission was to pick up 500 military personnel and their dependents and fly them back to Yokota.

We loaded everyone on board and took off for our destination. The weather was good, with clear skies on the return trip. When we were over Japan and I could see Mount Fuji ahead, I made an announcement over the PA system that the passengers on the left side will be able to get a good view of Mount Fuji as we pass by off to the right.

After passing Mount Fuji, we started our descent to the airbase. I made a left turn on our approach and descended into an overcast cloud layer. Almost

747 Captain Thomas E. Constable in 1989

immediately our TCAS system sounded a warning of traffic and a possible collision. The dot went from green to yellow and then red.

The traffic was below us and climbing into us very rapidly. I immediately initiated a climb by pulling all the way back on the yoke and jammed the throttles to full power. We climbed rapidly and this was enough to avoid the collision with the unknown aircraft, which passed underneath, barely missing us.

We were in contact with Yokota Approach Control but they did not report the traffic or warn us of the impending danger. We told them what happened but all they did was to immediately hand us off and told us to contact Yokota tower. We reported the near-miss to the tower and they only replied, "Roger, you are cleared to land."

We landed and all were safe on the ground, all 500 plus the crew. A high ranking officer on the base came to see me after landing and said, "Wow, I saw

Military personnel disembarking a 747

your escape maneuver through the window of my office." Apparently it was a Japanese commercial jetliner that was handled by the civil air traffic control that passed very close to us. I reported the incident with local authorities but I never received an answer.

I can't tell you how lucky we all felt to have survived that flight. I for one am a big proponent of that little safety system! What really gave pause for that was that by pure chance we happened to be on Flying Tigers' sole TCAS-equipped passenger 747. With the number of passengers we had aboard, if we'd had the other ship that day, the loss of life would have been a tie for the worst single-aircraft disaster of all time, along with Japan Airlines 123 that claimed 520 lives only a few miles from our position, two years earlier.

53

Monkey Business

Captain Rudi Kohlbacher (FTL, FDX)

Rudi Kohlbacher, The Belgian Tiger

It was April 21, 1988, and I was still a junior 747 flight engineer working a scheduled trip, flight 75 from Anchorage to Tokyo Narita aboard N820FT. As is often the case, not all went as scheduled on this Tigers flight with the live animals that were frequent flyers with us.

After reporting to the ramp office with Captain Bob Saunders and first officer Larry Weeks, they informed us that we would be delayed because monkeys on the main cargo deck had broken out of their cages. After the inbound flight arrived from the Lower 48, the ramp had found that several monkeys were running loose on the main deck. The live cargo had apparently become bored with the lack of inflight entertainment enroute and as intelligent critters, a few of them figured out how to reach out to a buddy and have some fun before getting deplaned in Japan.

The cages had been loaded in two adjacent pallet positions, all close together so they could be comforted and secure I guess. What the loaders didn't consider was monkeys' reach and smarts and neglected to notice their cage doors facing each other. Sure enough, one bright primate in the group got the party started, reaching that long skinny arm through his cage to reach over and fiddle with the cage door latch on the adjacent pallet. Voilà, jailbreak! Naturally, the 'monkey see, monkey do' trait kicked in and the 747 main deck became a jungle gym of fun.

So, the ramp plan was to close all the cargo doors and the L1 door, and power off APU/ground power, hoping the dark and cool interior would coax them to huddle back to their remaining caged buddies. No doubt they also did not want any jumping ship for escape on airport property. That would really be embarrassing.

So, they called out the experts, a Department of Fish and Game (DF&G) agent, to handle a professional recapture. I'm pretty sure the guy never dreamed he would be handling monkeys in the Alaska bush!

The crew plan was to perform our normal preflight duties, hoping the round-up would be successful, without too much delay. I was warned about the dark jet and to be careful and quick to open and secure the entry door after doing my walk around. Entering a pitch dark and quiet main deck on the 747 was certainly a different routine and my ears were on full alert as soon as I had rotated the door handle closed. With my mag light in hand, the narrow beam scanned the cargo seeing nothing. But immediately my hearing senses became acutely aware of the sound of scurrying critters running across the main deck and bouncing off pallets! Sitting in a long dark aluminum tube with monkeys bouncing off the freight was a bit concerning. Now, I just had to make my way up the crew stair to get up into the cockpit without getting jumped!

Clearly, the dark and quiet jet plan wasn't working too well. The DF&G guy now had a new plan. Power up the jet, get the lights and heat back on and he would be setting out grapes to entice them back to their cages. Now I got to see a few of these scurrying monkeys on the main deck in the full light. They seemed to be loving their freedom, leaping from pallet to pallet. But what really got my attention was watching a few use the control cables along the ceiling! Then, while setting up the engineer panel, I saw the control yokes making small movements from these swinging primates and I knew this wouldn't be an ideal situation if it occurred inflight. So after Bob and Larry arrived into the cockpit, we all agreed a positive head count and no unaccounted monkeys was a good plan.

I made a trip back down to the main deck to see how things with the game warden were working out. "Like herding cats. But worse!" His new plan was to inject the grapes with a sedative and place them all around the main deck. Bad plan, I thought. So I asked him, how would we account for these guys when they're passing out in all sorts of places in our aircraft? Obviously, an on-time departure were the least of his priorities. So, back at my panel, I updated the crew. and Bob had a good chuckle about the plan. Meanwhile, as Larry sat relaxed with his legs up on the panel, I saw the beady eyes of a monkey sitting on top of his rudder pedal, just starring at us! "Hey, Larry, ah, don't look now, but..."

Well, needless to say, now we started reconsidering the "drugged" monkeys going to sleep plan. Since this guy came up into the cockpit via avionics tunnels and not through the crew stair door that remained closed. After a short discussion with DF&G and the ramp about our visitor and concerns about where these drugged monkeys could hide and fall asleep, the spiked grapes plan was wisely abandoned.

Now, behind the scenes, Tigers was trying to get an accurate manifest head count, facing curfews and duty times concerns and generally trying to make sure the shipment would arrive and we didn't mess up any bigger. Then with typical Tigers Can Do Spirit, the ramp had a real game plan. It's Alaska! Everyone hunts and loves fishing. So, someone at the ANC ramp came up with the brilliant idea to get everyone to bring in their fishing nets and then went hunting and netting monkeys like salmon!

And that's how they eventually rounded up the monkeys. But, it did take a while. The delay conflicted with Narita's curfew, so we were sent back to the hotel for a legal rest and launched the next day and had an uneventful trip with a bunch of well caged lives that were not going to pull any more monkey business!

OLIVER: SPECIAL 747 CARGO

In 1976, Oliver, a stocky humanoid creature whose man-ape characteristics have made him the object of study by noted scientists and anthropologists traveled in the upper deck of a Flying Tigers 747 from New York Kennedy to Tokyo and back. Four feet six inches tall and weighting in at 120 pounds, Oliver was displaying some man-like characteristics such as a bi-pedal posture (walks only on two legs) that has the experts baffled with posture like a man, appeared to possess a higher degree of intelligence than the usual primate and had a distinct bone structure unlike that of chimps and other primates. Oliver was believed to come from the Congo River region in Zaïre (now D.R. Congo).

Accompanied by a handler, Oliver steps off the plane in Tokyo
photo Flying Tigers Club Archives

54

Ammonia In The Cockpit

Captain Rex Cotter

I carried just about any animal from spider, monkey, sheep, cattle to reindeers. In 1989, I was first officer on a 747 charter from Auckland, New Zealand to Vancouver, Canada. We were taking little reindeers up to Canada as they are bred in farms to be later eaten. They were about 30 in cage so there was about 800 of those little reindeers stacked on top of each other on the main deck of our 747.

En route, we had a stop in Honolulu, Hawaii for a scheduled crew change. Soon after reaching cruising

Inside a 747 loaded with reindeers   photo Captain John Tymczyszyn

Triple-deck pens of 118 in high with reindeers are ready to be loaded onto the 747   photo Captain John Tymczyszyn

altitude in our eight and a half hour flight from Auckland to Honolulu, reindeers started urinating on top of each other and progressively urine started turning to ammonia smell. About two hours into the flight the smell started reaching the upper deck of our 747 aircraft through the cabin air circulation. We started feeling our eyes burning. The second officer lowered the temperature in the aircraft zones in an attempt to decrease the impact of the smell.

The smell became simply unbearable. So, we decided to start putting our oxygen masks and our smoke goggles. I was worried because oxygen masks are designed to be used in emergency situation such as a rapid descent to 10,000 feet in case of decompression and we were cruising at 41,000 feet. We still had several hours to go to Honolulu and typically, crewmembers only have 10-15 minutes of oxygen for an emergency situation. The oxygen supply depends on altitude, number of crew using the oxygen and the temperature. So, we started taking turn with oxygen masks.

After long excruciating hours, we started our descent and landed in Honolulu. Fresh air at last! The ramp crew started to open the cargo door and soon after ramp handlers started scattering on the ramp, moving away from the plane and wondering aloud, "What's that smell?"

We came down the stairs and the continuing crew to Vancouver approached the aircraft and immediately could smell the ammonia coming out the open doors. So, the captain and first officer said to the second officer "You got up for the cockpit set-up, load the INS, do the external walkaround and then when everything is ready, you turn the landing lights on and we will go to the cockpit."

We got to the crew van to go to the hotel. At this stage, our noses were ruined and we could not smell anything. We reached the hotel reception and received our room keys like plague victims. We got to the elevators with two elderly couples and a lady started sniffing, turned around and said "What the hell happened to you guys?". We smelled so bad with this ammonia that we had to get our uniforms dry-cleaned before taking the next trip.

At the end of the journey, when offloading the little reindeers in Vancouver, the smell and the urine went down and dripped through to the lower bellies and stayed in the plane for weeks. The morale of this story if you are carrying little reindeers is: put your suitcase in a plastic bag and do not wear your uniform. (Editor: And don't eat meat.)

First Officer Rex Cotter on the 747 in 1988 together with Captain Jim Levrett and Second Officer Henry Andor   *photo Captain Rex Cotter*

As she relaxed, she started to look around at her fifty or so shipmates. Most appeared to be very poor Chinese with packs on their backs, chickens and other goods hand carried. All were dressed in somber black workers' clothing. They looked like weary workers and many appeared hardened. She saw immediately she was the only blonde American girl onboard. She was certainly the only tourist. She quickly surmised there would be no beverages, snacks or music on this trip, and she would be very happy to catch up with her friends on Lantau Island and the sooner, the better.

The water was very calm in the harbor, but once out to sea, beyond Hong Kong, it turned somewhat rough. No problem, Kristi was a good sailor, owning her own sailboat in southern California. In fact, she was enjoying this short cruise on the South China Sea as time passed. Finally, several small islands hove into view. The ferry entered a small harbor with a little fishing village. The ferry drew close to a dilapidated looking pier and stopped. A crew member quickly placed a narrow heavy, long, wooden board between the vessel and the pier.

There were no announcements made upon arrival but the entire boatload of people, chickens and heavy bags arose in unison and started their customary frantic push-and-shove procession, again sweeping Kristi along with them. With no handrail to grasp, it looked like a circus balancing act, watching the mass crossing over the single, fully utilized, wooden board. Miraculously, no one fell into the sea.

"Well, this must be my transfer point to Lantau Island". Kristi was thankful she had not arrived dripping wet! She looked back to see that the haphazard gangplank had already been removed and the empty ferry was backing out of the little harbor.

Kristi followed the crowd along the pier, on what appeared to be the main street, which was just a long dusty road along the waterfront. There were a few low-lying buildings, but no signs suggesting where the ferryboat office might be. She looked around. Not a hotel or café. The few people around were staring at her as she walked. She was beginning to wonder when the next boat would arrive. She had been advised in Hong Kong that there might be a little wait.

Kristi saw a small, peasant women near the corner, and walked toward her. The woman tried to avoid her, but stopped abruptly. In very basic sign language, she motioned about her boat, without success. Well then, she knew most islands had their own temple, so she motioned with both hands where might that be? The old women acknowledged immediately and pointed in the direction she should walk. Kristi smiled and replied, Sia sia (thank you in Mandarin).

The Chinese woman looked glumly at her and walked away. Kristi headed in the direction given, along the dusty road, and she still noticed people weirdly staring after her. It was a very rural area, very much like the interior of mainland China. Here she was, dressed in white shorts, her blonde hair blowing about her face, a tourist where there were no tourists. This was such a rural island that she knew it was not the place for her to be, unaccompanied. And she was very sorry to have missed the direct ferry.

Thinking she would be able to get some information at the temple, she hurried along the road. As the buildings began to disappear, the dusty road began to grow very narrow and she could stretch both arms out to touch the entire width between the remaining structures. Now, the road was only a dusty alleyway as she continued on. Soon she was surrounded by trees and the landscape was now a dark and ominous forest. She looked back over her shoulder, with a feeling she was being followed. She took another quick glance and now she was certain, she caught a fleeting sight of a silent, dark, shadowy figure behind her, moving along and drawing closer. She began to walk much faster now, and took another quick look over her shoulder. A man, dressed in dark clothing, was most definitely following her.

Now, she began to feel scared. No other people were in sight, and this was a very unfriendly foreign island she was on, all alone, and worse, this strange man was following too close behind her. She should have stayed in her nice safe bed in the hotel. Too late now.

She hurried up the switchback path over the hill that was ahead of her. At the summit, she spotted the big temple below her, in a wide open area. At last, she thought. The man was still silently approaching behind her. Quickly, she began to race down toward the temple, a tall pagoda. Once reached, she started climbing up many steps to go to the very top.

At the top stood two women, who did appear to be tourists, with cameras. They were Chinese, and were startled by this blonde girl's breathless, unexpected appearance before them. At least, they seemed somewhat friendly. Again, there was no English to be spoken, but with sign language, they smiled and proceeded to reach out to stroke Kristi's long, blonde hair. She understood this gesture as it was common, when she met most oriental people who had never seen a blonde person close up.

By now, the stranger had, also reached the top of the temple. Staunchly, she dared to face him, with the two women behind her. She boldly looked directly at him. It was a shock! The stranger returned her suspicious gaze with one glaring dark eye and a horribly disfigured, milky white eye, a grotesque sight to behold, and much too close to her now. It scared her, but she tried to remain calm, as she stood there, planning what she should do next.

Kristi turned and gave half a look to the two tourist women, who were no help, then she turned and raced back down the steep old temple steps. Rushing out across the wide field that led back toward the big trees, she did not look back.

Running into the dark forest once more, she was moving at a very fast pace, hair flying in the wind, still not looking back. She knew she was in a potentially dangerous situation and it was not over yet. She was a good runner, but feeling out of breath once more, she started to slow down. Still not daring to look behind, but feeling the strange man was still pursuing quickly behind her. She was, almost shaking with fear, when suddenly, there was some terrible noise in the bush in front of her, "Oh no, stop!" she screamed out loud.

There, before her, stood a snarling big dog or maybe a wolf. It seemed to have jumped out of nowhere. It startled her and she trembled. It was vicious and his grayish black fur was standing straight up on his back, his mouth was foaming and his big teeth were a frightening sight. Kristi stood, literally frozen, on the path.

She was shaking with fear now. The big wild dog was poised to attack her as she stood there, so she attempted to be perfectly still. The big animal, ready to jump, gave out a terrible howling sound, and just as sudden, the mysterious stranger with the grotesque milky white eye, that had been following her, pushed her hard, hitting her away from the path. He held up a big bamboo stick in a halting maneuver, to confront, not Kristi lying there, helplessly with arms stretched high above her head, but the completely out of control, snarling wild animal.

It worked, and there was an agonizing silence, as the big, frightening, mad dog laid down with a sudden understood obedience. Kristi could hardly believe what she had just witnessed. So relieved, she started running as fast as she could, never looking back toward the dark forest, the stranger or the dog. Soon she was on the now-familiar path back to the fishing village.

Finally, the road grew wider and she could see the village once more. She did not care who might be staring at her, as she rushed along the dusty road that led to the dilapidated old pier. There was a ferry and board gangplank there, and she hoped, with all her heart, it was her boat to Lantau Island. It was not, but with relief, she found the destination, in sign language, was the second-best option: a long-overdue voyage back to Hong Kong and civilization.

The ferry made good time back to Hong Kong. It was getting late now. Driving back to the hotel, she was thinking that this had been enough adventure for this one little stew. On arrival, she picked up her room key at the front desk, while looking about the lobby for her friends. No friendly faces in sight, so she hurried to the elevator and up to her room. Clearly appreciating the immaculate room, she dropped down on the big bed and reached for the telephone and immediately called room service, requesting a large carafe of white wine and a bowl of rice. She placed the tray bedside and seated herself close by. She hungrily ate the rice with chop sticks, then poured the wine and took a comforting swallow. Relieved and very tired, she was glad to have the long day over. Wild dogs trying to attack her, the disfigured stranger chasing her all over that unfriendly Chinese island (and then actually coming to her rescue!) and all of those dark glaring eyes staring after her. Kristi finished her wine quickly, pulled down the bed sheet, fell into the soft bed and literally covered up her head. A long sleep this night in Hong Kong was more than welcome.

The next morning, Kristi took her place on the jumpseat and fastened her seatbelt, after making the important flight announcements and checking each passenger once more. Kristi always made a point to look out of the airplane window and remember how her pilot father had once shown her the beautiful velvet blue sky on her first trip on a jet when she was a little girl. Finally, she had a little time to give this layover in Hong Kong further thought. Her next assignment was to be an all-volunteer airline crew flying from Los Angeles to Ethiopia, a charter with actor/singer Harry Belafonte for famine relief. That will be a real adventure, she thought.

Kristianne 'Kristi' Peake with her father Captain John H. "Jack" Bliss and First Officer John DeRier onboard a passenger 747

photo Kristi Bliss Peake

The Tiger Blues

Cathy Fune-Schinhofen, Flight Attendant #37719

Let me tell you a little story about an airline crew
Don't cover your ears, just need a minute or two
They're a crazy bunch of cats they fly high in the sky
Doin' what they do best and that is fly, fly, fly!
Once you hear their name, it'll make you proud
Flying Tigers! Flying Tigers! Always pleases the crowd
Since 1941 they've been kickin' ass
Shootin' those Zeros into the grass
And after World War II, Prescott rounded up the gang
He got the best flyboys to fly those planes
He struggled to make money shipping all kinds of junk
Even though his Connies went clunk, clunk, clunk!
One day a bunch of sailors needed a ride
So we flew them home to Mama cuz that's her pride
We fly soldiers in war time and soldiers in peace time
When MAC says "GO" we Fly them anytime
Up and down all over this world
Tigers helped lots of friends and then danced with the girls
But after landing those silver birds the crews need a break
Lots of sleep, lots of beer, always sounded great
But in '78 deregulation's here to stay
What's that mean? It means a frickin' cut in pay!
The price of gas went up and our paychecks went down
The rumors started goin' around and around
Tigers bought Seaboard adding more 74's
We Fell deeper into debt, ooh talk about poor
The CEO's and Metro, they came and went
but the Wolfman, he hung around to see our spirit bent
He's a sinister man, he thinks he's got clout
We hope United boots his ass out!
Last year we gave the Tiger a goodbye kiss
And we found ourselves on planet Memphis!
Piss tests, purple planes, a form for this and that
How much longer can we take this crap?
Now we're up to our ears in paperwork
Cooter thinks he's cool, we think he's a jerk!
ALPA is out, Teamsters is in!

F Street has been hot for some union bustin'!
Screw control is up to their same old tricks,
Hells Angels, church boys, man, they just don't mix
Purple-lized with koolaid eyes some folks have gone that way
Now it's Absolutely Positively Overnight they say
I know I should be patient it's a game of wait and see
All I really want is a pilot's salary!
Been furloughed only once, no make it more than twice
Guess that's why I drink lots of vodka just with ice
We miss the Circle T and we miss the Tiger face
Man if Bubba hears this rap of mine
We'll all be Dubai based!
I know, I know, I know I shouldn't complain
But ever since T day, I got this certain pain
The days of the Tiger are gone, gone, gone
But they'll always be days of which I'm very fond…

Cathy Fune-Schinhofen seated (centre) in Flying Tigers 747 upper deck with a few friends, left to right standing, Marilyn Breen, Deidre Dixon, me, Ann Ventouris, Judy Curtis, Ara Ghazarosian. To kill time on those long flights over the Pacific Ocean, we held an earring contest. The cockpit crew voted for the best pair of earrings, Deidre Dixon won big with her airplane earrings! photo Cathy Fune-Schinhofen

Captain Jim Hengehold

Captain Douglas Happ

James "Jim" Hengehold was hired by Flying Tigers on August 22, 1966 as a flight engineer. We were in the same class and although he had more hours than me, I was hired as a co-pilot and received a seniority number above his.

He had taken his flight engineer written exams and I had not. We lived in the same one-bedroom apartment in New Jersey with five other new hires. Jim and I became good friends and we both met our wives at that apartment complex.

He was the best man at my wedding and we both loved to fish. Together with Ralph Grella and Jim Levrett, Jim and I participated in big game tournament fishing including the Hawaiian Invitational once and the Bisbee's Black and Blue six times. We finished fourth in our first tournament with a 514-pound blue marlin. We hired a Mexican boat and lined up three mornings in a row at seven a.m. for a shotgun start with 180 other boats. We were competing against a billion dollars' worth of the latest, greatest, state of the art electronic equipment, and two million in prize money. Our boat had no compass, no radar, no sonar, no depth finder, no fish finder and the captain had no shoes, but we naively considered it a fair fight because the captain had seven brothers who fished those waters almost every day of their lives.

The Bisbees Black and Blue Marlin Tournament in Cabo San Lucas, Mexico was a particular favourite. At a gala after that tournament, where much alcohol was consumed, a raffle was being conducted. A Penn International reel was being raffled off and I coveted that reel. I told Jim that I would really like to have that reel and he said, "Too bad, I have the winning ticket." With that he stood up and started walking to the stage even before all of the numbers had been read. I thought I

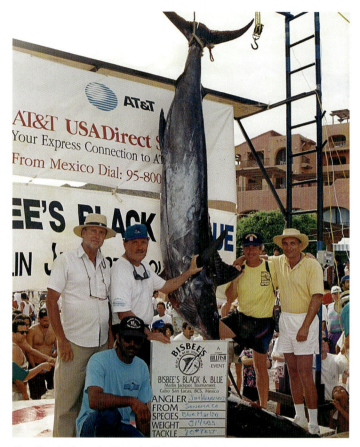

Kneeling in front is Captain Pancho from the Juanita fleet, standing from left to right are Jim Levrett, Jim Hengehold, Doug Happ and Ralph Grella   *photo Doug Happ*

would see him turn around when the last number was read but he kept walking to the stage and claimed that beautiful reel!

Several years went by and Jim developed a brain tumor which eventually took his life. Two days before Jim passed away a FedEx package was delivered to me. When I opened the package, I found that beautiful Penn International reel with a note attached. "Doug, I know how much you loved this reel and it is yours now. Your friend Jim." Needless to say I cried like a baby. What a wonderful friend he was.

Flying Tiger Line Pilots Reunions

H. Paul Rebscher

Susan and I have attended 25 consecutive Tigers reunions before and since retirement in 1995. Don Hassig had attended about 30 consecutive reunions before his passing a few years ago and we miss him.

During our span of 25 years we became involved in tending bar, no longer necessary, as a way of helping out at the reunions. We enjoyed our bar-tending duties very much and got to talk to a lot of Tiger folks who showed up for a drink or two or three – all free!

At a Seattle reunion a few years back, Chuck Westcot and I were "on duty" when one of our crew members who had a nasty personality when drinking came to the bar for his 20th free drink. Chuck leaned over to me and said: "Take care of so and so, but he shouldn't have any more booze."

Now this guy, who is really in his cups, is a big fellow, six feet plus and about 230 pounds says to me, "I want another drink." I looked him right in the eye and said, "Sorry B, no more drinks for you today."

In a very gruff voice, "Why not?" The only thing I could think of was, "Doctor's orders!" Without any argument he said: "OK," and walked away.

Paul Rebscher (left) with Mike Johnsen at the bar serving Rich Van Veen during the Seattle FTLPA reunion in 2014

photo Eliot Shulman, Flying Tiger Line Pilots Association

Hi Tiger (on the right) opened on June 15, 1973. Joe Baker dubbed the original two-storey building, Lo Tiger.

photo J. Eyerman, Flying Tigers Club Archives

59

7401 World Way West

Guy Van Herbruggen

Time has passed since Federal Express merged Flying Tigers into its operations, and that the Flying Tigers name passed into history (with the exception of two associations which have kept the memories alive – the Flying Tigers Club and the Flying Tiger Line Pilots Association).

All Flying Tigers aircraft were progressively retired starting with the DC-8-73 fleet in late 1990 followed by the Boeing 727-100 fleet by 1992. Only the former Tigers 747s had a longer career with FedEx, until 1997.

Today, some key original Tigers building remain at the Los Angeles International Airport on 7401 World Way West at the west end of the Los Angeles International Airport.

IN THE BEGINNING

The first roof over the heads of the Tigers (known as National Skyways Freight Corporation until February 1947, when it was changed to The Flying Tiger Line Inc.) was a suite at the Los Angeles Biltmore Hotel. The hotel's management got nervous about the lines of prospective employees crowding the hallways; a short

time later, the company moved to a one-room office with a two-car garage at the Long Beach Airport. The garage at Long Beach Airport contained a couple of desks, three chairs, a ratty sofa, a war surplus filing cabinet, and a bunch of phones that never stopped ringing.

It was to and from Long Beach that the Budd Conestogas marked history for the new all-cargo airline with three cargo shipments. One trip launched and one trip landed at Long Beach that very first day on August 22, 1945.

The first terminal at Long Beach in 1945

photo Flying Tigers Club Archives

The Los Angeles Biltmore Hotel depicted in a postcard

The first trip, flown by John Gordon, carried 10,000 pounds of flowers from Long Beach to Detroit; the second trip, flown by Paul Kelly, was the famous 10,000 pounds of grapes from Bakersfield to Atlanta (even though it technically took off before the first trip). The third trip was 10,000 pounds of furniture from Newark back to Long Beach. It was after Robert P. 'Duke' Hedman landed in Long Beach with this third shipment that all the company employees celebrated their good fortune at the Hilton Breakers Hotel Sky Room atop the hotel. This building still stands today on East Ocean Boulevard in Long Beach and was designated as a Long Beach Historical Landmark in 1989.

For a brief period, beginning in the spring of 1946, Tigers moved to Mines Field, today better known as LAX – Los Angeles International Airport. In late 1946 most airline flights at Burbank also moved to LAX.

At Mines Field, three large classrooms formerly used by North American Aviation Company were further augmented by a hangar – but one with no paved surfaces. Since Tigers didn't have a tow truck to its name in those days, in rainy weather, long-suffering maintenance personnel had to lay planks and pull a plane by hand inside the hangar, one foot at a time. The building at that location is still standing today, named Hangar One, added to the National Register of Historic Places in 1992.

It was after the company won the Air Transport Command's Trans Pacific contract that the cliff-hanging little airline began a desperate search for quarters to

The Lockheed Air Terminal in Burbank, note the second hangar under construction *photo Flying Tigers Club Archives*

house 42 C-54s furnished by Air Transport Command for the missions. That contract called for 28 weekly flights supporting U.S. military occupation forces in the Pacific.

LOCKHEED AIR TERMINAL, BURBANK

Just before the new year of 1947, Bob Prescott found a home for the airline at the Lockheed Air Terminal

Flag raising for the dedication of the new Flying Tiger Line office building at Lockheed Air Terminal *photo University of Southern California*

Hangar One was built in 1929 *photo Bobak Ha'Eri*

Helen Ruth Verheyden, first wife of Bob Prescott, putting a plaque on the wall of the company's new two storey office building in Burbank

photo Watson, Flying Tigers Club Archives

in Burbank, California, which had a big empty hangar and office space. In late January 1948, Tigers employees came back to work at Mines Field after the holiday to find a sign posted that read, "Your company has moved to Lockheed Air Terminal, Burbank. Park your cars and board the C-54."

In the spring of 1951 the company moved to its own two-storey, air-conditioned office building a couple of blocks away at 10811 Sherman Way. The company continued to grow and soon space became inadequate. In 1965 Flying Tigers undertook an ambitious project, a new headquarters back at Los Angeles International Airport.

LO TIGER, HI TIGER

In Spring 1965, ground-breaking ceremonies at Los Angeles International Airport for Flying Tigers' new $4,000,000 office and maintenance base brought out a large group of construction, airport, engineering and airline executives around Bob Prescott to turn the first earth on the 25-acre plot the Tiger base would occupy. The new facility was complete at the end of 1965, and

in early 1966, Flying Tigers moved into its new building (later called Lo Tiger), at 7401 World Way West, while the airfreight station moved into the cargo terminal area at 5720 Avion Drive, near the beginning of runway 25R. The cargo terminal went into initial operation in January 1964, enabling Flying Tigers to move from its temporary position at the SAS hangar on the field.

In addition to the new building, complete with its own cafeteria and what seemed an inexhaustible amount of space at that time, a large hangar was built. It was at that time one of the largest cantilevered structures of its kind west of the Mississippi was built, capable of accommodating three big Tiger Stretch Eights wing tip to wing tip.

Adjacent to the maintenance hangar, a training centre was constructed – later named after former company's founder Samuel B. Mosher. After breaking ground in late 1966, the training centre opened in 1968 and housed offices and student classrooms. The DC-8 Cockpit Procedure Trainer (CPT) was part of the school curriculum. It was a stationary reproduction of the

The Flying Tiger Line's brand spanking new administration building at LAX in July 1967   *photo Flying Tigers Club Archives*

LAX cargo terminal circa 1967

photo J. R. Eyerman, Flying Tigers Club Archives

The Flight Training Center opened in 1968

The maintenance hangar with two Stretched DC-8s and a CL-44

photos Flying Tigers Club Archives

DC-8 cockpit where student pilots learned to work as flight crews.

Next to the DC-8 procedural trainer was the DC-8 full-motion flight simulator, manufactured by the Link Group-Systems Division, General Precision Systems Inc. in Binghamton, NY. Flying Tigers took delivery of the simulator in 1968. It was only in 1973 that a visual display system was added.

But the building, as luxurious and spacious as it seemed, soon was bulging at the seams. In the spring of 1972, the board approved a proposal for the building of a 10-storey companion building to the existing two-story structure. The three-million-dollar decision to build on the airport was carefully weighed and considered in light of construction, occupancy, maintenance, training, operations and information technology requirements.

The construction of the new 10-story world headquarters became the tallest structure on the airport except for the LAX control tower. The new addition was named "Hi Tiger".

Joe Baker was Flying Tigers Director of Facilities and Equipment. Hired by Bob Prescott in Long Beach in September 1945, Joe had the responsibility for planning and execution of Lo Tiger and responsible

for the coordination and expediting Hi Tiger among his many accomplishments – and nicknamed both.

Situated on a 315-acre site, with its 104,040 square feet of floor space, Hi Tiger provided room for the operations control, sales, service planning, marketing, terminals, legal, finance, treasury, internal audit, banking insurance, computer, contracts and public relations departments.

Robert L. Barnett of Beverly Hills was the architect. Sheldon Appel of West Los Angeles was the general contractor. Hi Tiger was designed to complement and continue the basic design of Lo Tiger, repeating the clean off-white exterior with charcoal window trim.

Hi Tiger was directly linked to Lo Tiger by a glass-walled walkway. Lo Tiger hosted connecting departments such as personnel, industrial relations, employee benefits, employment, the controller's office, general cost accounting, the credit union offices and a spacious cafeteria with a patio for additional outside dining.

Hi Tiger Ground breaking on April 11, 1972, from left to right, Sheldon Appel (General Contractor), Bob Prescott and Al Cormier

The 10-storey structure was poured in two-storey high concrete panel units at the site. They were lifted by 100-ton cranes and affixed to the precision-bolted and -welded steel framework built to withstand earthquakes. Accelerographs were installed to measure earth disturbances. The decorators made use of carpeting throughout the building to reduce noise levels. Placing the three elevator shafts off-centre in the front corner portion of the building left office floor space entirely unobstructed. Typical of the 70s, cheerful tile elevator lobbies introduced each of the office areas decorated in warm tones ranging from brown, orange, and gold through red and cream, offset by charcoal doors and office furniture in blending colors.

The 10th floor was called the Night Club because of its warm atmosphere, soft lighting and custom decoration and furniture. This is where Bob Prescott's office was located with other vice presidents' offices and where the boardroom, facing the airport, was located.

The DC-8-63 Flight Simulator prior to the installation of its visual system. Note the Cockpit Procedure Trainer in the background.

photos Flying Tigers Club Archives

Office space on the sixth floor of the new Hi Tiger building

HI TIGER PRESCOTT DEDICATION

Following the death of Bob Prescott on March 3, 1978, Hi Tiger was dedicated to the memory of the airline's founder and president for 33 years. On August 14, 1978, bronze letters with Robert W. Prescott Building were placed on the building entrance and a ceremony with family, company founders, officers, board members and airport officials took place. Back row, left to right, Russ Emerson, Bill McKenna, Eddie Holohan, Bill Bartling, Dick Rossi, Bob "Catfish" Raine, Duke Hedman, Bill Caldwell, Jack Rosenthal, Nissen Davis, Laura Hoffman, Wayne Hoffman, Clif Moore. Walt Bernhardson, "Shad" Shadowens, Joe Healy, and Glenn Saxon. Standing in front, left to right, John McDonald, Houston Rehrig, family members Dick Smith, Kirchy Prescott Smith, Anne-Marie Prescott, French Prescott Reill, Peter Reill, and Charles Luckman.

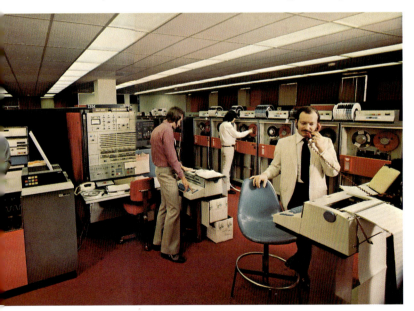

One of the stars of Hi Tiger was the computer centre on the first floor, Flying Tigers' brain and nervous system, connecting the airline's terminals, stations and off-line offices throughout the world

photos Flying Tigers Club Archives

Early 1979 saw the announcement of construction of a new $10 million air-cargo terminal at Los Angeles International Airport, next to the site where Flying Tigers operated for a short time in 1946 before establishing facilities in Burbank. Covering an area of more than 23 acres, the new terminal became the largest single carrier cargo facility at the airport and the largest of 28 terminal facilities maintained by Flying Tigers throughout the world, with nearly 110,000 square feet, including more than 82,000 square feet of warehouse

The air cargo terminal at LAX photos Flying Tigers Club Archives

space, 20,000 square feet of offices and 6,000 square feet for maintenance. The ramp area provided simultaneous parking positions for five stretched DC-8s and two Boeing 747s. Located at 5927 West Imperial Highway, the new facility also provided an extensive trucking area including 46 dock-high truck doors.

In the autumn of 1979, Flying Tigers announced a $3.7 million expansion of its flight training center located at World Headquarters in Los Angeles. The 45,000 square-foot, four-level structure was an extension of the initial Samuel B. Mosher Flight Training Center, housed 15 student classrooms for flight attendants, cockpit crew members, maintenance, terminal and management personnel. Construction started in January 1980 with completion set for the end of the year. RMA Architectural Group of Costa Mesa designed the building. The highlight of the new training building was the six million dollar 747 simulator built by Link-Miles Division of the Singer Company and installed in 1981.

The Hi Tiger building also became the nerve centre of the new Flying Tigers flight operations that was moved from the ninth floor to the third floor in March 1981.

The Flying Tigers six-axis Boeing 747 Flight Simulator

It was the heartbeat of the airline. Multiple departments worked on the third floor hand in hand including OpsCon (operations control), Maintenance Control Flight Planning and Traffic Services (known today at FedEx as FMC,

Freight Movement Center). Also called the Fishbowl because the room was enclosed by glass, its focal point was a 68-foot wide floor-to-ceiling, graphic display of two seven-day schedules for every Flying Tigers aircraft.

The flight board included a clock with a motorized cursor, as high as the board, always marking the current time of day. The board originated from the plan of Forrest Luff who came up from Braniff. Although he left Tigers soon after, it was nurtured by many in OpsCon over the next few years. The board would have to be manually rebuilt by 24-hour periods by OpsCon personnel using a ladder to move and rebuild the schedule one day at a time and about a week into the future using plastic strips with magnets on the back. Other flight operations related departments on the third floor (but not within the "fishbowl") included Crew Control, Flight Operations Analysis and Overfly and Landing Rights.

The 68-foot-wide, floor-to-ceiling board in the Operations Control Center. The left side of the room was the seven-day display of the domestic operation with the 727s and DC-8s. Even if the DC-8 had an international trip, it was still carried on the left side of the room. The right side of the room was the seven-day display of the 747 international operation.

photos Helena and John Burke, Flying Tigers Club

MERGER WITH FEDERAL EXPRESS

When Federal Express took over Flying Tigers in August 1989, various departments in Lo & Hi Tiger were progressively integrated by Federal Express. Many Flying Tigers employees were given the option to relocate to Federal Express World Headquarters in Memphis, and in the 90s, Lo & Hi Tiger buildings were taken over by the Los Angeles World Airports Authority, housing departments such as the Airport Police Division, Human Resources, and Security Badges.

The DC-8 flight simulator was sold around 1996 to Aero Service Aviation Center in Dayton. Even after the retirement of the last Federal Express 747 in December 1997, the 747 simulator continued to be used for simulator rides as part of the FedEx pilot interview process. Ultimately disposed by FedEx, it was sold to Northwest Airlines and moved to Eagan, across the river from Minneapolis St Paul airport.

The original Hi Tiger lobby featured an aircraft model display against the wall on the left as one entered the main door and across from the elevators. This was preserved and relocated to the nearby Flight Path Museum & Learning Center located on West Imperial Highway.

At LAX, FedEx Express is still the tenant of building 7401, the large hangar where McDonnell Douglas (now Boeing) MD-10 and MD-11 aircraft maintenance is conducted, and the original Flying Tiger Training Building, which is now the main entrance building leading to the

The original lobby planes display is preserved in the Flight Path Museum

photo Guy Van Herbruggen

Runway 24L

Ground Equip Maint

Employee Parking

Aircraft Maint Hangar

Flight Publicaitons

Sam Mosher Training Building

Cafeteria

Credit Union

Original Lo Tiger

Hi Tiger

Employee Parking

Employee Parking

Main Entrance

World Way West

Continental Airlines Headquarters/Training/Maintenance

The different locations on World Way West   *photo Google Earth*

FedEx hangar. It is still used for training, and even houses a Boeing satellite office. It also houses the unique Flying Tigers Museum, a two-room space where volunteers of the Flying Tigers Club are preserving aircraft models, manuals, a large 35mm slide collection, newspaper clips, magazines, pictures and other various archives.

The former DC-8-63 flight simulator bay is now a storage room but the former DC-8 flight attendant cabin evacuation simulator still sits on top of the FedEx screening facility of the maintenance hangar.

At 5927 West Imperial Highway, Federal Express quickly took over the large hub and sort facility. This is the place where a great scene was shot in the 2000's Cast Away movie, a scene where Tom Hanks (playing the role of Chuck Noland) receives a pocket watch from Helen Hunt (Kelly Frears in the movie) before boarding its aircraft. With the watch in his hands, he says "I am always going to keep this on Memphis time" – a line derived in part from a corporate custom that the FedEx pilots had of always referring to any time of meetup or "show time" on a layover using Memphis time.

Past and present cargo terminal facility locations

photo Google Earth

60

Friends For Life

Leigh-lu Prasse - Flight Planner/Aircraft Dispatcher

It doesn't seem like a big deal today but when I was hired by Flying Tigers in 1987, I was the first woman to step into the role as a dispatcher, one of the three FAA certified jobs at an airline: pilot, aircraft mechanic, and aircraft dispatcher, known as Flight Planners at Tigers.

While a female dispatcher may have been more common by then, it was novel at Tigers because they rarely hired dispatchers to begin with. I had transited through many airlines during the turbulent post-deregulation era, and it never really occurred to me that I had been the only woman working in operations at each one until joining Flying Tigers where I discovered it was the topic of the hour at OpsCon. They let me know I had joined the rank and file with Norah O'Neill as the first female pilot at Tigers, Sandy Szegetti as the first female captain, and Diana Nichols as the first female aircraft mechanic. I felt a great honour with the other female firsts, and even more so to be dispatching aircraft.

The flight planners consisted of a small group of just 18 guys, and a storied bunch they were! They represented many countries around the world emulating the international destinations that Tigers went to. Bent Rasmussen was originally a merchant seaman from Denmark, Hank Kwan a flight controller for Pan Am from Hong Kong, Richard Van Ardeen a former soldier and two-time POW in the Dutch East Indies from the Netherlands, Rick "Soup" Boulion from Cuba, Umberto De'Lugi from Chile, and Walter DeCunha from Goa, India. Ted Godek was a former Dispatcher for Trans-Ocean based on Wake Island and there was Jim Doyle noted for holding a CAA dispatcher license, predating the FAA (est. 1958). The other cast of characters included Art Lombardi, Ron Flynn, Tony Fiorelli, a prior dispatcher clerk from Pan Am, and Nick Cambria and Ed Bell from Seaboard. There were just five of us on the bottom in the same age group, Rich Bower, Dave Lusk, Steve Germain, Gary Goode, and me. (Calvin Goodale joined us at the merger in the middle of transitioning to Memphis.) And these gentlemen were just a few compared to the other notorious characters we worked with in Tigers flight operations (some of whom are no doubt in this book!).

When I began my aviation career with Capitol Airlines a week out of college in 1979, I knew with certainty I was in my destined profession. Although I went through airline bankruptcies, furloughs, a Teamsters strike, bankruptcies, loss of pay checks, mergers, and also had been the dispatcher on duty at one airline to take the FAA's phone call for the "emergency revocation of your operating certificate," it never occurred to me to do anything else but aviation. As a matter of fact, it was so ingrained in me (in all of us) that even working in Jeddah in the early 1980s with Overseas National Airways (ONA), renamed United Air Carriers, Inc. (UACI) and leased to Saudia, did not deter me in the least. I would be in Jeddah for five years (on the biggest adventures of my life) and would come to discover that friends I made there early on, I would find again flying the line at Tigers.

As I look back on the friendships I have made over a lifetime, it seems that those most endeared to me all have the common denominator of aviation, and especially so with those from Flying Tigers. Was it the culture of Tigers itself, or all of us working in the Fishbowl, maintenance control, and crew scheduling that made a close-knit group, or was it going through the merger and moving to Memphis that officially cemented us together?

Whatever the answer may be, we all became close friends; at work grappling with the many operational issues at every turn, yet savoring every crazy moment and occasion life offered us. None of our jobs were "just a job", but a common thread we shared, a type of survival mode of always living in the present with the mission of getting the plane in the air. It was aviation that bonded us together, the perfect proving ground for friendships like no other, unexpected and treasured, friends for life.

Notorious Tiger Characters! From left to right, Dave Lusk/FLT Planner, Erich Krueck/OpsCon, John Burke/OpsCon and Dave Stratton/Crew Scheduling

Ex-Tigers at Bent Rasmussen's retirement party: Tom Chisim in red shirt, Rich Bower, Dave Lusk standing on chair in the back, Glenn Van Winkle (next to Bent, cut-off by Chuck Byrkett in front), John Burke, Steve Germain in back on the right. Kneeling in front are Tiger NRT dispatcher and Dave Stratton.

Former Tiger flight planners at Ted Godek's retirement. Front Row: Ted Godek, Leigh-lu, Steve Germain (with beard) and Nick Cambria

Former Tiger flight planners & OpsCon. Behind Ted Godek: Umberto De'Luigi, Chuck Byrkett (OpsCon) and Ron Flynn

61

The Flying Tiger Spirit

Deborah Paul (McCoy)

The forward of my Flying Tiger yearbook says it best: "The Flying Tiger Spirit can never truly be defined in words. It can mainly be felt in the hearts of those who have experienced it."

I joined the company in 1974 as a maintenance records clerk. In the 1980 hiring spree I transferred to the in-flight service department to fly Cambodian, Laotian, and Vietnamese refugees out of Asia. I can't count how many times I've heard the question, "Flying Tigers had flight attendants?"

Yes, and Federal Express too! Even though Federal Express absorbed the Flying Tiger pilots, mechanics and other employees, they left unionised flight attendants to fend for themselves; the muck and mire of big business vs. Teamster politics. Federal Express honored the last Flying Tigers' three-year passenger charter contracts with the Federal government, then laid off its 250 flight attendants in 1992.

Flight attendant special assignments were a veritable feast of adventure. As well as countless tourist, student, or affinity group charter flights, early cabin attendants flew in the Korean and Vietnam wars carrying MAC charters full of soldiers, or orphans to adoptive parents in the United States. In the 1980s we fed caffeine-laden kola nuts and rice to Muslims traveling from Africa to Mecca on pilgrimages.

I remember a reunion of former Flying Tiger pilots, mechanics, administrative employees and flight attendants in Las Vegas. More than 350 ex-employees donning Flying Tigers wings, emblems and patches gathered to toast a company that everyone loved and truly misses.

Memories linger about the back-breaking labor involved in getting DC-8 and Boeing 747 cargo and passenger planes out on time. Company picnics, motorcycle clubs, fancy Christmas parties, exotic travel, worldwide shopping sprees, and lots of marriages and intrigue add flavor to the recollections.

Former employees turned authors are trying to capture Tiger escapades in books. Most of the flightiness is printable. Other stories can ruin lives. But one thing is certain – everyone has a Tiger Tale of their own.

It was delightful to see some of the retired pilots who used to mischievously heave young, girdled flight attendants into overhead bins to greet boarding passengers. It was fun back then.

Some of the retired guys could hardly walk. But the Tiger twinkle was still there as they remembered a pool party at the Pony Hotel in Tokyo, or a stolen kiss on the cable car going up to Victoria Peak in Hong Kong.

Screams of delight reverberated off the walls for each new arrival as they stopped by the hotels hospitality suite. (And spouses were pleasant, but tried not to look intermittently bored or overwhelmed when waves of Tiger talk swirled around them.)

"There's Dennis Ferraro in shorts – that old swashbuckler!" hollered one former flight attendant. "Oh my gosh, there's Judy Keown – God, she hasn't changed in 10 years," said another, eying the 50-year-old tennis buff in her little black evening dress.

Mild-mannered pilot Elgen Long, who still holds the world record for a circumpolar flight, told of helping Linda Finch rig her airplane for her recent retracing of Amelia Earhart's around-the-world flight.

During the final banquet at around 9 pm, we drank a toast to past Flying Tigers who have gone on to heaven's greener jungles. The rest of us vowed to keep aloft the Tiger spirit of camaraderie – as long as we are able to wag our tales.

References

WEBSITES

- flyingtiger923.com commemorating the crash of Flying Tiger Lines Flight 923 on September 23, 1962, by Fred Caruso
- n6914c.weebly.com dedicated to First Officer Thomas D. Hunt and the crash of Super H N6914C
- n6921c.com and flight739-14-1962.com honoring the 93 U.S. Army Rangers and flight crew who lost their lives on March 16, 1962 aboard Flying Tiger flight 739/14 enroute to Saigon
- www.flyingtigerline.org the official website of the Flying Tiger Line Pilots Association
- www.flyingtigersclub.org the official website of the Flying Tigers Club

OTHER REFERENCES

- Interviews with the following:
  - Lydia Rossi, August 12, 2018
  - Ann Ludwig, August 14, 2018
  - Ginny Dixon, January 17, 2019
- Quote regarding "Good Boss" came from Charles Erwin Wilson, an American engineer and businessman who served as United States Secretary of Defense from 1953 to 1957 under President Dwight D. Eisenhower.
- Various online obituaries and sources

BOOKS, PERIODICALS AND OTHER PUBLICATIONS

- Airliners magazine Spring 1993
- Curtiss C-46 Commando, John M. Davis, Harold G. Martin and John A. Whittle, Air-Britain Publication, 1978
- The Lockheed Constellation Series, Peter J. Marson, Air-Britain Publication, 1982
- Flying Tigers 1945-1989 pictorial history
- Flying Tigers Over Cambodia, Larry Partridge, 2001
- Hungry Tiger, Frank J. Cameron, 1964
- The American Magazine, January 1946, The Tigers Fly Again
- The New York Times Archives, 1978, Robert Prescott, Ex-Fighter Pilot and Founder of Airlines for Cargo #333
- The Desert Sun, Volume 39, Number 181, 4 March 1966, Probe Launched on Air Crash
- Tigereview, Tigertrack and Tiger Spirit publications

"The best stories we have you will not ever hear because we will take them to our graves."

Deborah Paul (McCoy)